►Going the Distance: Library Instruction for Remote Learners

Edited by
Susan J. Clayton

Neal-Schuman Publishers, Inc.
New York   London

Published by Neal-Schuman Publishers, Inc.
100 William Street, Suite 2004
New York, NY 10038-4512

Printed and bound in the United States of America.

The paper used in this publication meets the minimum requirements of American National Standard for Information Sciences—Permanence of Paper for Printed Library Materials, ANSI Z39.48-1992.

ISBN-13: 978-1-55570-592-3
ISBN-10: 1-55570-592-8

Library of Congress Cataloging-in-Publication Data

Going the distance : library instruction for remote learners / edited by Susan J. Clayton
    p. cm.
  Includes bibliographical references and index.
  ISBN 1-55570-592-8 (alk. paper)
  1. Libraries and distance education. 2. Library orientation. 3. Web-based instruction. I. Clayton, Susan J.
Z718.85.G65 2007
025.5—dc22

                   2006033013

▶Dedication

To my friends in
upstate New York and in Montana,
who are always supportive;
to my mom and my brother,
whom I depend upon;
and to my dad and my sister,
who are always in my thoughts.

▶ Contents

▶ PART I
DESIGNING DISTANCE INSTRUCTION

▶ PART II
DELIVERING DISTANCE INSTRUCTION

▶ PART III
COLLABORATING FOR DISTANCE INSTRUCTION

▶ PART IV
ASSESSING DISTANCE INSTRUCTION

▶ List of Figures

▶ Preface

Librarians feel a renewed commitment to satisfy the needs of their virtual patrons as the number of distance education programs multiplies and the number of students enrolled in them keeps pace. Once relegated to the sidelines as a relatively minor professional matter, meeting these students' information requirements has steadily grown into a major concern. Today we all are searching for smart and savvy answers for the best ways to

▶ provide the same access to resources through library instruction as for their counterparts on campus

▶ teach users how to use the library remotely yet effectively

▶ take away some of the mystery and sense of isolation that may still surround the online experience

▶ instruct students to think critically, evaluate Web sites, become knowledgeable about copyright, avoid plagiarism and confront all of the same information literacy issues that face their on-campus complements.

In *Going the Distance: Library Instruction for Remote Learners*, frontline professionals share some innovative solutions to everyday challenges. The idea for this collection followed the great audience response to a recent presentation on the subject of teaching library information distance education at a Computers in Libraries conference. I made a call for authors over the Off-Campus Library Services list and chose these 26 contributors. All are librarians currently working in the field, and all bring their varied, hands-on experiences to their writing. My goal in bringing them together is to offer an extensive range of real remedies and practical ideas from many expert voices.

Going the Distance explores and maps four main areas. It looks at the best ways to design, deliver, collaborate, and assess distance instruction.

Part I, "Designing Distance Instruction," features seven chapters that include information ranging from practical examples of various types of sessions to the nine most useful librarian tools, from a guide for the new off-campus librarian to how to create subject-specific Web-based learning modules. It also looks at basics such as copyright issues and examines the connections between adult distance learners with library anxiety and the lure of Internet plagiarism.

Part II, "Delivering Distance Instruction," examines the struggles and successes of many interesting experiments. Chapters delve into a variety of critical concerns, such as the incorporation of the newest technology tools: the creation of subject-specific online tools, from online catalogs to flash tutorials; and the formulation of online tutorials using the Blackboard Course Management System. Also considered in depth are issues such as the creation of surveys to determine which format is preferred by distance education students, faculty perspectives on library instruction, suggestions to alternatives to the traditional research paper, and virtual classroom software.

Part III, "Collaborating for Distance Instruction," includes chapters on finding faculty and information technology (IT) staff who are interested in collaborating with librarians. These chapters also discuss how we can become more involved in online courses. Also examined is the design of marketing plans for determining the target audience demographics and the best marketing strategies.

Part IV, "Assessing Distance Education," offers alternatives to traditional face-to-face library instruction courses for training in online environments, taking into account all of the complications that arise from this shift. Ideal means of collecting and responding to student comments and assessments also are detailed in this section, as are many resources available online and in print on the assessment of distance learning library instruction. Further, these chapters contain a history of library instruction assessment and stress the importance of assessment in the accreditation process.

In providing extensive, up-to-date practical information with current references, *Going the Distance* presents what librarians really want to know: how to deal with the real-life distance library instruction issues we face. I compiled this volume to give you solutions, insight, and encouragement. Given the diversity of the ideas presented here, I hope that these chapters have the same impact as attending a conference, infusing your own distance education practice with the current collective wisdom of a vital community. I also hope they renew interest in the issues surrounding the provision of library instruction to remote students and ignite an invigorated commitment to make it continually improve and expand.

►Acknowledgments

I would like to thank everyone who has made this collection possible, especially the contributors who have written such excellent and informative chapters. While I have not yet met most of these colleagues, I look forward to meeting everyone at some point at a library meeting or conference.

Thank you to my editors at Neal-Schuman Publishers: Miguel Figueroa for finding me at Computers in Libraries and suggesting that this collection might be a possibility and Michael Kelley and Christine O'Connor who patiently and painstakingly took me through the steps of editing this collection of chapters into a book on library instruction and distance learners. Also, thanks to my library director, Jean Swanson, for encouraging me to pursue this opportunity.

Last, but certainly not least, thank you to my family and friends who never stopped encouraging me even when there were setbacks and life events that seemed determined to slow everything down. Thank you so much!

▶Part I

DESIGNING DISTANCE INSTRUCTION

▶1

USING MODELS AND METHODS TO DESIGN LIBRARY INSTRUCTION

LUANN DEGREVE
JACK FRITTS
GRETEL STOCK-KUPPERMAN

Overview: This thorough examination of the different types of library instruction sessions also details two models of instructional design: responsive and structured. Examples of various types of library instruction sessions in use by a number of college and university libraries across the country, from Maryland to Washington State, are discussed. Particularly useful are the Instructional Outlines from four libraries, which are included in the Appendix.

INTRODUCTION

Institutions involved in distance learning have always struggled with the issue of providing strong support to distant learners. The ACRL "Guidelines for Distance Learning Library Services" state that "library resources and services in institutions of higher education must meet the needs of all their faculty, students, and academic support personnel, regardless of where they are located" (ACRL, 2004).With the current trend in higher education toward greater involvement in distance and nontraditional learning, academic librarians need to develop programs and processes to ensure that remote learners receive as solid a grounding in library and research skills as do local patrons. This includes library instruction in all its forms.

This chapter focuses on the models and methods used by six institutions to deliver instruction and related services to distance students. Each assessment is based on e-mail or telephone conversations with the distance education librarians at each institution. The librarians were asked to discuss how they designed and executed their instructional plan. Summaries of their responses are included. The instruction models and methods in this chapter reflect how the represented institutions meet the needs of their distance students.

LEARNING THEORY

Librarians offering instruction need to address both the traditional and the nontraditional student. While learning theories apply to all types of students, traditional and nontraditional students are in different places along the continuum and, therefore, require alternate forms of instruction. Professor Frances Stage, et al., the author of the ASHE-ERIC Higher Education report on learning-centered classrooms and professor of higher education at Indiana University, describes the best practices that promote learning for traditional undergraduate students:

▶ Social learning experiences, such as peer teaching and group projects, particularly those that promote group construction of knowledge, allow a student to observe other students' models of successful learning and encourage him or her to emulate them (social constructivism, self-efficacy, learning styles)

▶ Varying instructional models that deviate from the lecture format, such as visual presentations, site visits, and use of the Internet (multiple intelligences, learning styles, self-efficacy)

▶ Varying expectations for students' performance, from individual written formats to group work that includes writing and presentation; interpretation of theatrical, dance, musical, or artistic work; and performance of actual tasks at a work site (attribution theory, "conscientization," multiple intelligences, learning styles)

▶ Choices that allow students to capitalize on personal strengths and interests (self-efficacy, multiple intelligences, learning styles)

▶ Overt use of sociocultural situations and methods that provide authentic contexts and enculturation into an academic disciplinary community (social constructivism, conscientization)

▶ Course material that demonstrates valuing of diverse cultures, ethnic groups, classes, and genders (conscientization, learning styles) (Stage, 1998)

It is important to take these learning styles and practices of traditional students into account when creating and delivering library instruction. The development of instruction sessions and tools should meet the needs of students at their level and should incorporate a variety of learning theories to be most effective for all students.

Nontraditional students, commonly referred to as adult learners, now compose about half the student population at institutions of higher education. These students may be returning to school after a lengthy separation; they may have had no opportunity or access to higher education at the traditional age. They may be seeking to improve their skills in their chosen careers or to change careers entirely. Whatever the reason for their returning to school, adult learners have a different set of needs than traditional undergraduates. Because they are older than traditional students and have had different life experiences, adult learners have a stronger sense of direction and focus. They tend to be more self-directed and more motivated to succeed. Malcolm Knowles developed a seven-step process for adult learning, known as andragogy. This process requires educators to:

1. Set a cooperative learning climate
2. Create mechanisms for mutual planning
3. Arrange for a diagnosis of learner needs and interests
4. Enable the formulation of learning objectives based on the diagnosed needs and interests
5. Design sequential activities for achieving the objectives
6. Execute the design by selecting methods, materials, and resources
7. Evaluate the quality of the learning experience while diagnosing needs for further learning (Knowles, 1980)

These expectations are as important for library instruction as they are for classroom instruction. In a review of the literature about library instruction for adult learners, Helene Gold identified five themes:

1. Adult learners have unique social, physical, and cognitive characteristics that have an impact on learning.
2. A variety of barriers should be recognized and removed when creating library instruction for adults.
3. Traditional library instruction models are ineffective for the adult learner.
4. Andragogical learning theory should be used when creating library instruction and services for adult learners.
5. Multiple andragogical-based models and strategies have been successfully used to provide adult-centered library instruction (Gold, 2005).

These themes echo Knowles's process elements while leaving the exact approach open so that library instruction can be tailored to the specific program and student needs.

Learning theory should shape and guide librarians in their approach to instruction sessions and the development of instructional tools. The ACRL standards for information literacy are another important set of guidelines to incorporate into plans and practices. The standards call for instruction that enables the learner to achieve the following goals:

▶ Determine the extent of information needed
▶ Access the needed information effectively and efficiently
▶ Evaluate information and its sources critically
▶ Incorporate selected information into one's knowledge base
▶ Use information effectively to accomplish a specific purpose
▶ Understand the economic, legal, and social issues surrounding the use of information, and access and use information ethically and legally (ACRL, 2000)

These basic concepts of need, access, evaluation, and appropriate use are an important frame for all library instruction, regardless of age or learning style. The ACRL standards are utilized in several of the instruction programs described in this chapter.

INSTRUCTIONAL DESIGN

In examining library instruction outlines and practices from libraries that serve distance learners, two major models emerge. The responsive model represents instruction programs from one set of institutions that are based almost exclusively on user needs gathered in reference interactions or in previous instruction sessions. The structured model represents instruction programs from another set of institutions that are based on predefined goals, rubrics, and pedagogical outcomes. Structured programs go one step beyond responsive models by creating a set framework to address feedback gathered in reference and instruction interactions. This does not imply that responsive instruction programs do not have structured elements or that structured programs are devoid of user feedback. Instead, each set of instructional programs is founded on responsive or structured elements.

Instruction programs in the responsive model base instruction directly on user feedback and expressed user needs. Instead of using a rigid rubric, librarians listen to what users are telling them and focus on meeting those needs. As would be expected with this model, practices vary depending on the institution. The University of Phoenix, while incorporating institutional learning outcomes in its instructional philosophy, bases its formal tutorials on the rigorous examination of the content and quantity of reference questions (Bickford, 2005). Based on observations and instructor feedback, Fielding Graduate University developed tiered online tutorials to teach research skills, supplemented by open general research workshops, to meet the need for immediate instruction and promote long-term information literacy (Dussert, 2005). Responsive programs balance point of need help with in-depth instruction, mostly, but not entirely, in an online environment.

Structured library instruction programs differ the most from responsive programs in that they have fully articulated goals and learning objectives that are not specific to a particular instruction session or research need. The instruction outlines from the University of Maryland University College (UMUC) and Central Michigan University (CMU) (UMUC, 2004; CMU, 2003) focus on core concepts followed by topics that fall under those concepts. The Benedictine University outline goes one step further by providing expected outcomes for each lesson segment, followed by activities and handouts for each lesson (Benedictine, 2005). Structured programs also more explicitly state and employ information literacy concepts into their outlines and practices. The UMUC's model ties goals to specific ACRL standards and university instructional outcomes within each section, and Central Michigan University's and Benedictine's goals closely mirror the ACRL standards (ACRL, 2000).

The structured model enables librarians teaching in a variety of settings to cover the same concepts and provide a consistent level of instruction to all students. User feedback and session observations are incorporated into teaching styles and objectives on a periodic basis. However, all respondents using this model discussed shifting gears to another lesson component during an instruction session based on student needs. Interestingly, all the structured programs involve a heavy load of face-to-face instruction. Online tutorials and other forms of instruction play a variety of supporting roles.

Some libraries have based their instruction programs on a hybrid version of this model. They have broadly stated goals of what is covered in an instructional session but have no formal instructional objectives or outcomes. One such example is Gonzaga University (Kappus, 2005). Each curricular program is addressed differently, and the outcomes depend on varying levels of student abilities. The content and teaching format highly depend on student needs, and the way in which instructional objectives are articulated depends on class assignments and feedback.

There are similarities in the instruction approaches of both models. All respondents indicated that a rapidly increasing number of students and sessions in an off-campus learning environment forced them to examine their practices and decide on an instructional approach accordingly. Many also spoke of the challenge of addressing instructional needs in a variety of delivery formats, including in-person, online, and other distributed learning technologies. All approaches cover similar kinds of information, from how to access the library's Web site and off-campus services to constructing complex and effective search strategies. Finally, adherents to both models seek to address the need for an equitable and unified user experience that best fits student needs in their programs of study.

In designing a program, there are several factors to consider. What is being taught and what are the outcomes? How the program is executed will be driven by the answer to these questions. Another factor is the nature of the program or programs being served. Is the course online or off-site? Online courses may be served better by responsive models, while off-site offerings based on existing degree programs have more structured elements. How are similar programs supported in traditional delivery models? It is important to offer the same or equivalent services to students in off-campus programs, regardless of responsive or structured models. The needs and abilities of the user population also should be considered.

Closely tied to the nature of the program are the skills and availability of instruction librarians. Can librarians dedicate the preparation, teaching, and travel time to off-site or online programs while maintaining their other duties? Adopting a structured program requires consistent delivery in all programs offered, where responsive programs fill needs as they arise. An honest analysis of how instruction commitments will impact the individual librarian and related library staff is critical for deciding the right approach for a given institution.

Finally, consider the institutional climate and role of library instruction in the organization. Is the library responsible for instructional outcomes or other institutional standards, or is it a support organization? A structured program may get more institutional support in an outcomes-based environment but may not be as successful if the library is positioned in a support role. A responsive program can be designed to have measurable outcomes but by nature addresses needs reactively as opposed to proactively.

PROGRAM EXECUTION

Developing the outline and contents is only half of an instructional plan. The other half is the execution. Fielding Graduate University, which follows a responsive instructional model, uses a multitiered approach to reach its students. Several times a year, face-to-face seminars are held on online searching. Because not all students are able to participate in these seminars, the librarians have also developed an online tutorial ("Online Research Techniques for Graduate Students") which covers the building blocks of searching. The tutorial was designed to be viewed both sequentially and nonsequentially, allowing students to view topics of interest when they need the information (Dussert, 2005). The University of Phoenix, another responsive model institution, faced exponential growth at the turn of the twentieth-first century, which made face-to-face instruction impractical. As a result, the University of Phoenix created a series of online tutorials covering basic information literacy and research skills. Subject- and resource-specific tutorials were added on a "just in time" basis. The tutorials, combined with handbooks and assignments in introductory courses, help familiarize students with basic library research skills (Bickford, 2005).

The University of Maryland University College follows a structured model of library instruction and utilizes more than one method to reach its students. Face-to-face instruction and online tutorials are the two methods used to teach students, although much of the instructional growth has been in the online environment (UMUC, 2004). Central Michigan University, also following a structured model, allows for flexibility with the program. Librarians are free to present the concepts in their own manner as well as develop their own materials, whether in a face-to-face or an online environment (CMU, 2003). Benedictine University, with its structured program, relies primarily on face-to-face instruction, with only a handful of programs being offered in a solely online environment or at a considerable distance from the main campus. For those programs, the librarians are developing a series of online tutorials to meet the objectives of the instructional program (Benedictine, 2005).

The librarians at Gonzaga University use a hybrid approach to reach their students. The distance education population at Gonzaga consists largely of graduate students who live more than fifty miles from campus. Face-to-face instruction sessions are supplemented with handouts and online tutorials. Much of the instruction, though, takes place in face-to-face settings whether on the main campus or at the site (Kappus, 2005).

All of these institutions are similar in the execution of their instructional programs. The only apparent difference is in the degree to which the library relies on online tutorials as the primary method of instruction. Those libraries whose institutions have faced exponential growth and/or whose students are at a considerable distance must rely on online tutorials to reach the maximum number of students. Those institutions whose population is closer to home or has not faced such exponential growth are able to rely more on the traditional method of face-to-face instruction.

The six institutions studied are moving or have moved toward online instruction out of necessity rather than desire. Each would prefer to meet students in a face-to-face environment where all modes of communication are available as feedback. Online instruction removes or greatly reduces the personal touch from the instructional setting. On the other hand, there are many benefits to online instruction, such as meeting students at their point of need regardless of time and location, allowing for self-paced or nonsequential instruction as determined by the student, and so forth.

There are many guides available for designing face-to-face and online instructional programs and tutorials, each with its own set of tips and tricks. Based on their experiences, the authors would like to share their thoughts on the best practices for instructing students whether in person or online.

BEST PRACTICES

First, the key to good teaching is flexibility. This is true whether the students are across the room or across the country, whether the program is responsive or structured. The librarian must be able to adapt the materials and examples for the needs of the students. This may occur prior to the instruction, when the librarian meets with the instructor to discuss the library session, or it may happen on the fly as the librarian assesses the level of the students in the class. The librarian also needs to be flexible regarding the tools used to teach. In a face-to-face environment, the librarian must be prepared for the equipment not to work or the connections to fail. In an online environment, the librarian must take into account the technological skills and equipment of the users. In order to avoid additional barriers, online tutorials must download quickly and work correctly on a user's computer.

Second, it is important that the students know where to turn if they need additional help. As good as an instruction session may be, there are always areas that are not as clear as they could be or that do not work the way they did in the session. A student needs to know to whom these questions should be addressed and that questions will be addressed quickly. Lack of this type of information adds another barrier to the student's use of the library.

Third, try to meet as many learning styles as possible with the instruction session. It is important to attempt to incorporate the same information in a variety of ways for the students. If one is using a lecture format for a part of the session, have handouts available for those students who are visual learners. Add voice narration to online tutorials to aid auditory learners. Allow time for students to practice what is being taught to aid the kinesthetic learners.

Fourth, try to incorporate active learning into each lesson. This will allow students the opportunity to participate in the session rather than merely hear what is being said to them. There are a variety of articles in the education literature that provide samples of activities for active learning.

Fifth, grow as a teacher. While each person has his or her own style of teaching, everyone should strive for growth. Incorporate a new strategy into an instruction session. Assess what is happening in the learning environment, and strive to correct the problems. Update examples, let the students take a more active role in the process, or add technology to a presentation. There is a wealth of information available in the library and education literature to provide guidance for growth.

CONCLUSION

The challenge in distance library instruction is to provide an experience that is comparable to the on-campus experience. The Distance Learning Section of the Association of College and Research Libraries has developed a set of guidelines for distance learning library services that address all areas of service. The guidelines indicate the need for a strong support base at the home library (ACRL, 2004).

There are additional challenges in the delivery of high-level instruction and support to remote patrons, including communication channels and technology. Feedback is an important element in instruction, but it is not always available in distance learning situations. In some cases, instructional programs are delivered electronically and asynchronously rather than in person. This sort of delivery makes it difficult for the librarian to know whether the recipients truly grasp the concepts presented and whether the students' instructional needs are being met. To address this, many libraries have developed a series of communication tools and support links to help ensure success on the part of their users. For example, many academic library Web sites include links to tutorials designed to address confusion or misunderstanding about access to various resources or the use of specific tools.

Telephone and e-mail access also are vital elements of a successful remote instruction program. Some libraries are using chat or instant messaging as a supplement to the instructional offerings, and there are cases in which academic librarians are embedded into online academic programs where they can address library-specific issues when they arise. Regardless of the support options made available, the key to success in educating students in distance programs lies in the thoughtful construction and consistent execution of a strong library instruction program.

▶ FIGURE 1.1: Sample University Instructional Outlines

Instructional Outlines:	Benedictine University
	Central Michigan University
	Gonzaga University
	University of Maryland University College

Benedictine University
Information Literacy Program
Lesson Overviews
March 2005

Overview

Lesson 1: Orientation
Goal:
- ▶ Library users understand that the library is available to support them as they work through their program.

Objectives:
- ▶ Students are registered as library patrons and have completed the delivery preferences form as appropriate.
- ▶ Students can locate general information about the Benedictine Library.
- ▶ Students can identify three types of resources available through the Benedictine Library.
- ▶ Students can identify four services offered by the Benedictine Library.

Lesson 2: What Information?
Goals:
- ▶ Library users can determine the extent of information needed.

Objectives:
- ▶ The student can articulate his information needs.
- ▶ The student can determine types and formats of potential sources of information.

Lesson 3: Accessing Information
Goal:
- ▶ Library users can access needed information effectively and efficiently.

Objectives:
- ▶ Students can identify appropriate tools needed to access information.
- ▶ Students can determine when it is appropriate to use controlled vocabulary and keyword searching techniques.
- ▶ Students understand how to limit the results of searches.
- ▶ Students understand and can apply Boolean logic to searching.
- ▶ Students can construct effective and efficient searches.
- ▶ Students can correctly interpret the results of a search.
- ▶ Students can locate the hard copy of a citation.

Lesson 4: Evaluating Information
Goal:
- ▶ Library users can evaluate information and its sources critically.

(Cont'd.)

► FIGURE 1.1: Sample University Instructional Outlines *(Continued)*

Benedictine University *(Continued)*

Objectives:
- ► Student will describe a minimum of 5 criteria that can be used to evaluate information and its sources.
- ► Student will apply criteria to evaluate information and its sources.

Lesson 5: Citation Management

Goal:
- ► Library users will use RefWorks to manage citations.

Objectives:
- ► Students will register to use RefWorks.
- ► Students will maintain citation database by entering citations manually and by importing citations.
- ► Students will use RefWorks to prepare papers and theses as well as bibliographies in appropriate styles.

Central Michigan University
Off-Campus Library Services [OCLS]
General Bibliographic Instruction Outline

I. OCLS overview—tour of services
   a. Hours
   b. Contact information
   c. Overview of services and how to use them
   d. Using OCLS website

II. Defining/refining a topic statement
   a. Analyzing a topic statement to generate related concepts
   b. Narrowing/broadening a topic
   c. Knowing when to use a book, a journal, and the web
   d. When to call a reference librarian

III. Finding books/materials owned by CMU Libraries
   a. Description of library's online catalog
   b. Using the library's online catalog
      i. Keyword
      ii. Author
      iii. Title—journal and book
      iv. Limits—general collection, sort by date
   c. Saving/Exporting records
   d. Requesting materials through Document Delivery

IV. Finding journal articles
   a. Using a library database versus the web to search for information
   b. Databases and what they contain—e.g., citations, abstracts, full-text
   c. Selecting the appropriate database for your topic
   d. Telling the difference between research/scholarly/peer-reviewed, etc., articles and popular/trade/news articles
   e. Searching the library databases for Information
      i. Specific subject databases
      ii. Keywords
      iii. Subject headings
      iv. Limits
      v. Explanation of search interfaces
   f. Saving/Exporting records
   g. Requesting articles through Document Delivery

V. Specific internet resources and sample capstone projects available from the OCLS website

(Cont'd.)

▶ **FIGURE 1.1: Sample University Instructional Outlines** *(Continued)*

Central Michigan University *(Continued)*

VI. Citing sources/plagiarism
   a. Style manuals
   b. Examples of complete citations

Instructional Objectives

At the end of an OCLS bibliographic session, students should:

- ▶ Be aware of Off-Campus Library Services, including how to access databases and request assistance
- ▶ Understand tools for refining a research topic
- ▶ Able to identify and select materials and resources available for finding information on a variety of research topics
- ▶ Understand how to critically evaluate information
- ▶ Be aware of resources available for assistance in avoiding plagiarism and properly citing information sources

Further Explanation of OCLS Instruction Program

The goals behind the Off-Campus Library Services (OCLS) instruction program are to re-acquaint non-traditional adult learners with the academic library system, inform them that the service is available to offer support throughout their academic program, and provide them with tools to begin their library research projects. While there is no formal way the information covered in the outlines needs to be presented, and each OCLS librarian tends to create his or her own materials, the unit is in agreement regarding key points and objectives that the instructional sessions need to include.

The outline and objectives have been formulated and revised through a variety of means. Librarian and faculty perceptions of student needs and analysis of student reference questions and student survey results have all influenced the focus of the instruction. The instruction program continually evolves as technology advances and Central Michigan University's off-campus programs develop and change. Periodically, OCLS librarians meet and review what each individual is teaching in the classroom (face to face and online), ensuring that everyone is covering similar material and addressing the key objectives. Librarians continually share feedback from students and faculty members and discuss potential changes to the library instruction sessions informally through email or regularly scheduled department meetings as well.

The OCLS instruction program targets specific courses within the different degree programs offered through the university. These courses require some level of library related research. Librarians monitor course schedules and syllabi and make arrangements with faculty to attend the courses and deliver tailored library instruction.

Gonzaga University

Foley Library / Gonzaga University
Theresa Kappus /ILL & Distance Services Librarian
509-323-3820 / 800-498-5931 / kappus@gonzaga.edu

Library Services for Distant Students in Education

Library Main Menu

- ▶ **Catalog—Search** for books and other materials located in the Foley library collection (approx. 400,000 titles). You can also check your library account, renew books and place books on hold.
- ▶ **Indexes & Databases—www.foley.gonzaga.edu/indexes.** Search for articles on your topic in full-text databases or subject specific indexes. Databases are grouped by general topic areas.
- ▶ **Periodicals at Foley**—(see below)
- ▶ **Interlibrary Loan / ILLiad**—Request books and articles not available through Foley library or one of our full-text databases.
- ▶ **Hours**—Check here for the library's operating hours, including holidays and semester breaks.
- ▶ **News & Events**—A link to the library's newsletter *Foley Front & Center.*

Periodicals at Foley—www.foley.gonzaga.edu/periodicals. Periodicals at Foley is your gateway to finding journals available to you as a student at GU. Foley Library subscribes to over 1200 print journals and has access to over 18,500 electronic journal titles.

(Cont'd.)

▶ **FIGURE 1.1: Sample University Instructional Outlines** *(Continued)*

Gonzaga University *(Continued)*

▶ Identify journals owned by Foley Library *and link to full-text options* if available.
▶ *Always* check this first *before* requesting an Interlibrary Loan for an article.
▶ Distance Students, if you find a journal that is *not* available online, but *is* available in print format at Foley Library, fill out an article request form using ILLiad and we'll send you a copy of the article electronically.

Logging in
▶ **Foley Library Catalog** requires your Gonzaga ID number and your last name in order to access your library records or make a request (place a hold) on a book.
▶ **Databases** require a login for off-campus use. The default login is: User Name: first initial + first 7 letters of your last name / Password: first initial + last initial + last four digits of your social security number. Example: User name: dcopperf Password: dc1234

Interlibrary Loan/ILLiad—www.foley.gonzaga.edu/ILL If Foley Library doesn't have a book or a journal you need we may be able to get it for you from another library.
▶ Register for an ILLiad account, then use the forms provided by ILLiad or place your request through the ILLiad link on our databases.
▶ Please limit your interlibrary loan requests to 10–15 per week or call 800-498-5941 and let the ILL Office know if you need to do more.
▶ Always check Foley Library's Catalog (for books) or "Periodicals at Foley" (for articles) *before* placing an interlibrary loan request!
▶ Distant students may use ILLiad to request articles from print journals held at Foley.
▶ Articles are sent electronically and usually arrive within a few days.
▶ Books may take several weeks. Lending libraries mail them to us and then we mail them to you. You are responsible for return postage.
▶ Due dates *and* renewals are at the discretion of the lending library.

Suggested Databases:
ERIC • *Professional Development* • *Psychology & Behavioral Sciences Collection* • PsycInfo • *Sociological Abstracts* • *Academic Search Premier* • *ProQuest · WorldCat (for books)*

Full Text Databases—ERIC, ProQuest & others
▶ Limit to Peer Reviewed/Scholarly journals.
▶ Look for a link to the database's list of "Subject Terms," "Thesaurus," or "Topic Guide" to identify additional keywords or recommended subject terms related to your search.
▶ Click on subject headings within a record to search related topics.
▶ Narrow your search. Limit by subjects, dates, "Boolean operators," etc.
▶ Limit to Full Text only (not recommended).
▶ Create a "marked list" (Ebsco: put items in a "folder").
▶ Options: Print, save or E-mail articles.
▶ Take the Ebsco tutorial: http://support.epnet.com/CustSupport/Tutorials/basicSearchingAcademic.html
▶ Create a MyEbscoHost account to save your ERIC searches.

First Search Databases—PsycInfo, SocAbs, WorldCat, etc.
▶ There may be limited full text access depending on the database or index you choose.
▶ Use WorldCat to search for books in other libraries "worldwide."
▶ Use limiters (language, dates, etc.).
▶ Use truncation: bicycl? (retrieves bicycle, bicycles, bicycling).
▶ Use subject headings within a record to search related topics.
▶ You can submit Interlibrary Loan requests by using the link to ILLiad within most databases.

What's a Boolean Operator? That's the terminology describing the limiting and expanding capabilities of the words "and, or, not" in electronic database searching.
▶ AND – retrieves documents with both terms. (teenagers and literacy)
▶ OR – retrieves documents with either term or both terms. (teenagers or adolescents)
▶ NOT – retrieves documents containing one term but not the other (motorcycle not Harley)

(Cont'd.)

▶ **FIGURE 1.1: Sample University Instructional Outlines** *(Continued)*

Gonzaga University *(Continued)*

Other Resources
- ▶ **NetLibrary** on the Indexes & Databases page. Provides electronic access to selected books. These may be quite useful depending on your topic. Create a username and password to "check out" these online books.
- ▶ **SUBJECT GUIDES**—Click on Subject Guides on the left menu of the Foley homepage, then select a topic for links to some great print and online resources selected by Foley librarians.
- ▶ **ERIC**—In addition to the database, you can search through the ERIC website http://eric.ed.gov/

Web addresses & Help
- ▶ **Foley Library:** www.foley.gonzaga.edu
- ▶ **Distance Services:** www.foley.gonzaga.edu/distance or kappus@gonzaga.edu
- ▶ **Indexes & Databases:** www.foley.gonzaga.edu/indexes
- ▶ **Reference Help:** 800-498-5941 / foleyweb@its.gonzaga.edu
- ▶ **Reference Live Chat:** Available when the library is open. Select the "Contact Us" link on the Foley Homepage and then select "Questions? Click for live help" and start your chat.

University of Maryland University College

Information and Library Services
Core Concepts for Library Instruction

The University of Maryland University College (UMUC) is the Open University of the state of Maryland and of the United States with a focus on the educational needs of the nontraditional student. UMUC provides higher education both online and in face-to-face settings throughout the world.

Over the past few years, UMUC has experienced a tremendous growth in enrollments. As a result, between spring 2000 and 2004, library instruction at UMUC grew by more than 800%, with most of the growth occurring in the online environment.

In order to handle the growth in library instruction requests, and demand of myriad modalities, including online sessions and off-site and on-site face-to-face sessions, UMUC instructional librarians at the Information and Library Services (ILS) formed a team in spring 2003 charged with developing a structured and scalable library instruction approach. The team reviewed concepts and materials covered in library instruction sessions and developed information literacy objectives mapped to the School of Undergraduate Studies standards, which in turn were adapted from the ACRL Information Literacy Competency Standards for Higher Education.

Based on its work, the team developed a set of core concepts to be covered in a library instruction session. The core concepts became a framework for a template that presents the information in the online classroom environment and serves as a guide for face-to-face sessions. While a template presents the core concepts, librarians are free to modify it to fit the needs of particular classes or assignments. In addition to the core concepts and the template, a standard exercise was also developed that could be assigned as either required or optional by the instructor.

Outline: Core Concepts

1) **Introduce the ILS Web site and provide virtual presentation of information and library services.**
   Topics included:
   a. Online access to research resources.
   b. 24/7 research help via telephone, e-mail, and live chat.
   c. Online guides and tutorials to help with research and proper citations.
   d. Reference hours for drop-in research help or appointments.
   e. Electronic delivery of articles not found in full-text in the library databases.
   f. Delivery of library books to distance education students.
   g. Virtual Library Classroom—a self-study class available online.
   h. Audio/visual presentation of library services and resources.

   IL standards: determine nature and extent of information needed; access needed information effectively and efficiently.

(Cont'd.)

▶ FIGURE 1.1: Sample University Instructional Outlines *(Continued)*

University of Maryland University College *(Continued)*

2) **Discuss use of library and non-library Internet resources for research and the importance of critically evaluating sources.**

Topics included:

a. Evaluation criteria.
b. Identifying types of sources.
c. Determining if an article is scholarly.
d. ILS Guides:
    i) Searching the Internet.
    ii) Using the Web for Research.
    iii) Evaluating Electronic Resources.
    iv) Identify and Locate Scholarly Journals.

IL standard: evaluate information and sources critically.

3) **Outline a research process and strategies for developing topics and effective searches.**

Topics included:

a. Research Skills Tutorial
b. Deciding types of information needed and available (Web sites, articles, books).
c. Gathering background information.
d. Search basics:
    i) Select topic.
    ii) Identifying search terms.
    iii) Keyword vs. subject searching.
    iv) Boolean operators.

IL standards: determine nature and extent of information needed; access needed information effectively and efficiently.

4) **Introduction to specific search tools and skills.**

Topics included:

a. Effective ways to access library databases.
b. Using the database descriptions.
c. Finding full-text articles.
d. Explaining a citation and reading a database record.
e. Using "find it" (or ExLibris SFX).
f. Using the Journal Finder (ExLibris Citation Linker) and Jake.
g. Getting full text articles via the ILS' document delivery service.
h. USMAI library catalog (reading a record, basic searching, requesting an item (signing in), my account, saved items and searches).
i. Guide to finding electronic books.
j. Guide to Find Articles: Using Library Databases.
k. Technical help accessing a library database.
l. Signing in to databases.
m. Show basic search.
n. Refine a search.
o. Basic navigation.
p. Known item search.
q. Manage results (e-mail, save, mark list, etc.).

IL standards: determines nature and extent of information needed; accesses needed information effectively and efficiently.

(Cont'd.)

▶ **FIGURE 1.1: Sample University Instructional Outlines** *(Continued)*

University of Maryland University College *(Continued)*

5) **Citing according to MLA or APA standards.**

Topics included:

a. UMUC Effective Writing Center plagiarism tutorial

b. ILS' APA citation tutorial.

c. APA and MLA guides to citing electronic resources.

d. UMUC's Virtual Academic Integrity Laboratory (VAIL) portal for students.

e. VAIL citation guide: Citation! Citation! Citation!

IL standard: understands many of the economic, legal, and social issues surrounding the use of information and access, and uses information ethically and legally.

REFERENCES

Association of College and Research Libraries. 2004. *Guidelines for Distance Learning Library Services: Final Version Revision.* Chicago: ACRL.

Association of College and Research Libraries. 2000. *Information Literacy Competency Standards for Higher Education.* Chicago: ACRL. Available: www.ala.org/ala/acrl/acrlstandards/standards.pdf.

Benedictine University Library. 2005. *Information Literacy Program: Lesson Overviews.*

Bickford, David. Personal communication, August 2005.

Central Michigan University Libraries. 2003. *Off-Campus Library Services: General Bibliographic Instruction Outline.*

DuCharme-Hansen, B. and P. Dupin-Bryant. 2005. "Distance Education Plans: Course Planning for Online Adult Learners." *Tech Trends* 49, no. 2: 31–39.

Dussert, Alain. Personal communication, September 13, 2005.

Gold, Helene. 2005. "Engaging the Adult Learner: Creating Effective Library Instruction." *Portal: Libraries & the Academy* 5: 467–481.

Kappus, Theresa. Personal communication, July 25, 2005.

Knowles, Malcolm S. 1980. *Modern Practice of Adult Education.* Chicago: Association Press.

Stage, Frances K., et al. 1998. "Creating Learning Centered Classrooms: What Does Learning Theory Have To Say?" ASHE-ERIC Higher Education Report, 26, no. 4. U.S.; District of Columbia.

University of Maryland University College Information and Library Services. [2004?]. *Core Concepts for Library Instruction.*

►2

LEARNING AND MASTERING THE TOOLS OF THE TRADE

KAREN ELIZABETH JAGGERS

Overview: A toolbox full of tools to help librarians who are preparing library instruction sessions for distance learners is the topic for this chapter. The author presents and describes nine tools that are useful for the distance instruction librarian. Some of the tools included are determining learning objectives, engaging the students, planning, communicating, and assessing the instruction sessions.

INTRODUCTION

Each profession has tools; some are for everyday use, and some are kept for special occasions. Library instruction also has tools upon which one can draw while preparing educational materials for the distance learner. While a successful program can be set up without looking into all of the areas addressed below, the program can be enhanced and the learners will benefit from their use.

TOOLBOX FOR INSTRUCTION TO DISTANCE LEARNERS

Preparing a toolbox for instruction to distance learners is challenging because of the wealth of material that is available. Although the written record on library instruction had a slow beginning (Lorenzen, 2001; Hardesty, 1989), a brief review of the literature today produces so many articles on instruction in general and, more to the point, for the remote user, that it is difficult to remain current in the field. In addition to the articles and studies there are bibliographies and Web sites that point to the information, and discussion lists and blogs in which practitioners share experiences. For the beginning or the experienced librarian there is a world of expertise from which to draw.

One toolkit will not fit all instructional programs. Tools should be developed and utilized as needed. A librarian may work alone, or with a large staff; may be on-site at a branch campus; or may provide support from a main-campus library to one or multiple sites. There are as many variations as there are schools providing distance programs. This toolkit will address generalities and approaches to information or elements of instruction.

Tool 1—Develop a Working Definition of Instruction within Your Work Space

Gather the information to define the elements of instruction that will work best within your environment. Identify what is already in place, using a broad view to encompass all of the activities or interactions between the library and the end user that inform or teach. Think globally. Some of the elements to consider are instruction or point-of-need assistance on the Web site, brochures or handouts, contacts at a reference desk, presentations in classrooms or at orientations, chat sessions, tutorials, and interactive instruction through Web conferencing software, including links placed or pushed to the user within the software.

Library instruction does not begin in a vacuum. It develops out of a perceived need, expressed by the patrons, by the faculty, or by the librarians. Create a file of your institutional or library goals and how instruction fits within those goals. Include a brief historical overview of how instruction has been presented in the past, what has worked, and what has not worked. Look for an environmental scan that covers the makeup of the student body you serve, with demographics, age of students, diversity, and distribution. Create a list of teaching centers, classrooms, equipment, access, contacts, travel distance, and accommodations. Each site will be different; make notations for future reference.

Tool 2—Determine the Learning Objectives and Create the Learning Outcomes

There are different ways to approach what to teach. Student assessments or focus groups reveal gaps in student knowledge (Carter, 2002; Quarton, 2003). A literature review will help clarify why instruction is important and what the instruction should entail. An emphasis can be placed on what the students need to know about the library, including services and resources that are offered, with the goal of equipping them to choose appropriate articles indexes, to be successful in searching and retrieving information from remote locations, to construct complex searches, to effectively conduct literature reviews, and to become independent searchers (Casey, 2002). Or a review can be made of the learning outcomes developed by academic departments to see how collaborations can be developed to enhance student learning. Another approach would be to start with the goals and objectives outlined within educational literacy standards (ACRL, 2003). For an in-depth discussion of elements to consider see the research agenda identified by the Association for College and Research Libraries ("Research," 2003).

Become familiar with the academic programs of your institution. Study the course offerings that will be targeted. Collect syllabi or link them electronically to departmental Web pages. Meet with the faculty, set up lines of communication, and establish areas in which collaboration will occur.

Consider the location of the instruction and the mode in which the classes are taught. What is appropriate? Step back and look at how instruction is being done now; consider the alternatives. What is the audience, what are the learning objectives, what is available in your toolbox in the way of technology, what staffing is available, how do your students learn?

Explore teaching methods and how they work in particular circumstances. For example, online instruction delivered over the Internet is accessible from remote locations and can be used at the student's convenience. Information placed on the library Web site is available at the point of need and can incorporate interactive teaching methods or link to an FAQ. It can also provide contact with a librarian from the home institution or one contracted to provide the assistance. Oral presentations provide personal interactions. No one method will work for all situations. Build the box of tools and use the ones that fit the task at hand.

Tool 3—Engage the Students

Adapt presentations to the age, ethnicity and abilities of the learners. The literacy levels, technological skills, and library knowledge will vary from class to class, from semester to semester. Pursue the literature on left-brain and right-brain preferences and on visual, auditory, and kinesthetic learning. Become conversant with instructional theories and strategies, with learning styles, and with how to deal with diverse populations. Invest time in workshops or webcasts on why, how, and what to instruct.

Decide whether to have a broad program that will meet the needs of current and future students, addressing a diverse, international clientele involving different languages and cultures, second-language learners, or multiple cognitive styles. Or will the instruction be focused on the current, immediate needs of the existing students and be adapted as need arises? Will instruction be limited to information literacy? Whichever decision is made, the toolbox should contain information on how the distance learner differs from the on-campus counterpart. Consider learners within driving distance, for which face-to-face instruction is possible, and remote users, those across town, out of state, across the nation, or international. An institution may involve any or all of the student groups.

Build a knowledge file, drawing information from articles, discussion lists, and workshops. Trial-and-error experiences from colleagues will enrich the file. As class instruction is developed, it will be shaped by the knowledge you have or that you collect concerning the best way to work with a distance class. Share your knowledge with your colleagues. Online discussion lists ("Off-campus," 2006; Regional, 2003) are a good venue for learning from other librarians.

Tool 4—Plan in Advance

Traveling to a remote site involves arranging for transportation, filling out travel authorization forms, working with a contact person for room preparation, and allowing for driving time. The instruction itself involves numerous components that need to be put in place (Cybela, 2002). While preparing slides or handouts for use with an interactive television class, add in transmission time for getting the handouts to the remote locations. Whether you prepare chat sessions or tutorials or set up informational links within a Web site, time for organization, development, and evaluation is needed. Allow time to learn how to work with the technology, and build in time for the remote learner to become familiar with the software.

Prepare a checklist of tasks with target dates for completion. Some items on the checklist will need to be done well in advance. Some can be checked off at the last minute. Do not take anything for granted; check out the details. Once the instruction has ended make notes of changes to implement for the next class, drawing on the student reactions or comments on assessment forms.

Tool 5—Establish Lines of Communication

Maintain a list of faculty with a means of being notified when new faculty are hired. Have an introduction to library services become part of faculty orientation. Include basic library information about library services. Provide forms on the Web site for faculty requests for instruction. Faculty that are comfortable with library services are more likely to utilize the services themselves and build library resources into their classes. When the faculty inform their students of the availability of library resources and utilize the resources in their classes, a primary part of the instruction program is addressed (Caspers, 2000; Fraser, 2002). Too often distance students complete a large portion of their coursework without knowing the resources or services that the library offers (Quarton, 2003; Kenny, 1997). Pursue opportunities to co-teach, a collaboration that increases your knowledge of teaching and the faculty member's knowledge of the library resources and how to access them.

Be informed of decisions made within the academic departments, and in other campus departments, that will impact what you instruct. For example, if the campus is utilizing a bibliographic manager for citations, the library will receive questions on how to download information from the library databases. Attendance at training offered within the academic departments can increase the librarian's knowledge and visibility. If possible collaborate with the faculty and the Web-course designers to create templates to assist faculty in adding library instruction and resources into their classes.

In institutions with multiple campuses, collaboration among libraries, with cross training among campuses, can ensure that each can point the students to the right information or contacts. Library Web sites within the system should support one another.

Contact academic advisers at multicampus sites to decide on the best way to distribute the library information. Advisers often know when students or faculty need assistance and can give users library information. Provide brochures to share with new or potential faculty and students. Information can be shared within the local campus newsletter, in faculty packets or posted in electronic mailings, or within Web courseware.

Often classes are offered in other institutions, including community colleges, high schools, vocational schools, public libraries, and private schools. Keep a file with contact information for the person or persons to work through to set up the classroom. Network with librarians, faculty and administrators, other distance education library instructors, and librarians at the sites where the students take the classes. Provide information on resources that are available at the local site and in the local area, and if there are reciprocal borrowing privileges.

Tool 6—Incorporate Technology

Because of the growing numbers of distance learners, shrinking library staffs, tighter budgets, and the need to provide information 24/7, librarians have embraced technology as a tool to enhance the teaching and learning experience. The toolbox should include software that can be utilized as needed. High-tech and low-tech solutions abound. Among them are handouts, fliers, printed guides, slide programs, phone calls, help sessions, library skills classes, videos, and tutorials. Communication is promoted through toll-free phone lines, e-mail, and Web forms. The personal touch is presented through instruction at sites or through Web conferencing or chat software. Sophisticated software may take more startup time and require a greater learning curve—for the librarian and the end user.

Challenges that will shape the instruction include the number of users, user abilities, distances involved, and amount of information that needs to be transmitted. Technology can assist in overcoming these challenges. Much material has been created for the distance learner utilizing technology, including learning objects, tutorials, computer-assisted instruction, Web conferencing software, and chat and instant messaging systems. Web pages and tutorials can be enhanced with simulations, animation, or video.

Keep abreast of what is new, realizing that some technologies will fade quickly and others will continue to be utilized. What you will use will depend on your institutional goals, funding, and available personnel. A library with access to instructional designers and staff who can develop games and create media-rich presentations will choose an instructional program different from that of a one-person regional campus library. Libraries serving large programs with multiple campuses or classrooms will develop programs that are scalable and easily revised.

Be aware not only of the technology used by the library but also by the other units on the campus. These technologies may become part of your instructional program, or you may be called on to teach them.

Tool 7—Include Assessment

Although this tool is falling late in the list, assessment should be applied throughout the instruction process. Pretests illustrate the need for instruction and indicate the skills that need to be developed. Posttests measure the learning outcomes. Focus groups provide insight into the user's viewpoint and can expose gaps in the learner's grasp of library processes. Information can be gathered through surveys, comments pages on Web sites, or questions added to faculty or course evaluations. Since reference desks and AskALibrarian services receive questions that indicate users do not understand library services and resources, utilize their statistics and comment forms in preparing instruction.

Assessment tools are also used for accreditation purposes. They may measure qualitative or quantitative output. Assessment forms are readily available within the literature, with discussion of the advantages of particular instruments.

Tool 8—Plan for Marketing within Your Program

A good marketing campaign will alleviate some of the need for instruction. Consider utilizing the campus newspaper, handouts within faculty orientation packets, and mail or e-mail announcements concerning new library resources or services or instructional sessions. Plan your strategy for letting your clientele know what is available and how to use it. Again, make a checklist; plan in advance.

Tool 9—Maintain a Service Attitude

The ultimate tool is having the desire to work with the distance learner to remove barriers that prevent the efficient and timely use of library resources and services. Pursue a goal of assisting students to become independent learners, providing them with the skills for successful research.

Conclusion

The toolbox is never full. While overused and redundant resources may be removed from the box, new approaches to instruction will be added. If you keep the tools polished through use, you will have a resource that will support your endeavors and that you can share.

REFERENCES

ACRL Distance Learning Section Guidelines Committee. 2002. "Guidelines for Distance Learning Library Services." *College & Research Libraries News* 61: 1023–1029.

ACRL Instruction Section. 2003. "Guidelines for Instruction Programs in Academic Libraries." Available: www.ala.org/ala/acrl/acrlstandards/guidelinesinstruction.htm (accessed January 24, 2006).

"Blackboard and WebCt Are One—Blog." 2006. Available: http://blog.scs.sk.ca/mt/blackboardwebct/ (accessed January 24, 2006).

Carter, Elizabeth W. 2002. "Doing the Best You Can with What You Have: Lessons Learned from Outcomes Assessment." *Journal of Academic Librarianship* 28, no. 1–2: 36–41.

Casey, Anne M. 2002. "The Library and the Development of Online Courses." In *Library Services for Business Students in Distance Education: Issues and Trends.* Edited by Shari Buxbaum. New York: Haworth Information Press.

Caspers, Jean S. 2000. "Outreach to Distance Learners: When the Distance Education Instructor Sends Students to the Library, Where Do They Go?" In *Library Outreach, Partnerships, and Distance Education: Reference Librarians at the Gateway.* Edited by Wendi Arant and Pixey A. Mosley. New York: Haworth Information Press.

Cybela, Joan E. 2002. "Enhancing the Educational Impact of Distance Learning Experiences at the Local Level." Available: www.uwex.edu/disted/cybela.htm (accessed January 24, 2006).

Fraser, Mary G., Shari Buxbaum, and Amy Blair. 2002. "The Library and the Development of Online Courses." In *Library Services for Business Students in Distance Education: Issues and Trends.* Edited by Shari Buxbaum. New York: Haworth Information Press.

Godwin-Jones, Bob. 2003. "Blogs and Wikis: Environments for On-line Collaboration." *Language Learning and Technology* 7, no. 2: 12–16.

Hardesty, Larry, and John Mark Tucker. 1989. "An Uncertain Crusade: The History of Library Use Instruction in a Changing Educational Environment." In *Academic Librarianship Past, Present, and Future: A Festschrift in Honor of David Kaser.* Edited by John Richardson, Jr. and Jinnie Y. Davis. Englewood, CO: Libraries Unlimited Inc.

Kenny, Dallas. 1997. "Teaching the 'Net without a Net: Custom Simulations Boost Freshmen's PC Skills." *THE Journal* 24, no. 7: 87.

"LMS Learning Management Systems Options and Comparisons." 2006. Available: http://ctlet.brocku.ca/webct/LMS_Options_and_Comparisons (accessed January 23, 2006).

Lorenzen, M. 2001. "Brief History of Library Instruction in the United States." *Illinois Libraries* 83, no. 2: 8–18.

"Off-Campus Library Services List." 2006. Available: http://listserv.utk.edu/ (accessed January 23, 2006).

Old Dominion University. 2005. "Resources for Distance Learning Library Services." Available: www.lib.odu.edu/distance/dersrcs.htm (accessed December 15, 2005).

Quarton, Barbara. 2003. "Research Skills and the New Undergraduate." *Journal of Instructional Psychology* 30, no. 2; June: 120–124.

"Regional Campus Libraries Discussion Group." 2006. Available: RCL-DG@pc.fsu.edu.

"Research Agenda for Library Instruction and Information Literacy." 2003. *Library & Information Science Research* 25, no. 4: 479–487.

Slade, Alexander L. 2005. "Library Services for Distance Learning: The Fourth Bibliography." Available: http://uviclib.uvic.ca/dls/bibliography4.html (accessed December 15, 2005).

Sloan, Bernie, and Sharon Stoerger. 2005. "Library Support for Distance Learning." Available: www.lis.uiuc.edu/%7Eb-sloan/libdist.htm#gen.

University of Washington Information Literacy Lab. 2005. "Information Literacy Learning: An Approach for the 21st century." Available: www.lib.washington.edu/Ougl/instructors/uwill.html (accessed September 13, 2005).

University of Wisconsin-Extension. 2006. Distance Education Clearinghouse. Available: www.uwex.edu/disted/home.html (accessed January 25, 2006).

USDLA. 2005. USDLA—United States Distance Learning Association Homepage. www.usdla.org/ (accessed December 7, 2005).

▶3

SCHEDULING AND VISITING OFF-CAMPUS CLASSES

LADONNA GUILLOT
BETH STAHR

Overview: Planning, scheduling, and working with the course instructor are all parts of a successful library instruction session at an off-campus site. This chapter is a helpful guide for those off-campus librarians who are beginning their off-site visits or for those who are looking for ways to make their off-campus library instruction more effective.

INTRODUCTION

Pedagogical design for distance learning and library models of service interact at the institutional level to determine how best to provide library services to regional centers. Librarians are challenged to serve patrons in remote facilities, which vary from fully equipped branch campuses to sometimes sparsely furnished high school classrooms. Success depends on a number of factors. Effective planning and scheduling with the flexibility to adapt for the unforeseen are crucial. Increasingly, technological competencies and troubleshooting skills assist in successful presentations and delivery of services. Collaboration with teaching faculty, site coordinators, instructional technology staff, and administrators ensures implementation of the institution's mission to serve all learners. Above all, the needs and concerns of the learners must be understood and addressed to provide a successful remote-site library instruction program.

While developing effective library services for distance learners is primarily a library issue, it cannot be successfully implemented without the support of campus administrators and faculty. Administrators must be convinced that providing library services in support of educational opportunities at off-campus sites affords all students a comparable educational experience. Lebowitz (1997) delineates four realities that must be recognized by campus administrators: the increase in the number of distance learning students, the expectations of regional and discipline-specific accrediting bodies, the value added to the educational experience by library services, and the need for instruction in academic research by off-campus students.

FACULTY PARTICIPATION

Faculty participation is important in order to schedule library instruction and make library instruction valued by distance learners. John Butler (1997), project director of a grant, in "From the Margins to the Mainstream: Developing Library Support for Distance Learning," emphasized the need for faculty "buy-in": "Faculty awareness and involvement remain critical factors in the delivery of library services. For many distance learners, the faculty member is the main channel of communication to students for information about campus services, including those of the library. It is strongly believed that raising faculty awareness of library resources and services will, in turn, raise that of students."

It seems that distance learners, who are already disassociated from the main campus, need even more faculty reinforcement about the significance of library instruction. It is crucial to the success of library distance learning services programs and distance student success that librarians foster relationships with faculty who teach at remote sites. Jill S. Markgraf (2002: 351) provides useful suggestions "to build and nurture relationships with faculty, to promote and market services, and to provide reliable, timely responses to requests and demonstrated need for service" based on her effort as a distance learning librarian at the University of Wisconsin–Eau Claire. "Capturing the moment is not exclusive to the marketing and sales professional; it also applies to us—remote campus librarians" (Lockerby, et al., 2004: 250).

SCHEDULING LIBRARY INSTRUCTION

To build success into a remote-site instruction program, librarians need to create a convenient and obvious system to schedule instruction sessions. Web forms are often used for reservations. The librarian should provide immediate feedback so that instructors sense the importance placed on this library service. If Web forms are used, they need to clearly request the location, date, time, number of class participants, and scope of instruction. Furthermore, the Web form should request the details of specific class research assignments and types of resources the instructor wants presented and used by the students.

The librarian needs to establish who will be responsible for scheduling the class location at the off-campus facility. If the session is to be held during the normal instruction period, the classroom meeting space will already have been assigned. If the faculty has access to a computer lab or classroom with Internet access different from the normally scheduled class location, the librarian should confirm who will be reserving the space and equipment.

Timing is a key element in scheduling library instruction. Sessions held too soon or too late in the course duration may fail to sustain student interest if the relevancy of the instruction is not immediately apparent. The service is clearly most useful if timed to coincide with the beginning of a research assignment. It must allow students ample opportunity to take advantage of other library services, such as interlibrary loan and document delivery. Also, students frequently have the need to follow up on group bibliographic instruction sessions once they have delved into a research topic. One-on-one reference assistance may be available to remote campus users through a variety of reference services emanating from the main campus library. These include online virtual reference, e-mail queries, telephone consultations, and individual research consultations.

PLANNING THE INSTRUCTION SESSION

Librarians who present library instruction sessions at off-campus locations must plan adequately for each session (Clayton, 2004). Faculty typically schedule one class period for the instruction, and the librarian will need to include information critical to the research needs of the class. Remote access procedures and distance learning services also must be covered in the single session. This limited contact time and possible unpredictable complications of teaching in an unknown environment require preparation, polish, and poise.

Planning includes some very practical concerns, such as the distance from home library to the class site. For greater distances, the librarian could investigate video-conferencing networks that might replace travel to a remote site. Busy instruction and distance learning librarians need to plan ahead to schedule travel and time away from other library duties in order to respond to requests for remote-site sessions. Library administrators need to budget funding for travel expenses (mileage) and acknowledge the time commitment to supporting remote-site courses.

Although planning for each session is important, there is also a need to anticipate unforeseen complications. The librarian who teaches off-site may find the need to adapt to a dynamic environment. New or unfamiliar equipment, room changes, Internet connectivity failure, and a variety of other problems occasionally occur. A good sense of humor and an ability to improvise will serve well in instances when Murphy's law strikes.

TECHNOLOGY RESOURCES AT THE SITE

When scheduling the instruction session, the librarian will need to learn what technology resources are available at the location. Sometimes instructional technology staff will be able to provide assistance, but often a facility manager or office personnel will be the only one available to answer basic questions. Possible resources include networked or wireless Internet access, computers without Internet access but with a projector for class viewing, and videoconferencing capabilities. Even simple accessories like projection screens, network cords, and extension cords might be needed. The librarian will then know whether to bring along her or his own technology (laptop, projector, "canned" slide presentation) or whether to go "live" with a presentation using the Internet and showing library resources. Every librarian providing instruction at remote locations should have access to a traveling laptop and portable projector for backup.

INSTRUCTOR ATTENDANCE

Instructor attendance at the session is important for several reasons. First, the instructor can augment your instruction based on previous class instruction and assignments. Second, this individual will be aware of exactly what was covered in the session and can hold students accountable for the information presented. Finally, the instructor's presence reinforces the value of the bibliographic instruction and library services. Part of the planning process should be to confirm that the instructor will be present at the session. At the same time, the librarian may want to request a copy or description of assignments used in the course in order to properly address the research needs of the learners. Often a specific library-related assignment is beneficial for reinforcing research skills covered.

Careful preparation can also ensure that the lessons are flexible enough so that each student learns something from the session. Novice library users might learn about remote access and how to use the library catalog to retrieve electronic books. Experienced users with more complicated research problems can gain insight into good search strategy in proprietary databases. Since distance learners often take several classes at remote site campuses, some may have already participated in an earlier instruction session. With each iteration of instruction, these students will understand increasingly more content. Librarians need to be cognizant of the different levels of ability and experience of remote-site learners.

VISITING THE SITE

Bibliographic instruction should proceed smoothly if the instruction site is familiar to the librarian and if sufficient planning for content and delivery has taken place. If the site is new or unfamiliar, however, the librarian should arrive early to find the correct room, check out expected technology access, and set up equipment. As a practical matter, it might be necessary to find a building custodian to gain access to the classroom, to locate additional equipment such as projection screens or extension cords, or to log on to computer systems. Proper planning and early arrival on-site can diminish the possibility of complications.

The librarian may want to schedule a library orientation for off-site learners that is not yoked to a specific class but open to all students who take classes at the location. The librarian should identify the facility coordinator, learn who is responsible for the facility during evening and daytime hours, and select times for the orientations that will reach both day and evening students. It is essential to market the sessions. Brightly colored signs in elevators, on bulletin boards, and on information kiosks can capture students' attention. Ask faculty who teach at that location to announce the sessions in their classes. During these orientation sessions, the librarian should be prepared to answer technology questions as well as traditional library questions. Students often confuse a technology specialist with an information specialist, since so much information comes to us through technological tools. Through diligent and thorough preparation, the librarian can serve as a supportive representative from the main campus.

HANDOUTS FOR THE STUDENTS

Whether conducting a single-session, a course-yoked instruction session, or a general library orientation session at a branch campus or remote site, the librarian will need to provide some type of leaflet or brochure to students. The brochure should provide follow-up library contact information for students who may need additional help after the session is complete. It should also supply helpful hints such as remote access authorizations (PINs, Logins, UserIDs, or Usernames) for the library resources presented. For the course-specific instruction session, the handout can also include research suggestions for specific library resources (databases, e-books, e-journals) and vetted Web sites.

Consideration should be given to using an assessment tool to evaluate the effectiveness of instruction at the regional center (Espinal and Geiger, 1995). Many institutions are now using online forms for evaluation. In the absence of a formal assessment, anecdotal information is useful in planning subsequent instruction. Learners are generally willing to discuss the usefulness of the session and offer suggestions for improvement. The evaluation should include opportunities for students to comment on both instructional delivery and technological applications.

STUDENT CONCERNS

Student concerns vary according to their age, prior educational experience, academic major, technological competencies, and educational goals (Veal, 2002). It is not uncommon to encounter students on remote campuses who are completely unfamiliar with the vast array of academic technology, including library technology. For many, a single course at a remote campus may be their first attempt at college-level courses or may signal a return to academia after an extended absence.

According to Kirk and Bartelstein (1999: 42), "These returning students, while highly motivated and self-directed, may be insecure about their library skills or lack experience using new technologies." Apprehension often develops as students are bombarded, not only with ever-evolving library technology but also with online registration and instructional courseware. What appears easy or intuitive to the librarian may not be to the learner. Perplexed looks on the faces of students indicates the need to slow down the instruction session, encourage questions, and plan follow-up opportunities. It is important to keep the library instruction session a student-centered experience. The remote services librarian has a unique and often singular opportunity to convey a positive, user-friendly image of the entire library system.

CONCLUSION

The regional center approach to scheduling and visiting off-campus classes presents a number of challenges to ensure the successful delivery of library services and instruction to the distance learner. Cultivating collegial relationships with teaching faculty, university administrators, remote-site coordinators, and instructional technology staff lays the necessary groundwork. Administrators set the philosophical stage and broad distance learning policy for the institution. Faculty are the single most influential factor in conveying the value of library user instruction and services to distance learners. Librarians must schedule and plan remote-site instruction with the instructional goals of the faculty foremost in mind. Planning should also involve consultation with site coordinators and instructional technology support staff to maximize the use of available technology. Librarians need contingency plans in the likelihood of technology and infrastructure glitches. Integrating the needs and goals of the learner into off-campus instructional sessions is a challenging but manageable service for academic libraries.

REFERENCES

Association of College and Research Libraries. 2004. "Guidelines for Distance Learning Library Services." Available: www.ala.org/ala/acrl/acrlstandards/guidelinesdistance-learning.htm.

Association of College and Research Libraries. Distance Learning Section. Instruction Committee. 2005. *Collaboration for Distance Learning Information Literacy Instruction:* SPEC Kit 286. Washington, DC: Office of Leadership and Management Services, Association of Research Libraries.

Butler, John. 1997. "From the Margins to the Mainstream: Developing Library Support for Distance Learning." LibraryLine 8, no. 4. Available: http://staff.lib.umn.edu/Library-Line/LLvol8no4.htm.

Clayton, Susan. 2004. "Your Class Meets Where? Library Instruction for Business and Education Graduate Students at Off-Campus Centers." *Reference Services Review* 32, no. 4: 388–393.

Curtis, Donnelyn, ed. 2002. *Attracting, Educating, and Serving Remote Users through the Web*. New York: Neal-Schuman.

Espinal, Jack, and Sharon J. Geiger. 1995. "Information Literacy: Boole to the Internet and Beyond [Library Instruction for Off-Campus Students at National-Louis University's Branch Campus in Virginia]." In *The Seventh Off-Campus Library Services Conference Proceedings*. Edited by Carol J. Jacob. Mt. Pleasant, MI: Central Michigan University.

Goodson, Carol. 2001. *Providing Library Services for Distance Education Students*. New York: Neal-Schuman.

Kirk, Elizabeth E., and Andrea M. Bartelstein. 1999. "Libraries Close in on Distance Education." *Library Journal* 124, no. 6: 40–42.

Lebowitz, Gloria. 1997. "Library Services to Distant Students: An Equity Issue." *Journal of Academic Librarianship* 23, no. 4: 303–308.

Lockerby, Robin, et al. 2004. "Collaboration and Information Literacy: Challenges of Meeting Standards When Working with Remote Faculty." *Journal of Library Administration* 41, no.1, 2: 243–253.

Markgraf, Jill S. 2002. "Collaboration between Distance Education Faculty and the Library: One Size Does Not Fit All." In *Tenth Off-Campus Library Services Conference Proceedings*. Edited by Patrick Mahoney. Mt. Pleasant, MI: Central Michigan University.

Markgraf, Jill S., and Robert C. Erffmeyer. 2002. "Providing Library Service to Off-Campus Business Students: Access, Resources and Instruction." *Journal of Business & Finance Librarianship* 7, no. 2, 3: 99–114.

Veal, Robin. 2002. "The Relationship between Library Anxiety and Off-Campus Adult Learners." *Journal of Library Administration* 37, no. 3, 4: 529–536.

►4

DESIGNING AND IMPLEMENTING WEB-BASED LEARNING MODULES: A CASE STUDY FROM THE HEALTH SCIENCES

ULRIKE DIETERLE
DENISE K. DIPERT
PAULA A. JARZEMSKY

Overview: In this chapter on Web-based modules for health science courses, the authors provide an in-depth history of the development of the online modules. Much thought is given to the process, the communication, and the goals of the four final modules. Of particular interest is the section titled "Lessons Learned," which discusses building the team and customizing the content.

INTRODUCTION

Health sciences librarians and clinical nursing faculty at the University of Wisconsin–Madison collaborated to design and implement four Web-based library instructional modules for two undergraduate nursing courses. Integrated into the first-year clinical curriculum, the modules focus on strengthening the essential information-seeking skills of nursing students. These modules were assigned at various points throughout the academic year by fifteen faculty teaching a total of twenty beginning-level clinical course sections. The online modules are accessible to both local and distance students through the campus course management system and from the library's Web site.

Design and implementation benefited enormously from the rich working relationship that evolved between librarians and clinical faculty in this multiyear process. The fertile ground of collaboration and discovery brought instructional pieces together in a meaningful way and led to the development of the successful end products described here. The development team consisted of four librarians and three nursing faculty. All were active participants in the innovation, communication, and commitment that led to the attainment of a common goal, which was to provide more effective library instruction throughout the nursing curriculum. Trends in health-care education and library instruction significantly influenced the instructional design and content of the project. This chapter will focus on both this collaboration and, ultimately, the implementation of four online learning modules.

TRENDS IN HEALTH-CARE EDUCATION

The body of knowledge in the health sciences is increasing and changing at a rapid rate. Students face an overwhelming number of information sources that are themselves ever changing and must be continually evaluated for accuracy, reliability, and currency. The acknowledgement that this bewildering information milieu will remain challenging throughout the careers of health-care workers has resulted not only in teaching specific information resources but also in emphasizing critical thinking and information literacy skills necessary for continued professional growth and lifelong learning (Kasowitz-Scheer and Pasqualoni, 2002). The Association of College and Research Libraries (ACRL) in its "Presidential Committee on Information Literacy: Final Report" crystallizes the definition of information literacy: "To be information literate, a person must be able to recognize when information is needed and have the ability to locate, evaluate, and use effectively the needed information" (American Library Association, 1989: 10). While information literacy and information technology intersect at many points, they are not the same. ACRL's *Information Literacy Competency Standards for Higher Education* describes the difference between information technology and information literacy as follows:

> "Fluency" with information technology may require more intellectual abilities than the rote learning of software and hardware associated with "computer literacy," but the focus is still on the technology itself. Information literacy, on the other hand, is an intellectual framework for understanding, finding, evaluating, and using information— activities which may be accomplished in part by fluency with information technology, in part by sound investigative methods, but most important, through critical discernment and reasoning. Information literacy initiates, sustains, and extends lifelong learning through abilities which may use technologies but are ultimately independent of them. (ACRL, 2000: 11)

Effective use of information technologies is one of the essential competencies for health-care professionals, as noted in reports by the Institute of Medicine (Committee on Quality Health Care in America, 2001) and the Pew Health Professions Commission (O'Neill, 1998). Information literacy has long been a staple of health-care education; but its association with the health-care trends of informatics and evidence-based practice has, in recent years, generated new interest in how and when this content should be integrated into health sciences curricula. In addition, public access to health information via the World Wide Web has increased pressure on health-care professionals to assist consumers with selection and evaluation of useful information. Health-care consumers often look to professionals as they navigate an expanding quantity of information that is of uncertain quality and origin. In other words, information literacy—the ability to find, evaluate, and use information to make decisions—is essential to support new directions in health-care education.

Despite such realities, a survey of three thousand registered nurses across the United States revealed that many in the workforce are not ready to meet the challenge of accessing information to guide the best clinical practices (Pravikoff, Tanner, and Pierce, 2005). Over one thousand nurses (37%) responded to this survey which shows that, in large part, they turn first to colleagues or the Internet when seeking professional information, rather than using bibliographic databases. Summarizing numerous studies, Verhey (1999) cites inadequate time and preparation as barriers to nurses using professional literature in their workplace. Verhey asserts that nurses are not likely to view information literacy skills as necessary for lifelong learning, unless this content is integrated across their nursing curriculum and visible in their practice settings. As nurses attempt to move from practices based on past traditions to those supported by current research, information literacy is becoming an essential competency in their education.

TRENDS IN LIBRARY INSTRUCTION

For decades, library instruction was, and too often still remains, a largely passive endeavor. Librarians frequently wait for faculty to initiate contact, which results in sessions that are hurriedly scheduled with limited ramp-up time and little chance to customize content to enhance the curriculum and to support assignments. In fact, busy librarians have resorted to developing generic "scripts" and "one-size-fits-all" packages to address library instruction needs. To maximize the allocated time spent with students, these face-to-face, all-purpose sessions are often jam-packed with as much information as possible to take full advantage of the one-time opportunity. Well-intentioned librarians often overwhelm both students and faculty with information that is untimely and unnecessarily complex. The impact can be information overload and premature introductions to critical resources. Library instruction of this type has the tendency to become a mere supplement instead of an integrated learning component available on demand at the point of need. As observed by Dorner (2001), library instruction can easily become a singular, haphazard event on the academic landscape without meeting students' information needs.

A more effective approach recognizes the importance of incorporating library instruction into the curriculum at the point of need. Smaller, more-focused nuggets of information, when attached to specific learning applications, typically result in deeper learning. The growing maturity of instructional technology software has made it much easier to design discrete online "learning objects" from the desktop. Production of online instructional objects is now within the reach of librarians and faculty with minimal technology skills. In contrast to traditional face-to-face library instruction, online modules benefit the curriculum overall by establishing a common base of knowledge from which to build more sophisticated information-seeking behaviors. Whether used for local or distance students, they provide educators the flexibility to interject learning and skill-reinforcement opportunities at various points throughout the curriculum whenever appropriate, thereby greatly increasing the likelihood that students will be exposed to relevant instruction at the most opportune learning time. Finally, online modules free librarians from some of the time previously devoted to face-to-face contact and allow them to direct energy toward collaborative projects or more customized consultations as requested by students and faculty.

The concern of librarians and health-care educators is not whether students need library instruction to become information literate, but how to make instruction most effective. This question has resulted in best-practice guidelines, such as those outlined by the ACRL's "Characteristics of Programs of Information Literacy that Illustrate Best Practices: A Guideline" (American Library Association, 2005), which describes and categorizes the elements of exemplary information literacy programs.

PROJECT ENVIRONMENT: THE COLLABORATIVE NURSING PROGRAM

The School of Nursing at the University of Wisconsin–Madison offers accredited baccalaureate and graduate programs and in 2005 enrolled approximately 340 undergraduate and 130 graduate students. The School of Nursing has a strong tradition of reaching out beyond the borders of the Madison campus to teach, train, and share expertise. An active Continuing Nursing Education program offers numerous online courses to health-care professionals and has thrived at the university since 1985. Since 1991 five schools of nursing within the statewide University of Wisconsin System have collaborated to offer the innovative Collaborative Nursing Program (CNP), which provides individuals with prior nursing preparation the opportunity to pursue an academic nursing degree through distance learning. In 2002, the University of Wisconsin–Madison School of Nursing partnered with the Gundersen Lutheran Medical Center in La Crosse, Wisconsin, ninety miles to the northwest, to establish a western campus. Innovative use of distance learning technologies and proactive outreach activities to nursing educators have contributed to the growth and vitality of the distance learning options. Nursing faculty and outreach specialists in the School of Nursing have a strong tradition of involvement in state and federally funded projects that provide coursework in nursing education to registered nurses throughout Wisconsin and beyond by way of distance education programs.

The baccalaureate nursing degree requires courses in basic science, humanities, and social sciences. These studies build a foundation for nursing courses that emphasize clinical decision making and application of theoretical knowledge. Undergraduate nursing students, generally as juniors and seniors of a four-year undergraduate curriculum, complete clinical coursework in hospital and community settings during each semester of their two years in the nursing program. Students spend a considerable amount of their course hours working alongside licensed health-care professionals. Fifteen clinical faculty supervise twenty sections of the beginning level clinical course in five Madison area hospitals. Distance learning options provide convenient and effective learning applications for a diverse group of students and faculty in clinical settings, whether three miles across town or one hundred miles up the interstate.

The School of Nursing and other health disciplines are served by Ebling Library, which resulted from the 2004 merger of three separate campus health sciences libraries. Renamed and reorganized, Ebling Library is located in the heart of the new Health Sciences Learning Center, which is among the most sophisticated, technologically advanced educational facilities in the country, with distance learning classrooms that deliver curriculum to more than two hundred local hospitals, clinics and classrooms (Farrell, 2000). The building boasts wireless technologies, distance learning suites, and the latest in digital delivery systems. The library and its staff are ideally positioned to foster rich, interdisciplinary partnerships and collaborations that previously had been logistically difficult to initiate. It is in this setting that the collaboration to change the direction of library instruction began.

PROJECT GOALS

As the nursing school curriculum became more vested in creating online courses, librarians observed with interest as students and faculty spent increasingly more time in these digital learning spaces. As faculty became increasing proficient at developing and populating their online courses with syllabi, course readings, Web links, quizzes, graphics, chats, and more, links to library resources were often not included.

After analyzing past practices and looking toward a future filled with new possibilities, both clinical faculty and librarians were ready to introduce change. By maximizing the advantages of existing information technologies and focusing on just-in-time learning, librarians could invest more development time up front and reallocate saved time to other teaching endeavors. By developing a number of generic online learning objects, librarians believed they could make a positive contribution to online learning and, as an added benefit, produce reusable products that would be available to both on-campus and off-campus students, other courses, and possibly even other disciplines. Nursing faculty were delighted at the prospect of having flexible learning objects that could be brought into their online course environments and would serve students working locally or at a distance. From the start, all agreed on the ultimate goal of designing and implementing online learning modules and, at least in the beginning, all agreed on the projected content, which was largely based on scripts used in the past.

As the collaboration moved forward, it became painfully obvious that both groups had, over many years of working together, developed incorrect assumptions about what constituted useful library instruction. These assumptions were, through much discussion, more closely scrutinized, dissected, and, ultimately, adjusted to more clearly identify the actual information needs. The faculty assumed that librarians intuitively understood the course objectives and the best juxtaposition of course content to library resources. Library instruction of the past presented a broad array of library resources and services not necessarily focused on specific assignment goals but, rather, on broader literacy concepts. Sessions were often scheduled when time was available, instead of being determined by the course activities. Team members probed, prodded, and pondered to better understand one another and, almost unknowingly, embarked on a path to shared discovery and an innovative approach to integrated learning.

PROCESS FOR CREATING LIBRARY INSTRUCTION MODULES

Identifying actual instructional needs as opposed to assumed needs was the first step toward a successful outcome, as the collaborative group learned through candid, sometimes uncomfortable discussions. The group thought it had planned carefully and appropriately but ended up turning the plan on its head when it moved beyond assumptions and confronted real-world information needs of students working in their clinical environments. As the example that follows illustrates:

For many years librarians had worked with clinical faculty to conduct in-class instruction on the best uses of nursing databases. One of these, the Cumulative Index to Nursing & Allied Health Literature (CINAHL), served as the centerpiece for nursing research. Librarians and faculty traditionally focused on the CINAHL as the database of choice for nursing students.

Initially the development team agreed to convert the in-class instructional script used in the past to a Web-based format, thereby making it much more accessible, flexible, and reusable. While the CINAHL is helpful for topical research, and while it may be possible to find the information the students needed, it is not the best resource for basic queries about diseases and conditions found in clinical settings.

Librarians and faculty both spoke from the vantage point of their own base of academic knowledge. The clinical faculty felt that their students were lacking in library search skills and, over the years, had come to believe the CINAHL to be an appropriate tool to improve student performance. Librarians, in turn, without full awareness of the course demands, believed that the CINAHL provided the best information and that proficiency with this tool was essential to their academic and professional well-being. Year after year librarians had been asked to teach the CINAHL and, being service-oriented, were responsive to these requests. The special librarian with the School of Nursing, who joined the group of a few months into the project, brought the unique vantage point of understanding both the school's curriculum and the library's information resources. She questioned why library instruction focused on the CINAHL, since clinical students were not writing research reports at that point in their studies but were instead focused on patient conditions and patient care. This simple question marked the beginning of "bridging" the communication gap between the two academic disciplines and, ultimately, more succinct understanding of actual learning needs. At this point the direction of the collaboration shifted from information sources as the starting point to first examining the course requirements and, only then, identifying appropriate information resources. The clinical faculty then described in detail assignments that students are expected to complete, and the librarians used their expertise to match the demands of those assignments to the appropriate information tools. The pieces of the puzzle began to move together and align to form a more clearly defined picture.

PRODUCT—THE MODULES

Before embarking on the detailed design of the modules, it was unanimously decided that all would be Web-based for easy access, short (fifteen minutes), and focus on limited content dictated by the curriculum. Each module would have its own learning objective(s) that reinforced existing course objectives. Each also ended with an assignment created and evaluated by clinical faculty. Storyboards were constructed using Microsoft (MS) PowerPoint, which could easily be shared among team collaborators for input. Graphics and screen captures were generously incorporated using SnagIt, and video clips were added selectively using Camtasia. All modules went through multiple phases of evaluation, with librarians providing both technical software support and library content. Nursing faculty provided the clinical content, helped to tie module objectives to course objectives, and generated each related assignment. Development time for each module varied but spanned approximately six to eight weeks. The evolution of collaborative discovery between two very different academic groups (clinical faculty and librarians) with a singular purpose resulted in four online learning modules implemented during the 2004–2005 academic year. Modules discussed here will be available in their revised versions from the Ebling Library Web site (Ebling Library, 2006).

1. Virtual Tour of Library Web site

Since students were beginning to study more extensively in digital spaces, it seemed only logical to develop a virtual tour that would illustrate the library's Web site and access to its many resources and services. A virtual tour is of special importance to distance users, who may never walk through the library's doors, and is a great adjunct tool for local students who need a brief refresher. The learning objectives of this module are to 1) find and navigate the Ebling Library Web site to locate course reserves, databases, online and print journals, and online and print book; and 2) to locate online assistance or get help from our library staff. The program was built using HTML (hypertext markup language) with Macromedia's Dreamweaver and Fireworks software packages. Unique features include many screen captures that simulate and condense the Web pages. Call-out graphics draw attention to content and provide navigational cues.

2. Information Literacy in Nursing—MDConsult

This module represents the result of the first significant communication breakthrough. Instead of using more generic content, the group focused on specific tasks students would be performing and applied an information tool that would directly support performance. The module is interjected at a point in the semester when nursing students are introduced to a variety of clinical environments and patient conditions. Students review patient charts and interact with clinical staff. Since students must have an understanding of the conditions and diseases they encounter, they require medical reference materials, practice guidelines, and consumer health information. MDConsult is an online product that provides all of these resources. Learning objectives for this module include 1) using MDConsult to identify appropriate information resources and 2) retrieving information relevant to clinical patient care. The technology used was the same as in the virtual tour modules, but in fall 2005 the content was converted, using Macromedia's Captivate, to include improved navigation, audio, and more-engaging graphics. The unique features include the verbatim audio of text in the revised version, as well embedded links, sidebar navigation, and a little introductory music to catch students' attention.

3. Expanding Your Knowledge of Databases

This module provides a brief example of how to formulate a simple search. The search strategy evolves from the clinical question of how to properly insert a naso-gastric tube to the formulation of a well-constructed search query. Students are introduced to Boolean search logic. A number of databases are demonstrated through video clips with audio for a series of sub-modules describing specific databases appropriate for this topic. The objectives here include the following: 1) the use of a patient scenario to formulate simple search strategy with Boolean logic; 2) the identification of four additional health sciences databases; and 3) the ability to distinguish differences in content and application of databases presented. The technology used was the same as that in the prior two modules. Unique features include the meshing of real-world patient-care issues with various sources of information. Unfortunately, the demanding bandwidth of the video software made viewing difficult for distance users without a high-speed Internet connection. This was corrected in the revision a year later, which again utilized Macromedia's Captivate.

4. Finding the Right Needles in the Information Haystack

This module was developed for the second-semester clinical course in which students, in addition to seeing patients in clinical settings, begin writing papers based on nursing research. Their information toolkit becomes more complex and challenges decision-making and critical-thinking skills by bringing together various elements from previous modules. Students are asked to carefully analyze a patient case and extract both nursing and medical terminologies to be used later in constructing searches in appropriate databases. The stated learning objective of the module is to locate information in planning nursing care of assigned patients. Various decision points throughout highlight the complexity of the process and the importance of looking at a variety of resources. The technologies used included MS PowerPoint to create the storyboard and then Macromedia's Captivate for the final production version.

LESSONS LEARNED

Descriptions follow of the lessons learned and specifically include lessons on communication, team-building, generic vs. customized content, and replicability of design.

Communication

Most emphatically, the group learned how important clear communication is to the collaborative process. A particular challenge to curriculum-based library

instructional programs is that both librarians and course professors must understand something of the other group's base of knowledge in order to develop a
product together. Time spent at the beginning of a multidisciplinary collaborative
project discussing the specifics of what students do is critical. Librarians must have
knowledge of these specifics in order to apply their expertise in the selection of appropriate information resources. In this particular experience, each group came
to the collaboration with incomplete information or incorrect assumptions about
the demands of the other's academic disciplines. Each group failed to account for
how specialized its own discipline is and, therefore, how difficult it is for the other
group to understand specific details, terminology, and intent. Only after weeks of
probing questions about specific student assignments did the natural compatibility of online information resources and assignments come into focus and the instructional modules begin to take shape.

Building the Collaborative Team

A successful collaborative project requires a team of individuals who, when expertise is combined, can conceptualize a product and efficiently and effectively turn
those ideas into reality. The collaborative team consisted of four librarians and
three clinical nursing faculty who had expertise in content areas, project management, and assessment as well as distance learning practices and principles. One
member had previous experience in designing and implementing online learning
resources. Unfortunately, no member of the team had in-depth knowledge of the
instructional technologies needed to smoothly develop online modules. One librarian was fluent in HTML, but had only limited knowledge of other design tools.
No one was proficient in a broad spectrum of online tools. The omission of technical design skills was problematic in terms of time, stress level, and the design limitations of the finished product. Technical decisions not only influence the design
and development of the current project but also create issues for future revisions.
It is project-critical to assemble an appropriate mix of skills at the beginning of a
project and incorporate them at the right time during development. Additional
strengths of the team members, which added to the successful outcome included
1) the School of Nursing special librarian, who brought to the table library knowledge as well as specific knowledge about the nursing curriculum; 2) two clinical
course professors who had the authority to implement changes in the courses; 3) a
common goal; and 4) a high degree of motivation and enthusiasm.

Generic vs. Customized Content

Generic content in library instructional modules appeals to both librarians and administrators because it can be applied to a broad base of patrons and requires less

staff time overall. The librarians on the team began the project with generic models in mind; however, as the large goals turned into more specific learning objectives, the team concluded that generic instructional modules would not serve the information needs of clinical nursing students. This conclusion was based, in part, on the fact that nursing students had been given in-class generic presentations over the years, with the recurring complaint being the same—the students felt that they already knew "how to search" and yet the instructors could not see evidence of that skill in completed assignments. Nursing crosses multiple disciplines, and students needed to learn how to manipulate multiple information resources to answer the real-world questions posed by their assignments. They worked with complex medical conditions of which they needed a general understanding. At the same time, they needed to educate themselves about the issues related to nursing care of their patients. The challenge centered on matching the appropriate information tool to the task. The collaborative team also came to believe that a "stepped" or "tiered" approach to library instruction requires customized content in order to respond to the increasing complexity faced by students as they progress through the curriculum.

Replicability of Design

One major problem in developing online learning modules is that, whether a generic or customized design is used, database interfaces change frequently, requiring repeated maintenance. Any technical design should in part be based on the ability to quickly and easily incorporate these changes. Revisions of last year's modules are currently under way. These revisions, while necessary, are labor-intensive, requiring a collaborative team that is invested in working together over the long term and administrative units that understand the need for their staff to continue on these projects.

CONCLUSION

The importance of integrating information literacy skills in nursing curricula is well established by the research. Delivering such instruction to students who work in small groups under numerous instructors and in a variety of settings, however, was a difficult challenge. Librarian-led presentations to a general assembly of students resulted in an overload of information, without an apparent curricular context. A distance education approach seemed best suited to meet this need, even though the majority of learners in this setting were traditional, on-campus students. Online modules that were geared to assist students with specific course assignments would offer help at the point of need. But the "generic script" could not be expected to fare any better online than in front of a classroom. Only through collaboration did librarians and faculty in this setting reach a common understanding of the learning objectives and appropriate tools to assist students in meeting them. The collaborative process unveiled assumptions that interfered with previous attempts at library instruction. In this instance, closer scrutiny for the purpose of consulting information sources allowed for a more tailored response by librarians. Once the end point was clearly articulated by faculty, librarians were able to work backward from that point of need. Even in a setting well appointed to serve the needs of distance education, the expertise of a technical designer proved important to creating an attractive end product that could be readily adapted to changes in database interfaces over time. Rather than wait for schoolwide recognition of the need to integrate information literacy skills across the nursing curriculum, those willing to go the distance have done so. Without knowing when or if programwide support would ever occur, the team chose to embark on this collaborative effort, believing that success would generate broader enthusiasm. As word of this success travels through both the library and the School of Nursing, there are indications that more collaborative projects will follow.

REFERENCES

American Library Association. 1989. "Presidential Committee on Information Literacy: Final Report." Available: www.ala.org/acrl/legalis.html (accessed November 2, 2005).

American Library Association. 2005. "Characteristics of Programs of Information Literacy That Illustrate Best Practices: A Guideline." Available: www.ala.org/ala/acrl/acrlstand ards/characteristics.htm (accessed January 29, 2006).

Association of College & Research Libraries. 2000. *Information Literacy Competency Standards for Higher Education.* Available: www.ala.org/acrl/ilcomstan.html (accessed September 14, 2005).

Committee on Quality Health Care in America, Institute of Medicine. 2001. *Crossing the Quality Chasm: A New Health System for the 21st Century.* Washington, D.C.: National Academy Press.

Dorner, Jennifer L., Susan E. Taylor, and Kay Hodson-Carlton. 2001. "Faculty-Librarian Collaboration for Nursing Information Literacy: A Tiered Approach." *Reference Services Review* 29, no. 2: 133.

Ebling Library. Nursing—Ebling Library. 2006. Available: http://ebling.library.wisc.edu/nursing/index.cfm (accessed January 29, 2006).

Farrell, P. 2000. "Integrated Health Sciences Learning: A Dream Becomes a Reality." *Wisconsin Medical Journal* 99, no. 3: 79.

Kasowitz-Scheer, A., and M. Pasqualoni. 2002. "Information Literacy Instruction in Higher Education: Trends and Issues." Available: www.ericdigests.org/2003-1/information.htm (accessed January 29, 2006).

O'Neill, E. H., and the Pew Health Professions Commission. 1998. "Recreating Health Professional Practice for a New Century." Available: www.futurehealth.ucsf.edu/pdf_files/ recreate.pdf (accessed January 29, 2006).

Pravikoff, D., A. Tanner, and S. Pierce. 2005. "Readiness of U.S. Nurses for Evidence-Based Practice: Many Don't Understand or Value Research and Have Had Little or No Training to Help Them Find Evidence on Which to Base Their Practice." *American Journal of Nursing* 105, no. 9: 40.

Verhey, M. 1999. "Information Literacy in an Undergraduate Nursing Curriculum: Development, Implementation and Evaluation." *Journal of Nursing Education* 38, no. 6: 252.

▶5

TEACHING AN ONLINE LIBRARY INSTRUCTION COURSE

SRIVALLI RAO

Overview: To create an online library instruction course takes both dedication and organization. This chapter takes a step-by-step look at how to plan and develop an online library instruction course. The author clearly and thoughtfully outlines the creation, successes and challenges of the online course LISC 260 "Using Electronic Resources for Research" at Mercy College.

INTRODUCTION

The Web has revolutionized information access and retrieval. With the plethora of full-text resources available on the Internet and through proprietary databases accessible through the Web, academic libraries have been focusing on organizing these resources in a meaningful way on their Web sites for users to access. Software packages such as ERes by Docutek have made it possible to access library reserve material online through the library's Web page or by providing a link to it from the instructor's online course page. "Virtual" reference service has been in existence for some time through the use of toll-free phone numbers. Software packages developed to provide online reference, e-mail, instant messaging, and so on have taken reference services to new dimensions.

The Web offers a variety of educational and communication tools. Surfing the Web for recreational purposes or for casual research differs greatly from using the Web as a tool for one's education. Students need to learn skills in online searching so that they can use the Web effectively to glean quality information.

The Web is also becoming a viable vehicle for delivering courses entirely or partially online, and the virtual campus environment has seen a steady transformation of traditional methods of bibliographic instruction in the past decade. Faculty-librarian collaboration in delivering library instruction online has been on the increase at many institutions. Librarians have participated by designing and developing online pathfinders, tutorials, and information literacy courses.

This chapter will focus on the librarian as instructor in teaching a credit-bearing information literacy course online to distance education students at Mercy College in New York, as well as the successes and challenges faced by both the instructor teaching the course and the students taking it.

NEW VENTURE IN LIBRARY INSTRUCTION

Mercy College's distance education program began about fifteen years ago and is aimed primarily at students who need the flexibility to take courses at any time, anywhere, something other modes of course delivery, such as videoconferencing, do not provide. Students live or work within the geographic vicinity of one of the college's five campuses, and most of them also take courses in traditional classroom settings. The college offers undergraduate degrees in business, computer science, and psychology entirely online over the Internet using WebCT software for delivery of instruction and communication between the instructor and the students. Online bibliographic instruction to students enrolled in distance education courses is not a regular feature—even today.

Mercy's Online Learning Campus has been recruiting small groups of international students, living outside the United States, to register for these online degree programs. Most of these students do not have access to major academic or research libraries in the countries in which they live. When the first such cohort was recruited, the provost and the director of Online Learning approached the librarians to develop a course that would introduce students to online sources in psychology, business, health, current events, literary criticism, and statistical information—to help them in locating quality information using the Web and the databases subscribed to by the libraries. Hence the first three-credit online library course was born, and it is still the only undergraduate course offered by the college that does not have an on-site equivalent. It was decided that phrases such as "library instruction," "bibliographic instruction," or "information literacy instruction" would be avoided in the title of the course, since these phrases, it was felt, are better understood by professionals in the library field and not necessarily by students. Therefore the course is called "Using Electronic Resources for Research," which puts the emphasis on "research" and "resources" rather than on "library." At least five sessions of this course are offered every year. Librarians at Mercy College hold faculty rank, and full-time librarians at the college teach this course as an "overload"—in addition to their normal 35 or 40 hour week.

Initially, the course was open only to students registered in the online overseas grouping. Now any Mercy College student who satisfies the basic computer and English course requirements can take this course as an open elective. Classes tend to have a mix of local and online overseas students, which makes the course interesting to teach.

COURSE DESCRIPTION

The course runs for eight weeks and is divided into eight modules so that information is given to students in manageable quantities. Because online students read all the information provided to them, making the modules too long will only overwhelm the students. The instructor introduces one module each week, and the modules are presented in a prescribed sequence. The course begins with general topics—Internet, the Web, browsers, and so on—which students invariably find interesting and which capture their attention. This is followed by a discussion on search engines. Next, students are introduced to search techniques—Boolean, free-text, and natural language. Then it is time to move on to library catalogs and e-books, followed by journal databases. At this point students are given an assignment that compares search engine results with full-text database results; this helps in understanding that subscription databases yield quality resources, which is not always the case with the Internet. This is a good place in the course to educate students on the formats for citing sources such as APA and MLA and the criteria for evaluating resources on the Internet. The course starts winding down with a discussion on topics such as plagiarism, intellectual property, copyright, and security of information. No discussion on the Internet and the Web is complete without mentioning topics such as e-mail, listservs, news groups, and Web logs (blogs), which are used to transmit information and communicate with others. The course ends on a lively note with a discussion on the use of the Web and the Internet for business, finance, and marketing, and these topics always spark very lively participation from students.

The structure of this course plays an important role in the successful delivery of instruction. Course syllabus, outline, and grading rationale are posted a few days before class begins. Lectures notes and readings are posted each Monday, with additional course material, if any, posted a day or two later. Discussion is based on the lecture notes and a special topic for the week based on the week's course content, which the instructor assigns.

It is advantageous to give a pretest before posting the first module to determine the level of knowledge and understanding students have about libraries, databases, and the Internet. This will help the instructor in tailoring the course in such a way that students are neither lost in nor bored by the content. A simple question such as "How often have you used a library of any kind?" will result in interesting responses from students. Usually more than half the class has not used a library for quite some time!

Lecture notes deal with the basic information. Students are expected to contribute additional material in the discussion forum, based on factual information they have gathered from the course content, suggested readings for the week, work experience, or any extracurricular activities in which they are involved.

The main course page is organized into folders under clear and simple headings, each with an appropriate icon:

- ▶ *Course Information*—course syllabus, course outline, grading rationale, instruction for navigating through the course, and classroom etiquette are posted here.
- ▶ *Lecture Notes*—has content module for each week in separate sub-folders labeled Week I, Week II, and so on.
- ▶ *Quizzes and Assignments*—are posted here.
- ▶ *Communication*—includes course e-mail, discussion forums, and chat rooms.
- ▶ *Grades*—for quizzes, tests, and assignments are posted here.
- ▶ *Library*—links to Mercy College Libraries.
- ▶ *Online Tutoring Center*—for help with improving writing skills.
- ▶ *Help Desk*—connects to the college's Computer Services via e-mail, for technical help with course software, authentication, and so forth.

Students, especially those new to online learning, will appreciate instructions in navigating through the course, even if the course design is very simple.

The course does not require a printed textbook because of the nature of many of the topics covered and also because content in textbooks is quickly outdated. Since the Internet is fast developing into a rich source of reliable and authoritative information, readings consist of resources found on the Internet and material placed on the libraries' electronic reserve that supplement the lecture notes.

Widely available print sources are introduced so that it is possible for some students to find them in a neighborhood academic or public library. Depending on the students' interests or majors, subject-specific print resources that are well known in specific fields also are discussed.

Animation and streaming audio and video are used sparingly to ensure that the purpose of learning is not lost. It is important to use clear fonts and readable font sizes for the teacher's course pages. Screen captures to illustrate searching the library catalog, as well as databases and PowerPoint presentations, where appropriate, help in enhancing learning, especially for those students who are more visually oriented. Checking URLs (uniform resource locators) and links used in the module for currency a few days before posting is essential. Dead links will become an embarrassment for the instructor, since students will never fail to point this out, sometimes to the entire class! Each external link should open in a new window so that students are able to return to the module easily. If appropriate, online guest "speakers" are invited to enhance course content. As with any onsite library instruction session, repeating important information, and in more than one way, helps to reinforce learning.

Unlike a stand-alone library tutorial, course development software such as WebCT and Blackboard gives instructors the ability to put up course pages quickly and to revise pages for the next session when the instructor teaches the course again. Revisions do not have to be deliberated and approved in a library committee, nor does one need to depend on outside technical assistance to make the changes. This gives flexibility to the course and saves time because the instructor has control over the design and uploading of the pages.

Librarians are in many ways in the forefront of information technology and are therefore able to assist students who need technical help with the online course. Most institutions also recommend minimum software and hardware requirements for taking online courses. The user name and password the students use to gain access to the course may be different from the user name and password needed to access the library's resources, and it is important to make students aware of this at the beginning of the course. This will ensure that all hurdles to logging into the library will be ironed out before assignments are given using the library's resources. Ideally, and if time permits, the first session should be spent in introductions and resolving logging in issues (to the course page and to the library).

COURSE WIZARDS PROGRAM

In 2001 Mercy College's Online Learning Campus began offering online tutoring services for students. The college also has the Course Wizards Program. Faculty teaching an online course can request a "Course Wizard," who is equal to a teaching assistant or peer tutor and who can assist the instructor as well as students. Course Wizards are successful students who have taken online courses. Some of them have already earned their graduate or undergraduate degree, while others are still working toward their degree. Students feel a greater level of comfort in asking them for help. Wizards assist the instructors in tutoring students, facilitating discussions, locating resources, and providing the instructor technical help with the courseware as needed. They do not post course content or grade student assignments. Mercy's Course Wizards Program has received national acclaim.

QUIZZES, ASSIGNMENTS, AND GRADING

It was decided not to have proctored exams or term papers largely to avoid plagiarism and cheating and also because of the nature of the course. Short self-tests given at the end of each module reinforce student learning. These tests, which may be made optional and for review purposes only, help students test their own understanding of the material presented.

Students are given five quizzes that count for 60% of the final grade. As far as possible, quizzes are evenly spread throughout the course. There is no quiz in the first week of class, which allows students who enter class a day or two late to catch up with the material presented. Quizzes are posted on Thursdays. Students are given four days to complete them and e-mail the answers to the instructor before the next module is posted. WebCT allows instructors to monitor students' access to course pages, which helps in making sure they do not go to the quiz directly without reading the contents of the modules.

Each quiz is an extensive exercise in using search engines and the full-text databases subscribed to by the libraries to find information on topics chosen by the students and approved by the instructor. Students are encouraged to choose topics that they have to find information on for other courses they are taking. They can use the information retrieved to complete an assignment, a term paper, or a project for another course. This makes the search very meaningful to students; they take the quizzes seriously, and their answers are therefore well researched and more complete.

Quizzes and assignments are hands-on in nature, and students are asked to supply documentation of their search so that the instructor teaching the course can redo the search if he or she suspects that a student has cheated by not going through the research process. The other 40% of the final grade is assigned for participation in the online discussion forum. Students are expected to post at least two messages—one message on the lecture or recommended readings for the week and the other message on the special topic the instructor posts each week. Each week opens up a new discussion folder and closes and "locks" the previous week's folder. Once a folder is "locked," no more messages may be posted. This helps in managing the discussion forum efficiently and in making sure the discussion moves forward. However, all folders are available for viewing until the end of the course. Student participation in the discussion forum is assessed every two weeks, and grades are given to students along with instructor's comments. Students benefit from this frequent feedback, and their postings for future weeks improve in quality.

SUCCESSES AND CHALLENGES

Online learning fosters critical thinking and reflection on the material presented and strengthens writing skills. This is evident in the students' contributions to the online discussion and responses to messages posted.

The smaller size of the online class, which is set to a maximum of twenty students, enables the instructor and the students to develop a one-on-one student-teacher relationship that helps in addressing individual needs of students. It is pedagogically unsound to have too few students or two many students in an online class. Having more than twenty students will make the online class rather unwieldy, and having fewer than ten is not academically beneficial to them.

Lecture notes introduce the topic and give basic information. The assigned readings supplement the lecture by dealing with the topic in depth and also introducing and discussing advanced topics. Those who are familiar with the basics can contribute additional material in the discussion forum, which gives them a chance to participate in a meaningful way. This makes the weekly discussion very enriching. Since a high percentage of the final grade is reserved for participation in the weekly classroom discussions, students take this very seriously.

Timely feedback from students about the course helps the instructor in assessing how well the course has met students' research needs. The standard course evaluation forms that students fill out online at the end of the course and also peer evaluations of the faculty teaching the course are useful in getting feedback, but it may take several months before the instructor gets copies of these evaluations. Posing open-ended questions such as, "Did the course help to sharpen your research skills?" "What features of the course did you find most useful?" "Name one topic that the course did not cover that would have benefited you," and so on, will give quick feedback. This can be done in the last week of the course. Such informal feedback can help the instructor in revising and incorporating suggestions students make into the course content. The course is thus enriched every time the instructor teaches it.

Feedback received from students suggests that everyone benefited from taking the course. Even those students who are computer buffs and Internet savvy have responded that they were not aware of the large number of search engines available, the advantages of using Boolean logic and other search features, the vast amount of quality and relevant information found in the subscription databases, and the criteria used in evaluating Web sites.

For the instructor, the biggest challenge is bridging the "distance" and encouraging participation from students. Virtual classrooms lack the camaraderie and teamwork of a traditional classroom. Students should be motivated and challenged to participate in the virtual discussions. Learning online can be lonely, and the instructor should be able to play the part of a good facilitator who keeps the discussion lively and the students involved. Although most online students are highly motivated, some of them may still need individual encouragement from time to time to keep up with the class.

Cheating in exams is a major concern for all instructors who require students to take an onsite midterm or final exam for their online class. It is a challenge to find a proctor who will take the responsibility for administering and proctoring the exam at a remote site and sending the completed exams to the instructor. This is the reason why the course "Using Electronic Resources for Research" does not have an on-site exam requirement. All quizzes are hands-on. Students are asked to give the search strategy they used and the exact phrase or terms they typed in, the search limitations they used, the search engines or the databases they chose for their research (giving reasons why they chose them), bibliographic citations for articles retrieved from databases or the URLs for the Web sites located, and a summary of the information retrieved in two or three short paragraphs. Students are also asked to repeat the same search using different databases and search engines, compare the results retrieved, and explain the similarities and differences between the two searches. Answers to these quizzes and the messages students post in the discussion forum enables the instructor to evaluate not only students' understanding of the course content but also their language and writing skills.

WebCT provides instructors with the capability of tracking student course progress. Instructors can view the dates and number of times the students accessed the course material or quizzes. Students who are not "attending" class can be identified and contacted via e-mail.

Teaching online is more time consuming than teaching in a traditional classroom setting. From this writer's experience, it takes almost three times the amount of hours to develop and prepare an online course initially and an equal amount of time to teach it. On-site instructional materials do not easily translate to online ones, and a librarian who is good with on-site library instruction is not necessarily a good online instructor.

Since distance learning is "anytime, anywhere" learning, class is in session around the clock and students expect the instructor to be "visible" most of the time. Some online instructors have "virtual office hours" posted at the beginning of the course to inform students when the instructor will be "in." The office hours can also be turned into a regularly scheduled online chat so that many students can benefit from the exchange of information.

The Online Learning Campus at Mercy College has a very well-designed online tutorial that gives extensive instructions for logging in and using WebCT. Despite this, students who are new to the online learning environment have initial difficulties in logging in and navigating through the course pages, and the instructor spends some time in the first week of class dealing with these issues.

Not all students have high-speed Internet access. Many overseas students are logging in using slow-speed dial-up connections. Although the Online Learning Campus stipulates the minimum required software and hardware configurations for its computers in order to take online courses, many students do not take this seriously, cannot afford newer versions, or live in a rural area without high-speed Internet access availability. This can be very frustrating to them.

Timely feedback to students is important in virtual classrooms. Since students are given deadlines for submitting work, the instructor should also post grades and give feedback within a reasonable time frame.

The instructor must be sensitive to cultural and political differences between the United States and the student's country of residence in a class that has students living overseas. National and religious holidays observed in the student's country should be considered in giving deadlines for postings and assignments. It is wise to address these issues at the beginning of the course so both students and instructors are informed.

CONCLUSION

The role of academic librarians is being transformed. There are new opportunities to creatively deliver information to users. They are now co-teaching or have been partners in teaching along with course instructors.

Librarians' working week is usually 35 to 40 hours long, which leaves little time to teach a credit-bearing on-site class unless it happens to be part of their job responsibility. The flexibility of asynchronous online learning opens up a great opportunity for librarians to participate as course instructors not only for a credit-bearing library instruction course but also for courses in other disciplines in which they may have knowledge and expertise.

▶ **FIGURE 5.1: Mercy College Libraries Course LISC 260: "Using Electronic Resources for Research"**

Course Outline

Internet Basics*
1. Introductions
2. History of the Internet
3. Browsers—Netscape, Explorer, Mozilla, etc.
4. Glossaries

Module I   Search Mechanisms
1. Subject Directories
2. Search Engines—First and Second Generation
3. Invisible Web
4. Discussion Topic for Week I

Module II   Developing Search Strategies
1. Boolean versus Natural Language Searching
2. Boolean with Keyword Searching
3. Phrase and Proximity Searching
4. Discussion Topic for Week II
5. *Quiz I*

Module III   Library Catalogs Online
1. Mercy College Libraries' Catalog
2. Local Library Catalogs
3. WorldCat
4. Library of Congress Catalog
5. E-Books
6. Discussion Topic for Week III

Module IV   Indexes and Databases
1. Indexes Available on Mercy College Libraries' Website
2. Full-text Databases Available on Mercy College Libraries' Website
3. Other Fee-based Databases on the Internet
4. APA and MLA Formats for Citing Resources
5. Discussion Topic for Week IV
6. *Quiz II*

Module V   Using the Web for Research
1. Business Resources
2. Health Information
3. Social Science Resources
4. Education and Others
5. Discussion Topic for Week V
6. *Quiz III*

Module VI   Evaluating Websites
1. Criteria for Evaluating Websites
2. Discussion Topic for Week VI
3. *Quiz IV*

Module VII   Miscellaneous Topics
1. E-mail, Instant Messaging, Usenet Groups, Listservs, Weblogs, etc.
2. Security of Information on the Internet
3. Copyright, Intellectual Property, and Plagiarism
4. E-business
5. Discussion Topic for Week VII
6. *Quiz V*

Module VIII   Course Wrap-Up
1. Discussion for Week VIII

*Readings are assigned to cover these topics on ERes or as an introductory content page.

REFERENCES

Alberico, Ralph, and Elizabeth A. Dupuis. 1995. "The World Wide Web as an Instructional Medium." Paper presented at the 23rd Annual LOEX Conference, Denton, TX, May 4–6. Available: www.lib.berkeley.edu/~edupuis/LOEX/ (accessed January 15, 2006).

Arnold, Judith. 2002. "Bringing the Library to the Students: Using Technology to Deliver Instruction and Resources for Research." In Proceedings of the 10th Off-Campus Library Services Conference. Cincinnati, OH, April 17–19.

Behr, Michele D. 2004. "On Ramp to Research: Creation of a Multimedia Library Instruction Presentation for Off-Campus Students." In Proceedings of the 11th Off-Campus Library Services Conference. Phoenix, AZ, May 5–7.

Dunlap, Steven. 2002. "Watch for Little Lights: Delivery of Bibliographic Instruction by Unconventional Means." In Proceedings of the 10th Off-Campus Library Services Conference, 221–225. Cincinnati, OH, April 17–19.

Kelley, Kimberly B. 2000. "Library Instruction for the Next Millennium: Two Web-Based Courses to Teach Distant Students Information Literacy." In Proceedings of the 9th Off-Campus Library Services Conference, 191–197. Portland, OR, April 26–28.

Koenig, Melissa H. and Martin J. Brennan. 2002. "All Aboard the ETrain: Developing and Designing Online Library Instruction Modules." In Proceedings of the 10th Off-Campus Library Services Conference, 331–339. Cincinnati, OH, April 17–19.

Lindsay, Elizabeth Blakesley. 2004. "Distance Teaching: Comparing Two Online Information Literacy Courses." Journal of Academic Librarianship 30 (6): 482–487.

Rao, Srivalli, and Carol Ickowitz. 2001. "Developing a Distance Learning Course on Using the Internet for Research." In Proceedings of the InfoToday 2001 Conference, 413–421. New York, May 15–17.

Riedel, Tom. 2002. "Added Value, Multiple Choices: Librarian/Faculty Collaboration in Online Course Development." In Proceedings of the 10th Off-Campus Library Services Conference, 369–375. Cincinnati, OH, April 17–19.

Sax, Boria. 2001. "Brief Reports: New Roles for Tutors in an Online Classroom." Journal of College Reading and Learning 33: 62–67.

Sax, Boria. 2003. "The Wizards Program at Mercy College." Journal of Asynchronous Learning Networks 7 (2): 43–49.

Shannon, Amy W. 2002. "Integrating Library Resources into Online Instruction." In Attracting, Educating, and Serving Remote Users through the Web. Edited by Donnelyn Curtis. New York: Neal-Schuman.

Shannon, Amy W., and Terry A. Henner. 2002. "Providing Library Instruction to Remote Users." In Attracting, Educating, and Serving Remote Users through the Web. Edited by Donnelyn Curtis. New York: Neal-Schuman.

Tunon, Johanna. 2002. "Creating a Research Literacy Course for Education Doctoral Students: Design Issues and Political Realities of Developing Online and Face-to-Face Instruction." In Proceedings of the 10th Off-Campus Library Services Conference, 397–405. Cincinnati, OH, April 17–19.

▶6

UNDERSTANDING COPYRIGHT AND DISTANCE EDUCATION

JACKIE ALSAFFAR

Overview: For those who are unfamiliar with copyright and all of the issues related to it, this chapter is an excellent introduction to copyright concepts, the history of copyright, the legal aspects, the effect of technology on copyright, as well as the economic and global contexts.

INTRODUCTION

In days past, students may well have graduated from college never having heard of or learned about copyright. A student taking classes today cannot remain so oblivious. Copyright should be seen as more than yet another set of prescribed laws to be followed. A more useful understanding of copyright requires a consideration of the broader legal, technological, economic, social, and international contexts of which it is part. This chapter paints large the picture of copyright as it relates to distance education (DE), showing how the interrelated pieces fit together and interact in the digital environment.

COPYRIGHT IN THE DIGITAL CLASSROOM

Distance education is hardly new, but its reliance on the Internet is. Today's digital classroom is a departure from the traditional pedagogical model, with its shift from a teacher-centered approach to a learner-centered approach. This model of decentralized, individual, self-directed learning, with a great deal of learner autonomy, emphasizes and encourages knowledge building and knowledge creation. Such is exactly what copyright aims to promote and protect.

As both major users of and creators of copyrighted works, institutions of higher education have much at stake, especially in the increasingly digital environment in which DE operates. Educational institutions place great value on free inquiry, unfettered discourse, and open collaboration, "all based on a foundation of accurate and authentic information" (CIPR, 2000). Because so much of this information assumes a fixed format, and is therefore under copyright protection, it is easy to see why the entire college community must be educated about copyright issues.

Administrators and faculty are creating and/or reexamining existing policies and procedures, many of which relate directly to intellectual property. These include campus-wide copyright compliance policies, software policies, course ownership policies, and student privacy policies. Many day-to-day activities of librarians carry copyright considerations (for example, checking out a book, sending out an article via interlibrary loan, and accessing a licensed database). Now librarians must expand their knowledge of copyright as they negotiate license agreements for online databases; obtain permissions for works; provide guidance to faculty on copyright issues; provide research support to faculty and students; conduct training sessions for faculty and staff; and educate students about copyright law. This is the information age, and as such, librarians have a unique opportunity to promote an understanding of copyright. It is hoped that as students interact with information, they come not only to appreciate the vastness of the information landscape but also to gain a perspective that encourages them to contribute to that landscape.

THE LEGISLATIVE CONTEXT

Our founding fathers sought to establish a system that fostered the creation of knowledge. Although they did not stipulate how this should be accomplished, the Constitution gave Congress the power "to promote the progress of science and useful arts, by securing for limited times to authors and inventors the exclusive rights to their respective writings and discoveries." Thus, in 1790, the copyright system came into being. The system has undergone numerous changes over the course of more than 200 years, oftentimes in response to "disruptive" technologies. In the past half-century alone, photocopiers, tape recorders, and VCRs all emerged, each in turn threatening the delicate balance between those who create/produce/disseminate works and those in society who gain some benefit from accessing or using those works.

Today, the doctrine of fair use plays an essential part in maintaining this balance. It was codified into law with the U.S. Copyright Act of 1976. This major reworking of copyright law was due in part to technological changes. Congress saw fit to extend, for the first time ever, copyright protection to software, which, one could argue, paved the way for software's future success in the marketplace. This law also set into place important protections for libraries and educational institutions, allowing limited copying of works for scholarship, preservation, and interlibrary loan.

The most recent technological innovation to rock the world of copyright—the personal computer—became widespread in the 1980s to 1990s. "Probably no technology has had a more profound effect upon copyright, upon the creative process, or for that matter upon our lives, than the computer" (Samuels, 2000). The pre-Internet days of computers saw a number of copyright clashes, but the real battles began when the Internet took hold. Copyright law stipulates that everything captured in a fixed format is subject to copyright law, whether it is dominantly textual, auditory, or visual in nature. In theory, then, most everything on the Web is protected by copyright—including everything within a DE course.

Primo and Lesage argue that "[l]egislation and accepted practice must change and adapt in order to make the most out of the possibilities of distance learning" (2001). The heart of the issue is this: How can we encourage cross-pollination and collaboration to flourish in order to yield a rich flow of ideas in a DE course without eschewing the copyright protections afforded to content producers?

Two amendments to copyright law have already been passed that have great impact on DE: the Digital Millennium Copyright Act (DMCA), and the Technology, Education and Copyright Harmonization Act (TEACH Act). These two pieces of legislation add yet another layer of terms and conditions onto copyright's dos and don'ts in the DE classroom, and they are worthy of closer look.

The DMCA (passed in 1998) impacts online service providers (OSPs) and institutions of higher education that act as OSPs for their users. The act limits the institution's liability for infringing materials that faculty or students may transmit through their lines. It also makes it illegal for anyone to circumvent technological barriers designed to protect copyright, like the encoding found on most feature film DVDs, for example.

The TEACH Act (passed in 2002) is a significant piece of legislation in that it was the first time the law acknowledged that education has gone digital. This act permits the display and performance of nearly all types of copyrighted materials in the digital classroom, subject to a number of restrictions and exclusions. It allows for the display or performance of a nondramatic literary or musical work, in its entirety. Nondramatic works include such things as essays, photographs, charts, or symphonies. The act allows for "reasonable and limited portions" of dramatic works to be performed (as long as those works are lawfully acquired). That would include operas, plays, and DVD clips, which, prior to TEACH, were not allowed unless permission had been obtained. It also allows for the digitization of analog works if no digital version is available, subject to certain conditions.

In order for an institution to be TEACH Act compliant, however, several requirements must be met. The institution providing the materials must be a governmental body or a nonprofit educational institution accredited by the applicable state or national organization. It must promote copyright compliance through policies and disseminate informational materials to all faculty, students, and staff. The institution must restrict access of copyrighted materials to currently enrolled students, who must be notified that they are not to retain or redistribute the works.

Additionally, copyrighted works are to be used only under an instructor's guidance as part of the "mediated instructional activities" of the course. The TEACH Act brings into closer alignment that which may be done in courses online with that which has long been done in face-to-face courses. This gives many more options to distance educators.

DE and the Internet will continue to evolve and mature along side and in reaction to each other. We can expect that copyright law will be right there in the middle of it all, being reshaped and reformulated to address new issues that will inevitably surface.

THE TECHNOLOGICAL CONTEXT

There is little doubt we are caught up in a rapidly changing technological age. "Three technological trends—the ubiquity of information in digital form, the widespread use of computer networks, and the rapid proliferation of the World Wide Web—have profound implications for the way intellectual property (IP) is created, distributed, and accessed by virtually every sector of society" (CIPR, 2000). For a clearer sense of how much information is being produced, a UC Berkeley study (2002) calculated that the amount of data produced each year is enough to fill 37,000 Libraries of Congress (Lyman and Varian, 2003). This explosive growth shows no signs of stopping. Author John Battelle predicts: "For nearly every book, film, and television show, someone, somewhere, will come up with a reason to put it on the Web, assuming we can get out of our own way with regard to intellectual property issues" (2005). Therein lies the rub—what can be done technologically surpasses what can be done lawfully.

Distance education relies very heavily on the use of copyrighted works. The more wired we become, the more dependent we become on information in digital formats. Can copyright law continue to work in the digital age, or is it time to reconceptualize the law's basic tenets in light of these new technologies? The answer to this question has great import not only for DE but also on all sectors of society that rely on information.

THE ECONOMIC CONTEXT

In years past a student who wanted to go to college would literally go to college—meaning he or she would move into the residence halls, immerse him- or herself fully into college life, and experience all the social, cultural, and intellectual offerings on campus. While this mode of delivering education is still common (especially among the 18- to 24-year-old crowd), an increasing number of students who are "going to college" are never stepping foot on campus, opting to go online instead. Education today is being viewed ever more frequently as a product to be purchased, with "buyers" who wish to see a clear return on their investment. This commodification of education is changing the nature and the business model of higher education. Because education is going digital, students have more choices, and the numbers indicate that today's wired students are well aware of that. What students are probably not aware of, however, is that intellectual property considerations underlie what courses (and programs) are offered online, how those courses are constructed, what content is included in those courses, and how those courses are disseminated. Before an examination of those issues, though, a look at the numbers is in order.

"In 1999, 100 new university and college courses went on-line each month in the USA, and current production is keeping pace" (Oravec, 2003). Statistics from the 2000/2001 academic year show a total of 127,400 different DE courses offered (NCES, 2003). The online enrollment growth rate is over ten times that projected by the National Center for Education Statistics for the general postsecondary student population. That rate of 18.2% "greatly exceeds the overall growth rate in the higher education student body" (Allen and Seaman, 2005).

The fear that accompanies these numbers is that "change in higher education is too much focused on short-term gain and maximizing revenue at the expense of the longer-term purposes of higher education" (Mason, 2003). "The expectation of the critics is that learning will be reduced to 'serving the system' and not be of a kind that empowers learners" (Evans and Nation, 2003).

In looking at the underlying intellectual property issues surrounding DE, several key questions arise in regard to ownership of course content. Who owns the copyright to an online course (and the accompanying syllabus, learning objects, lecture notes, and presentations)? Who has the right to reuse, revise, adapt, reproduce, and distribute that content? Do faculty share in the proceeds from online courses? If a faculty member leaves an institution, can he take the content with him? The potential for a conflict of interest arises in the case of a professor who designs or teaches a course for a competing institution that is very similar to that offered by her employer's institution. A faculty member who invests time and energy developing learning objects wants to know where the payoff is. Caris argues that "[a]mbiguity about copyright laws and intellectual property has hindered the growth of learning object repositories. For example, if a faculty member develops a learning object with the help of technical support staff, who owns that learning object? Can the faculty member share it with others?" (2004). Clearly, institutional policies and contracts must spell out such things as whether online courses are considered works for hire, are created under contract, or are joint works.

The ACRL "Guidelines for Distance Learning Library Services," dated 2004, state that an institution of higher education "is responsible for providing or securing convenient, direct physical and electronic access to library materials for distance learning programs equivalent to those provided in traditional settings and in sufficient quality, depth, number, scope, currentness, and formats . . ." (ACRL, 2004) to meet their constituents' needs. Alas, providing quality materials to online students comes with a price. Librarians know firsthand that an increasing portion of libraries' materials budgets is going toward digital formats, much of it for licensing online databases. The benefits of online databases are many. Students enjoy 24/7 access to scholarly, peer-reviewed, full-text articles, many of which are not even available on the library's shelves. Online course designers can point to any number of articles in a database without hassle or payment of royalties if that database supports persistent, or stable, linking technology. The fact that so many libraries broker deals with a familiar slate of database providers makes life easier for the students too. No matter what institution they attend, they will have some degree of comfort seeing that old familiar EBSCO interface, for example.

Still, librarians are only too aware of the limitations of licensed resources. Licensing resources is a different model than owning resources. Licensing a resource is akin to renting it (Hoffmann, 2005). Librarians know that they are not gaining long-term access to the titles contained therein, but what is particularly problematic is that not even short-term access is guaranteed. Too many database users have experienced firsthand that a journal here today may be gone tomorrow.

Many educational uses of copyrighted works in the DE classroom go beyond what fair use allows. The fact that licensed resources can be used without violating copyright law makes them particularly attractive candidates for inclusion in an online course. Like it or not, the determination of what gets posted in a course often comes down to money. An article available full-text online may be selected in lieu of a better, more appropriate article that would require either permission to be sought and/or royalties to be paid.

A final observation in regard to licensed resources is more philosophical in nature: Given that libraries are somewhat invisible in distance education courses, do students perceive the same value in libraries when accessing collections digitally versus accessing them physically? Are we effectively communicating the value of libraries and of librarians within DE courses?

In addition to licensed databases, information producers have devised other methods to control access to copyrighted works, from e-textbooks with expiration dates to pay-per-view articles to click-wrap agreements. The cumulative effect of these electronic forays is decreased access to copyrighted works, since they are essentially "locked down" and outside the sphere of public access. Clearly, these electronic control mechanisms inhibit the widespread dissemination of information. This is certainly detrimental to students in a DE course; however, it has consequences beyond that for the general public too. How will a work enter the public domain once its term of copyright has expired if it is under lock and key and available only in a licensed database? This trend of licensing works over the sale of works could eventually diminish the body of works entering the public domain, which has large societal implications.

Educational institutions are finding that the costs associated with DE are greater than first anticipated. This is due in large part to intellectual property costs: the costs of negotiating licensing agreements for databases and the fees for using them; the link-resolvers necessary to navigate seamlessly across the many databases; the costs in time, energy, and money associated with securing permissions to other materials; and the fees associated with design and development of proprietary course materials. For for-profit institutions, the costs can be even greater. The TEACH Act, after all, allows for the display and performance of limited and reasonable amounts of audiovisual works but only for accredited nonprofit institutions. Institutions such as the University of Phoenix, Trump University, and their corporate brethren do not fall under that status, and are, therefore, required to ante up for each use of such a work.

The Internet has dramatically and forever changed the music business, the news business, the travel business, and the banking business, and it is now changing the education business in significant ways. DE is on the frontlines of this change, in many cases pushing the boundaries of what copyright allows.

THE SOCIETAL CONTEXT

"The net is all about connection" (Battelle, 2005), but all this connecting carries copyright considerations. As previously stated, a key provision of the TEACH Act is that institutions establish policies and procedures that encourage compliance with copyright law. An understanding of students' and educators' attitudes and behaviors toward copyrighted works is critical, since that serves as the starting point for education.

It has been noted "that a relatively small portion of the end-user population can be expected to read and fully comprehend all of the restrictions regarding intellectual property protection by which they may be legally bound, and in that sense the public is not well informed about what constitutes legal behavior" (CIPR, 2000). While professors make extensive use of copyrighted works for both their research and their teaching, they may nonetheless have a limited awareness of the laws governing those works. And then there are faculty who, even though familiar with the law, choose to take an overly liberal interpretation of fair use, as it serves their purposes. Finally, there are the part-time or adjunct faculty contingent, who often are not afforded the privileges of participating in college governance or curriculum development, much less the professional development opportunities offered to full-time faculty.

Part-time faculty compose no insignificant portion of the higher education workforce. In fall 2003, for example, of the 1,174,831 faculty members employed by degree-granting institutions, 543,235 of those were part-time faculty (NCES, 2004). Establishing points of contact with "face-to-face" adjuncts is difficult enough, much less designing a support model for "invisible" adjuncts who teach online. However difficult, though, it is critical to supply them with information regarding copyright.

Students may well come to the digital classroom assuming that anything on the Web that does not bear a copyright notice is in the public domain and is free for the taking. "The availability of this technology has bred a mind-set that seems to regard all copyrighted works as available for the taking without paying compensation" (CIPR, 2000). While some students may be flirting with copyright infringement, others have mastered the techniques. According to a recent survey (July 2005), 52% of American college students believe it is fine to download and swap copyrighted files (Roach, 2005). Alarmingly, 25% of faculty and administrators agree with them (Stat, 2005).

A review of the literature yielded few recently published studies on students' knowledge of and attitudes toward copyright. We can see, though, that copyright infringement seems to have gained a certain degree of social acceptability. During its heyday, Napster had somewhere in the neighborhood of fifty million registered users illegally downloading music. Young people especially "have an apparently less than rigorous respect for the protections of copyright" (CIPR, 2000). Although 60% of kids worry about getting a virus when downloading material online, it seems they are not overly concerned about the illegality of their actions (Ishizuka, 2004). Jones's questions cut to the heart of the matter: "Is this just a case of law-breaking en masse that can't be tolerated? Or is a law rendered obsolete if the bulk of the population don't [sic] see the unlawful act as unlawful?" (2005).

Thomas Paine penned long ago in *Common Sense* that "a long habit of not thinking a thing *wrong* gives it the superficial appearance of being right. . . ." Some infringement of copyright is due to simply innocent oversight. Other acts of infringement can be attributed to a lack of understanding of copyright laws. Let us face it: Sometimes copyright does not make common sense. Why a person's hastily written shopping list receives the same protection under copyright law as the Great American Novel is mystifying. Another problem is that copyright law is often less than intuitive. The concept of fair use serves as the perfect example. Fair use, as we know, is a legalistic construct that sets out four factors to be weighed in order to establish whether any particular use of a copyrighted work is permissible. Online students, though, may have an entirely different notion of fair use. They are probably not interested in the legal fine print, therefore going with their gut instinct of what seems fair. As long as they are not making a profit, they reason, any use qualifies as a fair use. Another explanation for noncompliance with copyright law is a perceived lack of equity in the system. A student may believe it is not fair to be charged hundreds of dollars for a piece of software that he or she believes takes just pennies to create (Kruger, 2004).

In a wired world, it is clear that our habits and behaviors change. One can choose to see the misuse of copyrighted works from a "glass half empty" perspective, as major corporate rights holders do. Alternatively, one can choose to see things from a "glass half full" perspective. Some see in the latest technology "the next, and perhaps ultimate, phase in copyright's long trajectory, perfecting the law's early aim of connecting authors to their audiences, free from interference by political sovereigns. . . ." (Jensen, 2003).

The Internet begat a whole new breed of people—the open-source community. Some of them are "copyleftists" (those who oppose the whole notion of copyright), but the majority are just average folks who see the benefits of openly sharing and improving on one another's works. Among the early products of these collaborative efforts were Netscape, Linux, and Apache. More recently, some prominent companies have gotten into the game. In 2004, IBM secured 3,248 patents, then turned around and pledged 500 of them to the open-source community (Open Secret, 2005). IBM is not simply being philanthropic; it sees this as a way (maybe a roundabout way) to boost the bottom line. How IBM, Sun, Nokia, and other companies can make money by giving away code is the stuff of another article.

In academia, the equivalent to the open-source movement is the open-courseware movement. Several years ago, MIT announced that it would make available two thousand of its courses online, open to anyone, free for the taking. It was called eye-popping, jaw-dropping, revolutionary, as well as altruistic and idealistic. Why would MIT do such a thing? What does it hope to gain? At a time when many institutions are hoping to cash in on online courses, MIT is doing the opposite. "Once you begin looking at college courses, course materials, and teaching as property, there are tremendous risks to the fabric of academic culture," explains Hal Abelson, co-chair of MIT's Council on Educational Technology. By giving its teaching materials away, MIT's President Charles Vest sees benefits both near and far. "We hope that our classes will become more interactive, our students will come to class better prepared, and our faculty members will use classroom time in ways we have yet to imagine. . . . But the real payoff of what we hope will become the open-courseware movement will be its effect on educators and learners around the world. . . . Ultimately, we believe that the trend toward open knowledge will help bring people of all backgrounds together and promote greater mutual understanding among nations" (Vest, 2004).

The ripple effect that Vest hoped for is happening. Johns Hopkins Bloomberg School of Public Health (JHSPH) and Tufts University have followed suit, adding their content to the initiative. Rice University has launched its own open-source project, called Connexions, which aggregates course materials from professors at any school. Elsewhere in education, scientists are pushing for open access to government-funded research. With the support of 25 Nobel prizewinners, they are requesting that journal articles be made publicly available online six months after publication. Since 59% of academic research is federally funded, (Swartz, 2004), it is only fair to turn it back to taxpayers, they say. Other variations on the open-source theme of interest to the academic community include the MERLOT Project, Creative Commons, and Science Commons.

What is important for this discussion is a consideration of how the copyright system as it exists today acts both to promote and to impede the creation of knowledge. The modern information infrastructure allows for the free exchange of information, ideas, and resources; however, the copyright system seems at times to get in the way, hindering instead of fostering the exchange of information that is so critical to knowledge building. This is one great dilemma of the digital age.

THE GLOBAL CONTEXT

Copyright concerns in the international arena manifest themselves most clearly in the commercial sector, as in the music business. The International Federation of the Phonographic Industry (IFPI) reported that in 2005, 85% of music sold in China was pirated. That number stood at 80% in Indonesia and over 60% in Mexico, Russia, and Ukraine. That report also indicated that thirty-one countries have larger pirated-music markets than commercial ones (Rupley, 2005).

In the educational arena, textbook piracy in developing countries is a major concern for publishers. Total losses to U.S. publishers for 2003 are calculated at $500 million. Among the top offenders were Philippines (with losses to publishers estimated at $45 million), Pakistan (with losses of $44 million), and China, Mexico, and Russia (each at $40 million in losses) (Bollag, 2004). A raid in Seoul in 2001 yielded six hundred thousand pirated books, with a market value of $14.5 million. A raid in New Delhi in 2003 uncovered seventy thousand books, among them pricey chemistry and medical texts. "The problem [of textbook piracy] is biggest in Asia, where it is fed by expanding economies and increasing college enrollments, the widespread use of English in education, and a weak tradition of respect for copyrights" (Bollag, 2004).

Although international treaties and trade agreements have come into place in an effort to align copyright laws internationally, significant differences remain not only in what laws are on the books but also in the degree to which those laws are, or are not, enforced. "The Indian government has an abysmal record when it comes to copyright protection. . . . Corruption plagues India's police forces. Indeed, the police are sometimes part of the pirating syndicates" (Overland, 2004). (This in a place where the price of Paula Bruice's *Organic Chemistry* is priced at $9 instead of the $139 U.S. list price.) China, too, has a reputation of turning a blind eye toward infringement, as well as aiding and abetting the infringement efforts, such as supplying students with counterfeited copies and illegal translations of textbooks.

It is important to recognize, however, that copyright, as a concept, is culturally constructed, and clearly not all cultures share the same concept of copyright as those of us in the United States. Stanford professor Michael Oksenberg, in commenting on the Chinese mentality, explains it this way: "What is regarded in the United States as an individual act of creativity would be regarded there as one person playing the role of scribe for ancestors and other contemporaries. As a consequence, one who expresses an idea has no right to it—it is a social expression, not an individual one, and part of the process of passing and extending a society's cultural legacy" (CIPR, 2000).

Similarly, the notion of copyright in India differs significantly from Western-held notions. "Until recently, the notion of copyright was a foreign one in India. Writing and publishing have historically been treated as charitable endeavors. India's sages were engaged in the selfless pursuit of knowledge. What they wrote was to be freely copied and shared. Today, that perception still persists. Few consider photocopying entire books to be wrong, let alone illegal. Professors freely reprint the works of others. Government scholarships give students a budget for copying" (Overland, 2004).

The Internet promises to greatly expand international markets for online distance education courses. Yet, it is apparent that exporting courses overseas is one thing and exporting the Western notion of copyright quite another. As we gaze into the crystal ball, we see Western universities partnering with Eastern universities, an increasing number of megauniversities with enrollments exceeding one hundred thousand students (most of which will be online), and an increasing presence of corporate universities that train and certify workers for particular jobs. Not only will issues regarding copyright surface again and again, but also a whole host of issues will greatly impact the teaching-learning process.

Information has already gone global and has transformed our culture and others' cultures. It is not unusual for a U.S. student studying abroad to access a database licensed in the States that is actually owned by a parent company headquartered in the Netherlands. Another sign of the digital times is China's concession to loosen the reins on information. "In the fall of 2002, the Chinese government began filtering out Google.com (and several other search engines) because those engines offered too many alternative routes to information that the government wished to keep hidden from its citizens. According to Chinese scholars in the United States, the loss of Google's service caused such a backlash among Chinese citizens that the government restored service within two weeks" (Battelle, 2005).

In spite of questions regarding the legal protections of copyrighted works, international jurisdictions, and applicable laws and enforcement of them, information continues to flow across national borders. As Nobel prizewinner Amartya Sen stated so eloquently in Thomas Friedman's book *The World Is Flat*: "Most knowledge is learning from the other across the border" (2005). Because we have come to live in a global world physically, technologically, increasingly culturally, and economically, one wonders whether we can continue to live in an isolated legal world. How copyright gets hashed out in the global context remains to be seen, yet the consequences for the emerging DE market are sure to be great.

CONCLUSION

Understanding that copyright is and always has been an invented means to an end allows us to see that it can be reinvented to further that end. What is the best way to promote the progress of science and the useful arts in a wired world? Yahoo! cofounder Jerry Yang states in Friedman's book that "[t]he democratization of information is having a profound impact on society. . . . People have the ability to be better connected to things that interest them, to quickly and easily become experts in given subjects and to connect with others who share their interests" (2005). Increasingly, the Internet provides the building blocks for creative works and in so doing seems to further copyright's goal.

Given that DE depends on a rich supply of information and that copyrighted materials permeate the digital classroom, it is imperative that educators and students alike grasp the purpose and value of copyright, understand the interests of the various stakeholders, and see the many forces at work shaping the copyright system. Distance education holds great promise and great challenge. Now more than ever in this information age, intellectual property issues are of paramount importance. The bottom line is that in order to make the most of all that is available, copyright and the information infrastructure must work in conjunction, rather than at odds, with each other.

REFERENCES

Allen, I. Elaine, and Jeff Seaman. 2005. *Growing by Degrees: Online Education in the United States, 2005.* Available: www.sloan-c.org/resources/growing_by_degrees.pdf (accessed January 4, 2006).

Ashling, Jim. 2005. "Internet Companies Invest in China." *Information Today* 22, no. 9 (October): 22–23.

Association of College & Research Libraries (ACRL). 2004. *Guidelines for Distance Learning Library Services.* Available: www.ala.org/ala/acrl/acrlstandards/guidelinesdistance-learning.htm (accessed January 12, 2006).

Battelle, John. 2005. *The Search: How Google and Its Rivals Rewrote the Rules of Business and Transformed Our Culture.* New York: Penguin Group.

Bollag, Burton. 2004. "Don't Steal This Book." *Chronicle of Higher Education* (April 2): A38–A39. *Academic Search Premier Database*, EBSCOhost (accessed December 23, 2005).

Caris, Mieke. 2004. "Obstacles to Using Learning Objects." *Online Cl@ssroom* (December 2004): 3, 7. *Academic Search Premier Database*, EBSCOhost (accessed December 23, 2005).

Cavanagh, Luke. 2001. "Singing a Different Tune: Napster's Numbers Fall; ABC Says Online Visitors Count." *Seybold Report: Analyzing Publishing Technologies* 1, no. 10 (August 20): 32. *Academic Search Premier Database*, EBSCOhost (accessed December 23, 2005).

Committee on Intellectual Property Rights and the Emerging Information Infrastructure. 2000. *The Digital Dilemma: Intellectual Property in the Information Age*. Washington, D.C.: National Academy Press.

Evans, Terry, and Daryl Nation. "Globalization and the Reinvention of Distance Education." Chap. 52 in *Handbook of Distance Education*. Mahwah, NJ: Erlbaum Associates, 2003.

Friedman, Thomas L. 2005. *The World Is Flat: A Brief History of the Twenty-first Century*. New York: Farrar, Straus & Giroux.

Goldstein, Paul. 2003. *Copyright's Highway: From Gutenberg to the Celestial Jukebox*. Rev. ed. Palo Alto, CA: Stanford University Press.

Hoffmann, Gretchen McCord. 2005. *Copyright in Cyberspace 2: Questions and Answers for Librarians*. New York: Neal-Schuman.

Ishizuka, Kathy. 2004. "Kids: Stealing Digital Data OK." *School Library Journal* (August): 18. *Academic Search Premier Database*, EBSCOhost (accessed December 23, 2005).

Jensen, Christopher. 2003. "The More Things Change, the More They Stay the Same: Copyright, Digital Technology, and Social Norms." *Stanford Law Review* 56, no. 2 (November). *Lexis-Nexis Academic Database* (accessed December 23, 2005).

Jones, Mike. 2005. "You Can't Stop the File Sharing." *Screen Education* No. 40: 88–89. *Communication & Mass Media Complete Database*, EBSCOhost (accessed December 23, 2005).

Kruger, Bob. 2004. "Failing Intellectual Property Protection 101." *T H E Journal* 31, no. 9 (April): 48. *Academic Search Premier Database*, EBSCOhost (accessed December 23, 2005).

Lyman, Peter, and Hal R. Varian. 2003. *How Much Information: 2003*. University of California at Berkeley. Available: www.sims.berkeley.edu/research/projects/how-much-info-2003/execsum.htm#summary (accessed January 20, 2006).

Mason, Robin. "Global Education: Out of the Ivory Tower." Chap. 50 in *Handbook of Distance Education*. Mahwah, NJ: Erlbaum Associates, 2003.

Moore, Anne H. 2002. "Lens on the Future: Open-Source Learning." *Educause Review* 37, no. 5 (September/October): 42–51.

National Center for Education Statistics (NCES). 2003. *Distance Education at Degree-Granting Postsecondary Institutions: 2000–2001*. Available: nces.ed.gov/surveys/peqis/publications/2003017/ (accessed January 4, 2006).

National Center for Education Statistics (NCES). 2004. "Employees in Degree-Granting Institutions, by Employment Status, Sex, Primary Occupation, and Control and Type of Institution: Fall 2003." *Digest of Education Statistics, 2004*. Available: www.nces.ed.gov/programs/digest/d04/tables/dt04_224.asp (accessed January 6, 2006).

"OpenCourseWare and the Mission of MIT." 2002. *Academe* 88, no. 5 (September/October): 25–26. *Academic Search Premier Database*, EBSCOhost (accessed January 10, 2006).

"Open Secret: Sharing Intellectual Property Can Be More Profitable Than Keeping It to Yourself." *Patent Commons Project.* October 20, 2005. Available: www.patentcommons.org (accessed September 6, 2006).

Oravec, Jo Ann. 2003. "Some Influences of On-Line Distance Learning on US Higher Education." *Journal of Further and Higher Education* 27, no. 1 (February): 89–104. *Academic Search Premier Database,* EBSCOhost (accessed December 23, 2005).

Overland, Martha Ann. 2004. "Publishers Battle Pirates in India with Little Success." *Chronicle of Higher Education* 50, no. 30 (April 2): A40–A41. *Academic Search Premier Database,* EBSCOhost (accessed December 23, 2005).

Primo, L. Heidi, and Teresa Lesage. 2001. "Survey of Intellectual Property Issues for Distance Learning and Online Educators." *Ed at a Distance* 15, no. 2. Available: www.usdla.org/html/journal/FEB01_Issue/article03.html (accessed December 23, 2005).

Roach, Ronald. 2005. "College Students Untroubled over Digital File Collecting." *Black Issues in Higher Education* 22, no. 12 (July 28): 30. *Academic Search Premier Database,* EBSCOhost (accessed December 23, 2005).

Rupley, Sebastian. 2005. "Global Piracy Factories." *PC Magazine* 24, no. 14 (August 23): 24. *Academic Search Premier Database,* EBSCOhost (accessed December 23, 2005).

Samuels, Edward B. *The Illustrated Story of Copyright.* New York: Thomas Dunne Books/St. Martin's Press, 2000.

"Stat." 2005. *Business Week,* no. 3958 (November 7): 12. *Lexis-Nexis Academic Database* (accessed December 23, 2005).

Swartz, Nikki. 2004. "Scientists Want Open Access to Research." *Information Management Journal* 38, no. 6 (November/December): 19. *Academic Search Premier Database,* EBSCOhost (accessed January 10, 2006).

Vest, Charles M. 2004. "Why MIT Decided to Give Away All Its Course Materials via the Internet." *Chronicle of Higher Education* 50, no. 21 (January 30): 20. *Academic Search Premier Database,* EBSCOhost (accessed January 18, 2006).

▶7

PREVENTING PLAGIARISM AND LIBRARY ANXIETY

NICOLE A. COOKE

Overview: This chapter on plagiarism and anxiety takes a careful look at types of plagiarism, the reasons for plagiarism, and the connection to distance learners. The author also examines the connections among library anxiety, adult learners who are distance learners, and the lure of Internet plagiarism.

◀

INTRODUCTION

The term *plagiarism* is derived from the Latin word *plagiarius*, which means "kidnapper" (MLA, 2003: 66). *The Merriam-Webster Online Dictionary* further defines plagiarizing as the act of stealing and passing off of the ideas or words of another as one's own, or the use of another's production without crediting the source. The definition even goes as far as to equate plagiarism with "literary theft" (Merriam-Webster Online, 2006). Cheating and plagiarism have long been a problem in the academic world, and the phenomenon continues to grow and cause concern, particularly in the Internet age. In today's society, where well-known historians have been accused of plagiarism (for example, Doris Kearns Goodwin and Stephen Ambrose), newspaper journalists are fired for falsifying reports, music is illegally downloaded, and musicians are routinely accused of lip-synching and illegal sampling, it almost seems that intellectual dishonesty and cheating are acceptable and forgivable, and occasionally profitable, offenses. This lackadaisical attitude is trickling down to students of all ages, and it is eroding the moral and intellectual development of future generations.

INTERNET PLAGIARISM

According to a June 2005 report released by Donald McCabe and the Center for Academic Integrity, 70% of students "admit to some cheating" and half of that percentage admitted to "one or more instances of serious cheating on written assignments"

(CAI, 2005). These statistics refer to students enrolled in traditional on-campus academic programs. Does this mean that distance learners do not engage in cheating or other forms of intellectual dishonesty? McCabe, a Rutgers University professor, the founding president of the Center for Academic Integrity, and perhaps the country's leading scholar on such issues, also uncovered significant information about the occurrences of Internet plagiarism: "Internet plagiarism is a growing concern on all campuses as students struggle to understand what constitutes acceptable use of the Internet. In the absence of clear direction from faculty, most students have concluded that 'cut & paste' plagiarism—using a sentence or two (or more) from different sources on the Internet and weaving this information together into a paper without appropriate citation—is not a serious issue" (CAI, 2005).

McCabe's study also found that 40% of students admit to participating in Internet plagiarism, which is up from 10% in 1994 (CAI, 2005). So while there may not yet be an epidemic of Internet plagiarism among distance learners, there is indeed a need for faculty and librarians to be concerned. Librarians need to be proactive in partnering with other faculty to raise awareness and educate students about plagiarism. Distance learners are a unique student population, and because they often lack access to a physical campus, the library, and other support services, not only are they susceptible to the same challenges and academic difficulties and questions as their on-campus peers, but also they are even more isolated and vulnerable. This chapter aims to examine several reasons why distance learners may fall prey to plagiarism and the ways librarians can help prevent these damaging occurrences of academic dishonesty.

ADULT LEARNERS

An appropriate place to begin is with a brief discussion of adult learners. Adult learners are increasingly participating in distance education because it meshes well with their time constraints and academic needs and preferences. Adult learners are multitaskers, with responsibilities of work, family, and school, and they have little time to waste with academic pursuits that are not relevant to them. These adult students are self-directed and self-motivated to improve their education, have a great interest in their course of study, and are open-minded to new ideas. Adult learners are practical and goal-oriented and also possess a wealth of personal life experience that they need to marry with their new knowledge. In this way, they seek to be cocreators of knowledge in the learning environment, instead of sitting back and passively receiving information from their instructors. With this in mind, it is to the library's advantage to present useful information and encourage participation without patronizing or alienating the learners, who most likely are not familiar with the academic research process, are overwhelmed by their assignment, and are not especially interested in the library and its services.

Adult educator Jane Vella states that "adult learners need to see the immediate usefulness of new learning: the skills, knowledge, or attitudes they are working to acquire" (2002: 19). The library needs to present itself and instruct learners in such a way that the research process is relevant and accessible. If it is not, these students will not consult the library, consequently making their academic endeavors more difficult than necessary and possibly placing themselves in a position to plagiarize or seek research and information in the wrong places.

FORMS OF PLAGIARISM

Plagiarism exists along a continuum, consisting of a variety of different forms. Plagiarizing can range from inadvertent improper citing or quotation placement to the purposeful cutting and pasting from various Internet sources to purchasing completely prewritten term papers from a paper mill. Other forms of plagiarism include improper paraphrasing, making up citations and references, and translating foreign articles into the English language (Harris, 2001). Whatever the form, plagiarism is becoming more prevalent and in some cases harder to detect and trace. Author Robert Harris discusses the complexities of plagiarism in his book *The Plagiarism Handbook*, stating, "Plagiarism is a complex issue that arises from several factors including ignorance, opportunity, technology, changes in ethical values, competitive pressures, perceived lack of consequences and even poorly designed assignments" (2001: vi).

In the aforementioned Harris quotation, reference is made to changes in ethical values; this is definitely a problem in today's society and one that makes the librarian's job even more challenging when trying to promote the research process. Academic librarian Vibiana Bowman likens this decline of ethical values and the increase in plagiarism to hip-hop music and its resultant culture. Like many of today's young rappers and musicians, today's students lack source knowledge and "cultural literacy" (Bowman, 2004: 9). Combine this lack of cultural literacy with poor research skills, lack of understanding about intellectual honesty and property, and the widespread belief that anything found on the Internet is free, and you have a ripe opportunity for plagiarism. Just as musicians such as Eminem and Sean Combs sample existing songs and create brand-new ones, students are "sampling" information from the Internet in an effort to complete their assignments. With the example set by the music industry, along with the examples set by journalists and writers such as Jayson Blair and James Frey, it is easy to recognize a culture that discourages intellectual honesty. When speaking of the recent debacle over author James Frey's book *A Million Little Pieces*, *New York Times* writer Michiko Kakutani described it as "a case about how much value contemporary culture places on the very idea of truth" (2006: E1). Frey is just the latest example of someone to profit from dishonesty. There is little wonder why some students resort to plagiarism, which ultimately causes them to cheat themselves.

REASONS FOR PLAGIARISM

Just as there are many forms of plagiarism, there are also many reasons that students resort to plagiarism. Some of the reasons for plagiarism come to mind easily, for example, ignorance of proper citing formats, deadlines, stress and peer competition, poor writing ability, perceived lack of punishment, the thrill of rule breaking, and poor time management skills (Harris, 2001: 2–13). Other reasons for plagiarism are less familiar and therefore more treacherous. An example of this is discussed by Harris, who refers to an affliction called "cryptomnesia": "Cryptomnesia, or 'unconscious plagiarism,' has been shown to occur when thinkers forget to monitor their sources closely. Ideas they have read or heard become assimilated into their pool of thought and later emerge under the guise of original ideas" (2001: 11).

A form of information overload, which is par for the course in the Internet age, the phenomenon of cryptomnesia underscores the importance of learning proper research methods and proper citing formats. Librarians can assist with this overload by teaching learners how to correctly and efficiently navigate quality information resources, thereby eliminating the inevitable overload that comes when using a general search engine such as Yahoo! or Google. Bowman concurs: "Good scholarship requires good work ethics, a working knowledge of accepted procedures, and the ability to recognize and keep track of the origins of numerous pieces of information. These we can teach. Our cultural, technological, and philosophical touchstones may be very different than those of our students. Still, we can effectively communicate if we approach them with an open mind, sensitivity, and a respect for their differing background knowledge and experiences" (2004: 10). The ideas of open communication, sensitivity, and respect for prior experiences are particularly important when reaching out to and instructing distance learners, whose information needs and library unfamiliarity may be more pronounced because of their lack of access to the physical library.

LIBRARY ANXIETY

As mentioned earlier in the chapter, there are many reasons why students may turn to plagiarism in order to complete an assignment. One reason that directly affects librarians and their outreach and instruction efforts is library anxiety. "Library anxiety describes having feelings of anxiousness about using the library and its resources. Library anxiety can stem from not knowing where to start, being hesitant to use the technology involved in the research process, and being reluctant to ask for help" (Cooke, 2006: 37). Academic librarian Esther Grassian remarks that only the "brave" and "desperate" students will ask for help (2004: 24), which means that there is a large percentage of students who remain confused and anxious and become susceptible to cutting and pasting their way to assignment completion. Librarians not only have to make information and research accessible and relevant, but also they themselves must be approachable and accessible. Librarians are on the frontline of access and must be proactive in marketing themselves, the library, and its services—becoming "more aggressive about letting people know what we can do for them" (Jones, 2004: 25).

Authors Washburn and Draper concur by stating, "Simply offering access through the library web page, however, is not the same as fulfilling and supporting the students' research needs" (2004: 510). In their study, which in part assessed students' needs and knowledge of the library, they found that "The vast majority of students were not aware of library services such as electronic reserve material, asking for help from a librarian via email or live chat, use of full-text databases . . . or instruction in the use of library resources. Being unaware of these services, the students did not use them." Imagine then, if on-campus students are not aware of library services, there is no doubt that the distance learners are unaware and are missing out on valuable information resources.

Once librarians get learners into the library, or in the case of distance learners, making them aware of the resources, they must often deal with the students' distinct lack of research and evaluation skills. Essentially, students are not information literate, and they are not "able to recognize when information is needed and have the ability to locate, evaluate, and use effectively the needed information" (ALA, 1989). In this age of the Internet and extreme computer technology, it is not uncommon for students to believe that their ability to surf the Web means that they know how to conduct research. The proliferation of technology and the instant gratification it provides also encourage what Professor Andrew Carnie refers to as "cyber-sloth," which is laziness for the computer age (Carnie, 2001). Therefore, students often believe that if certain information does not exist on the Internet, it does not exist at all. They have no knowledge of, or interest in, the invisible Web and library resources. Carnie goes on to say that faculty, and librarians, must "convince people that learning requires more than high-speed connections and a good search engine."

While the Internet does in some ways make plagiarism easier, it does not necessarily *encourage* plagiarism. And while distance learners may be more vulnerable because of lack of awareness and isolation, Internet plagiarism is not an automatic assumption for them. Like traditional, or on-campus plagiarism, there is ample room and opportunity for librarians and faculty to educate students, particularly in the distance learning environment. In this online environment, it is especially important that learners be comfortable and have a sense of trust, with their instructors and with each other. "Students need to trust their instructors in order to take the risks that can lead them to excellent work" (Henry, 2004: 81).

LEARNING ENVIRONMENT

In the study of adult education it is believed that the learning environment should be student-centered and that students should have a consultative voice in the educational process because the more they are involved in the process, the more they will take away from the learning experience. Vella advocates a holistic perspective of the educational process by stating, "The whole is far more than the sum of its parts. Learners learn more than what we teach" (2002: 30). Therefore, the class is more than just content and encompasses all aspects of the room, the information, and the people involved in the process; educators and librarians must be aware of the ever-changing dynamic that exists in a classroom, a delicate balance of many elements that can change at any time.

Librarians can also strive to create holistic learning environments when instructing students. Even with quality, plagiarism-discouraging assignments, students still do not know how to perform research or where to begin. They still do not know what a peer-reviewed journal is, or what a monograph is, or that there are more library resources than just the online book catalog. There are many ways that librarians can address these issues while still creating and maintaining a conducive learning environment. Some strategies require collaboration with faculty, while others can be done within the library. Grassian suggests that librarians offer one-credit library research classes, create Web-based tutorials for learners, post course-specific resources on the library's home page, set up and monitor library discussion boards (or participate in discussion boards set up by instructors), and create digital and interactive learning objects for use by students (2004: 24–25). The beauty of Grassian's suggestions is that they will work for both on-campus and distance education students.

CONCLUSION

Perhaps the most important thing librarians can do is to discuss plagiarism with students. It really is possible that students do not know what plagiarism is, even if they proclaim otherwise. D. Scott Brandt (2002: 41) suggests that when discussing plagiarism with students, librarians should make it a point to define plagiarism, give examples of plagiarism, detail the consequences of plagiarism, and promote all of the available alternatives to plagiarism. Librarians need to be explicit and open in their conversation.

Library instruction can make a remarkable difference in the academic achievement and satisfaction of students, especially with those students learning at a distance. Special attention must be paid in order for distance learners to be aware of library resources and in order for them to be less isolated and feel less library anxiety. If librarians are even moderately successful in these endeavors, they can create a positive learning environment and help prevent instances of Internet plagiarism.

REFERENCES

American Library Association. 1989. *Presidential Committee on Information Literacy. Final Report*, January 10, 1989. Available: www.ala.org/ala/acrl/acrlpubs/whitepapers/presidential. htm (accessed December 15, 2005).

Brandt, D. Scott. 2002. "Copyright's (Not So) Little Cousin, Plagiarism." *Computers in Libraries* 22(5): 39–41.

Bowman, Vibiana. 2004. "Teaching Intellectual Honesty in a Tragically Hip World: A Pop-Culture Perspective." In *The Plagiarism Plague*. Edited by Vibiana Bowman. New York: Neal-Schuman.

Carnie, Andrew. 2001. "How to Handle Cyber-Sloth in Academe." *Chronicle of Higher Education* 47(17): B14. Academic Search Premier Database, EBSCOhost (accessed August 15, 2005).

Center for Academic Integrity. *CAI Research*, June 2005. Available: www.academic integrity.org/cai_research.asp (accessed January 2, 2006).

Cooke, Nicole A. 2006. "Conquering Library Anxiety." In *Information Literacy Course Handbook for Distance and In-Class Learners*. Edited by Kate Manuel. Pittsburgh: Library Instruction Publications.

Grassian, Esther. 2004. "Do They Really Do That? Librarians Teaching Outside the Classroom." *Change* 36(3): 22–27.

Harris, Robert A. 2001. *The Plagiarism Handbook*. Los Angeles: Pyrczak Publishing.

Henry, Mallika. 2004. "Communicating Honesty: Building on the Student-Teacher Relationship." In *The Plagiarism Plague*. Edited by Vibiana Bowman. New York: Neal-Schuman.

Jones, Marie F. 2004. "Internet Reference Services for Distance Education: Guidelines, Comparison and Implementation." *Internet Reference Services Quarterly* 9(3/4): 19–32.

Kakutani, Michiko. "Bending the Truth in a Million Little Ways." *New York Times*, 17 January 2006, E1.

Merriam-Webster Online. *Merriam-Webster Online Dictionary*. 2005–2006. Available: www.m-w.com/dictionary/plagiarism/ (accessed January 2, 2006).

Modern Language Association. 2003. *MLA Handbook for Writers of Research Papers*. Chicago: University of Chicago Press.

Vella, Jane. 1994. "Learning to Listen/Learning to Teach: Training Trainers in the Principles and Practices of Popular Education." *Convergence*, 27(1): 17–21.

Vella, Jane. 2002. *Learning to Listen, Learning to Teach*. San Francisco: Jossey-Bass.

Washburn, Allyson, and Jessica Draper. 2004. "80 Miles from the Nearest Library with a Research Paper Due Monday: Extending Library Services to Distance Learners." *Journal of Library Administration* 41(3/4): 507–529.

▶Part II
DELIVERING DISTANCE INSTRUCTION

8

UTILIZING TECHNOLOGY

LANI DRAPER
MARTHEA TURNAGE

Overview: Technology and library instruction are viewed from every angle in this chapter. It examines the technology skills of students on, in particular, distance education students. The chapter looks at how librarians are incorporating technology into library instruction at a distance and examines the newest technology tools available for distance instruction.

INTRODUCTION

Librarians interweave technology into the planning and development of library instruction whether a student is on campus or at a distance. However, technology has become vital to bringing equal access to students that are at a distance. Librarians are bringing their services, collections, and themselves to distance students in order to facilitate assignments and integrate library information literacy into the curriculum. Moreover, as librarians plan and develop resources for distance education students using technology, they need to understand who their students are, how they can develop library resources for them, the roadblocks that might be in the way of a student's success in accomplishing a research goal, and continue to enhance the student educational experience through library information literacy.

Once I heard a librarian tell a student that finding something using a computer was like magic. When "non-techies" are thinking about distance education, necessary items such as computers, fiber-optic lines, browsers, IP (Internet protocol) providers, and so forth might give the appearance of these technological parts and pieces coming together like magic. Sometimes the providers of distance education themselves also might believe that to have all the pieces come together for a seamless learning experience, magic might be involved. Through anecdotal experience and a review of the literature, it appears to be evident that there are a lot of non-technical students who are using library resources from a distance with some difficulty. Who are they, what are they finding, and what is going on?

CHARACTERISTICS OF DISTANCE EDUCATION STUDENTS

Recently, Anna Sikora published a summary of the findings from the National Center for Education Statistics survey entitled "National Postsecondary Student Aid Study" (NPSAS). Some of the findings describe characteristics of students who migrate to distance education. Students who participate in distance education were found to be those with family responsibilities and limited time. They were more likely to be enrolled in school part-time and to be working full-time while enrolled. The study specifically noted that

> undergraduates usually with those characteristics associated with family and work responsibilities (such as being independent, older, married, or having dependents) were participating with higher rates in distance education. Gender was related to participation as well: females were more likely than males to participate. The participation rates of undergraduates attending public 2-year institutions and those seeking associate's degrees also tended to be higher than those of their counterparts in other types of institutions and degree programs. Undergraduates majoring in education participated in distance education at a higher rate than did those majoring in most other fields of study. (Sikora, 2003: 4, n4)

Moreover, from anecdotal librarian experiences, some full-time students at four-year or two-year institutions look for distance education classes from their current school or from any college or university around the country that will fit into their schedule, will add another credit, appear to be easier, or will replace a credit lost when they failed a class. Students who enroll in distance education, however, often do not have the technical skills necessary to succeed in the class. What are the computer skills of today's students?

Computer skills for these groups vary by the time they enter postsecondary education. According to several studies, students in public schools are using computers and the Internet at an early age. They do their homework using a computer at school and at home. According to the report entitled *Computer and Internet Use by Children and Adolescents in 2001*, the following Internet and computer usage was reported concerning age groups between five and seventeen years of age:

- ▶ 90% of children and adolescents aged five to seventeen (forty-seven million persons) use computers and about 59% (thirty-one million persons) use the Internet.
- ▶ Computer and Internet use is divided along demographic and socioeconomic lines. Uses of technologies are higher among whites than among blacks and Hispanics. Five- to seventeen-year-olds living with more highly educated parents are more likely to use technologies than those living with less well educated parents, and those living in households with higher family incomes are more likely to use computers and the Internet than those living in lower income households.

▶ A majority (59%) use home computers to play games, and over 40% use computers to connect to the Internet and to complete school assignments.

▶ About 72% of Internet users ages five to seventeen use the Internet to complete school assignments, while 65% use the Internet for e-mail or instant messaging and 62% of users use it to play games. (National Center for Education Statistics, 2004)

One group of students that is often forgotten when thinking in terms of accessibility consists of those students who live in rural areas. In the review of the literature, connectivity is one of the main problems for rural students and is often overlooked because students in urban areas complete most of the surveys. "The use of wireless, DSL and cable for broadband access has become increasingly prevalent in metropolitan areas. While these technologies are being successfully utilized in terms of both service quality and economics in densely populated areas, there are still vast geographic regions where broadband services are either prohibitively expensive or simply unavailable at any price" (Zhang and Wolff, 2004: 99). The "digital divide" is very real and continues to be an issue. "In rural America, it is clear that a digital divide, as measured by lower penetration rates of telephone usage, personal computer ownership, and Internet access and usage, still exists" (Kastsinas and Moeck, 2002: 207).

When students enter college, they assume they have the skills necessary to succeed. Students opting for distance education classes often do not have the technology skills to accomplish a Web-based course. The allure of taking classes at home on an "anytime" basis overwhelms the common sense of an individual. Indeed, according to a National Postsecondary Education Cooperative study, there were "127,400 distance education courses offered in 2001–2002 with about 3.1 million enrollments. Most 4-year college freshmen are computer literate. Almost four out of five freshmen reported using a personal computer frequently during the year prior to entering college" (NPEC, 2004). However, by definition, what does *computer literate* mean? Do these students understand about moving or sending files other than music files on their computers? According to many colleges and universities, students are having difficulty using the courseware presented in distance education courses. "Computer based learning can be difficult when previous exposure to the media is limited. Skill levels are varied and difficult to judge on admission to the classes. Hardware and software costs and compatibility were also issues" (Short, 2000: 56).

Many colleges and universities use a computer skills assessment survey offered to students before they register for a class. Most distance education Web sites offer information or orientation instructions about skill sets that are good to have to succeed in a distance education course, particularly if the course is Web-based. From experience, teachers know that many students expect a distance education course to be easier or the students expect that they can proceed through the course at their own rate. Students do not always realize that a distance education course also dictates time limits and requirements just like a face-to-face class. But do colleges and universities unintentionally place roadblocks in the way of students enrolled in distance education classes? "Librarians play an important role in facilitating the convergence of the growing number of distance education students and the growing complexity of information technology" (Turnage, Carter, and McDonald, 2004: 44). Librarians consider the connectivity issues involved with accessing library databases, often using software such as EZProxy or other authentication systems. If these systems require a student to know a password and pin, they might be one of many they must remember for campus activities. Librarians can be instrumental in working with the technology departments on campus to develop a one-password and one-pin access to campus activities and library functions. Moreover, if the computing entities on campus also installed on the network "backbone" firewalls or filters, off-campus users will have difficulty accessing the library or e-mailing full-text articles to their local e-mail systems. Communication between all computing departments and the library is necessary to work out any technology problems a student might encounter.

INCORPORATING TECHNOLOGY INTO LIBRARY INSTRUCTION

In order to support students at a distance, librarians are bringing more of their services online. They want to be wherever students will be on the Internet, so they apply all the current technology and applications that are available. The idea is for every student to have equal access. Historically, in around 1916 to 1920, reference librarians in higher education added a dimension to their service by going beyond the walls of the library and using a new invention, the telephone. Whatever the technology, librarians will use these methods to provide access and instruction online. Currently, librarians provide instruction through chat, e-mail, or course management software such as WebCT and Blackboard.

Internet Tutorials

One popular venue of teaching is a self-paced tutorial available on the Internet. Online tutorials provide students at a distance with the push they need for information literacy, often with instant answers to simple questions. The University of Texas at Austin in 1998 developed an award-winning tutorial called the Texas Information Literacy Tutorial (TILT). The UT librarians used some forward thinking and offered the tutorial duplicated or modified to fit any library's needs through their Open Publications License (University of Texas System Digital Library, 2004). Many librarians from across the country took advantage of this opportunity and adapted TILT to their own circumstances. Cuyahoga Community

College, for example, developed its Student Information Literacy Tutorial (SILT) based on TILT design (Jansen, 2002).

When librarians do not have the technology needed to create interactive tutorials such as TILT that use PHP scripting language, they can use a simple Web editor to create plain HTML/Web pages that provide critical answers to common questions posed by distance and local students. Simple Web pages can take the form of "how to" pages or FAQ pages because students in higher education appreciate a simple Web page. Web pages that actually say, "How do I find a book?" or "How do I find an article?" can be just as useful as complex interactive tutorials. Making Web pages to address issues such as access targeted especially for distance students is a good idea. A direct answer to a specific problem so that a student does not have to navigate through complicated modules can diffuse potential student frustration.

Another type of Web page that can be geared to a specific student audience is the course-specific page. Course-specific Web pages can be designed for either a distance education class or a face-to-face class. The type of information included on these pages might be items such as specific subject indexes, books, or articles that the students will find useful to accomplish a specific class assignment. Persistent links to full-text articles from databases may be placed on the Web page, as well as some text explaining how to use the library resources that have been highlighted. Moreover, Web sites evaluated by the librarian could be highlighted.

Virtual Tours

Virtual tours and streaming videos are good ways of introducing students to library resources and to librarians. Some students taking classes at a distance are often required to visit the campus once a semester or more. During this time students may find it easier to use the library if they are provided a virtual tour giving them familiarity with the layout of the library. The tour can be made simple with text and small graphics or it can be done with streaming video highlighting the key service areas and collections. The librarian can also tape an instruction session and publish it online through streaming video. However, it should be remembered that this technology should not become a student's roadblock to information. This type of technology might be for the high-speed networks and should not be the only means for students to get instruction or library help. Some students still do not have computers at home or have older versions with dial-up access to the Internet and will have problems viewing the video online. When the librarian is planning instruction on the library Web-site, a variety of helpful aids for students using a variety of technological tools must be developed.

LIBRARY SERVICES, LIBRARY COLLECTIONS, AND TECHNOLOGY

Distance students can also take advantage of interlibrary loan services. Current technology has changed the process involved with interlibrary loan. The old process of filling out a paper form and walking it to an office where someone had to handle it by hand and make a phone call has changed to computer applications handling a request without the help of an individual. An interlibrary loan form can be interactive over the Internet between the library and the student. Digitized articles can be passed through e-mail, while scanners can be used to deliver documents from print collections. Technology has also made this process more cost-effective. Most libraries do not charge students for material sent via e-mail.

Patron empowerment is the buzzword of the day because librarians are aware of customer self-service needs. If a student needs a book in the library's collection, the automated circulation applications can check out the book to the individual. Librarians are aware of value-added service enhancements. One of the ways to add value to current services such as interlibrary loan and document delivery is to digitize more library material. Digitizing projects are a growing trend in special collections and archives. Rare material once seen only in person can now be viewed online. Special imaging software can be used to manipulate objects in order to offer a real learning experience by the student. These types of projects are popular among grant-funding organizations. If a library does not have the support to apply for grants, it can start a simple digitizing project with an extra student, a scanner, and noncopyrighted material.

A large portion of a library's budget is spent on electronic access to information resources. Librarians must plan budgets well in advance of a budget year to spend money on electronic access to material such as e-books and e-journals. In the budget process, librarians are shifting the monies from journal titles in print to electronic resources. As libraries migrated to electronic full-text journals and e-texts, librarians noticed that many of the paper journal titles were available as database subscriptions; they discovered that they were paying twice for some journal titles. With the cost of print journals rising and legislatures cutting library funding, librarians no longer have the luxury of subscribing to print copies. In addition, publishers often provide an electronic rather than print subscription to higher education subscribers.

Therefore, with the myriad full-text electronic journals available from library databases and publisher subscriptions, librarians are faced with the task of not only coordinating collection development issues but also delivering these resources seamlessly to clients. To help coordinate the variety of electronic-type subscriptions and the continued paper subscriptions, there are some vendor solutions on the library scene. TDNet and Serial Solutions are products that attempt to create a portal for seamless access to electronic journals. The technology used by these vendors for locating an electronic form of a journal or magazine will also allow it to interface with the library's Online Public Access Catalog (OPAC). Students and librarians can search for a journal title, locate the full-text in a specific database, and link to the electronic version of the journal, or if it is not in electronic form, the service directs the user to the OPAC and a list of the holdings.

Another great use of technology and library services is the advent of electronic reserves. Electronic reserves are used by many faculty to create a hybrid course using face-to-face classroom experiences with the class reading materials available on the Internet. One of many ways to develop electronic reserves is by using management systems available such as Docutek ERes. In addition to allowing scanned material or persistent links, electronic reserves systems will also manage copyright issues. Docutek has a partnership with the Copyright Clearance Center so that a library can connect instantly to obtain electronic permissions for documents.

LIBRARIANS AND TECHNOLOGY TOOLS

"Many reference librarians could be described as chameleons discovering every venue to meet the information needs of students" (Turnage, Carter, and McDonald, 2004: 52). The great majority of librarians embrace new technology and certainly understand the importance of computing in libraries. They are developing online orientation and tutorials for distance education students. They also realize that they need to have a presence wherever clients are located on the Internet. Course management software used by faculty, such as WebCT or Blackboard, also is an avenue for librarians to be available for classes through the functions of chat, e-mail, and discussion groups. Another simple way to make the library presence known to students in course management software is to have a link in the navigation to the library.

An additional easy way to go online is through e-mail. E-mail, of course, is not a new technology, but it is one of the more effective ways to communicate with distance students and provide a simple form of instruction. As mentioned above, chat can be used through either course management software or some other means (AIM, Yahoo Messenger, and so forth) to provide reference and instruction services to online students. Librarians are not limited to chatting with students one-on-one. They typically can have access to student portals that offer access to school services. Often groups are set up inside the portal just for the purpose of exchanging ideas or information. In addition, as students and their professors join the group, it will provide tools such as calendars, chat, message board, and e-mail. Professors usually ask a librarian to join the group at a specific date and time for a chat with the class. This is beneficial for those professors who may not be using course management software for one reason or another. The discussion section is also open to anyone who wants to join the group, so students can get one-on-one help.

Librarians have also discovered instant messaging. Many libraries are moving to free instant messaging services for virtual reference owing to cost concerns over using other library vendor services. These instant messaging providers are free and are a good idea for a library that is just starting the service. They generally do not have all the bells and whistles of virtual reference software such as co-browsing, but for libraries that do not have heavy virtual traffic, paying for these extra services is not cost effective.

Discussion groups are another means to provide instruction to distance students. As discussed earlier, course management software often includes discussion boards in their product. Librarians can work with instructional technologists or other administrators of this courseware to create a separate library community, or they can collaborate with distance faculty in order to be a part of the class. Faculty may specify a certain time period for students to pose questions to the librarians, or the librarians could be embedded in the class so they can "lurk" in the discussion area and respond with help to appropriate questions. Discussion boards are a great way to communicate, but unless the campus community uses it often and is reviewed on a regular basis, the time and energy it takes to maintain may not be worthwhile. The librarian's energy could better be used in the technology that is popular currently on campus. If a library has a programmer and Web developer on staff, they can find freeware for discussion boards. A disadvantage of this open source software is that it needs someone with certain technical capabilities to get it working and keep it maintained. Two new communication tools that are rising in popularity are blogs and wikis. Many people in the library profession have seen the advantages of these resources but so far are using them only for professional communication. Priscilla Coulter and Lani Draper of Stephen F. Austin State University have conducted research that includes several surveys of members of the library profession in order to find out how librarians are using blogs as a means of providing instruction to their users. The findings will be published as part of the proceedings of the Off-Campus Library Services Conference (Coulter and Draper, 2007). One of the major advantages of using blogs is the fact that virtually no HTML or Web publishing skills are needed to create one. And blogging services are free online. One draw back, however, is the lack of use by or interest from students. Marketing any new service is a big issue, but librarians also need to know their users. If students are not blogging for their own personal interest, they may not want to blog with their favorite librarian, especially if it is not required.

Wikis are another quick (*wiki* means "quick" in Hawaiian) means of providing content online. In an article published in *College and Research Library News*, Rob Withers explains that Ward Cunningham, "in 1995, developed scripts for creating Web pages that could be created, edited, linked, deleted, or renamed without using HTML, software packages, or file transfer, which he named wiki" (2005: 775). Just like with blogs, there are many different types of services online that can be used freely or for a fee. The library can set permissions that will allow only certain individuals to make changes in content. A recent online Webcast, presented in wiki form, described the different ways wikis can be used and gave helpful information about where to start (Farkas, 2006).

CONCLUSION

As other computing venues "pop-up" on the Internet, librarians will be there to learn and help others to learn. The continuing collaboration with faculty and computing departments will aid librarians in acquiring the technical skills to develop current resources and ease of accessibility for distance education clients. Librarians' philosophy of free access and simple access will drive continued support for creative technological solutions.

REFERENCES

Coulter, Priscilla F., and Lani Draper. 2007. "Blogging It into Them: Weblogs in Information Literacy Instruction." In *The Twelfth Off-Campus Library Services Conference Proceedings*. Binghamton, NY: Haworth Press.

Farkas, Meredith. 2006. "Wiki World: An Introduction." Online Programming for All Libraries (OPAL). Available: www.opal-online.org/archivespecial.htm (accessed December 21, 2005).

Jansen, Ray. 2002. Cuyahoga SILT. Available: http://tili.tri-c.edu/students/library/SILT/ (accessed December 21, 2005).

Kastsinas, Stephen G., and Patricia Moeck. 2002. "The Digital Divide and Rural Community Colleges: Problems and Prospects." *Community College Journal of Research & Practice* 26, no. 3: 207–224.

National Center for Education Statistics. 2004. *Computer and Internet Use by Children and Adolescents in 2001.* (NCES 2004-014). Report prepared by Matthew DeBell and Chris Chapman. Department of Education Institute of Education Sciences. October 2003. Available: http://nces.ed.gov/pubs2004/2004014.pdf (accessed December 21, 2005).

National Postsecondary Education Cooperative. 2004. *How Does Technology Affect Access in Postsecondary Education? What Do We Really Know?* (NPEC 2004-831). Report prepared by Ronald A. Phipps for the National Postsecondary Education Cooperative Working Group on Access-Technology. Washington, DC. Available: http://nces.ed.gov/pubs2004/2004831.pdf (accessed December, 21, 2005).

Short, Nancy M. 2000. "Asynchronous Distance Education." *T H E Journal (Technological Horizons in Education)* 28, no. 2: 56–62.

Sikora, Anna C. 2003. "A Profile of Participation in Distance Education." *Education Statistics Quarterly*, 4 no. 4. Available: http://nces.ed.gov/programs/quarterly/vol_4/4_4/q4_3.asp (accessed December 21, 2005). (This article was originally published as the Executive

Summary of the Statistical Analysis Report of the same name. The sample survey data are from the NCES. National Postsecondary Student Aid Study [NPSAS].)

Turnage, Marthea, Wade Carter, and Randy McDonald. 2004. "Keep IT Simple: Internet Reference Support for Distance Learners." *Internet Reference Services Quarterly* 9, no. 3/4: 43–54.

University of Texas System Digital Library. TILT open publications license. 2004. Available: http://tilt.lib.utsystem.edu/yourtilt/agreement.html (accessed December 21, 2005).

Withers, Rob. 2005. "Something Wiki This Way Comes: An Interactive Way of Posting, Updating, and Tracking Changes in Information Used by Library Staff." *College & Research Libraries News* 66 no. 11: 775–777.

Zhang, Mingliu, and Richard Wolff. 2004. "Crossing the Digital Divide: Cost-Effective Broadband Wireless Access for Rural and Remote Areas." *IEEE Communications Magazine* 42, no. 2: 99–105.

►9

DEVELOPING DISTANCE LEARNING WEB SUPPORT

DENISE LANDRY-HYDE

Overview: This chapter presents a thorough review of distance education resources specifically for nursing, medicine, and the allied health fields. It reviews every type of resource tool available, from library catalogs to eLine (Electronic Learning in Nursing Education), from medical databases to flash tutorials.

◄

INTRODUCTION

The great challenge today for librarians teaching library research skills to distance learners is that we are working with students we will probably never see in person. Yet we must provide to these students the same level of support, both in terms of resources and services that we offer to students on our campuses.

The nursing and health sciences professions are perhaps even more challenging; as the American Association of Colleges of Nursing (2006) notes on its Web site (www.aacn.nche.edu/Media/FactSheets/NursingShortage.htm), approximately 32,797 qualified nursing applicants were turned away from baccalaureate and graduate nursing programs by U.S. nursing schools in 2004 owing to a lack of faculty, facilities, classroom space, budgets, and so forth. Yet the need for qualified nurses and health-care professionals is greater than ever as Americans rapidly age and live longer lives. By 2012, according to the U.S. Bureau of Labor Statistics, as noted in the above Web site, one million new and replacement nurses will be needed worldwide. So we must redouble our efforts to deliver quality instruction to a very diverse group of up-and-coming nursing professionals. We must be able to deliver anytime, anywhere instruction and training. According to the National Center for Education Statistics, only one-third of the more than sixteen million students in higher education are the full-time eighteen- to twenty-two-year-olds who used to dominate college campuses. The rest are part-time or older students who are juggling jobs, family responsibilities, and studies. They demand "flexibility in the educational process and marketability in the outcome" (Kirschner, 2005: 1).

RESOURCES FOR DISTANCE LEARNERS

Key areas in which libraries must provide support to distance learners and to distance faculty, as well, are in the areas of resources and services. From the learner's perspective, the distance learning environment requires information to be available "just in time" to wherever the learner might be located. From the library's perspective, it may not be sensible or feasible to acquire, house, and manage a growing physical collection that users will never visit but from which the library will need to pull and deliver items in some way to users at a distance (Distefano, Rudestam, and Silverman, 2004).

Web-based Resources

Most libraries today have Web-based catalogs revealing the materials owned by the library or to which the library has access, so even students who are at a distance are able to access these resources remotely. Catalogs contain records of all formats of materials—print, microform, and electronic. Catalogs such as OCLC's WorldCat provide users with information on the holdings of thousands of libraries, including those of libraries located nearer to the off-campus student's home. An ambitious trend is to try to catalog significant electronic resources available on the Web. Links to these resources are provided in the online catalog (ibid.).

Libraries also enable remote access to Web-based databases, often including the full text of journal articles and other documents, for their users. Many of these databases are proprietary. In the nursing and health sciences fields, core resources include CINAHL, Medline, and choices such as Gale's Health & Wellness Resource Center, and so forth. These databases, with the exception of Medline, which is government subsidized, cost a good deal of money; so legally binding license agreements with content providers typically specify that only currently affiliated students, faculty, and staff may gain remote access to these resources. Therefore, authentication, proving that users are who they say they are and not someone else, is required before users can get into these databases. Authentication procedures have gotten easier and smoother over time. Authorization also is an issue. Authorization establishes that a user has a right, as a student, staff, or faculty member, that others do not have (ibid.).

One of the most used methods of authorization is according to IP (Internet protocol) address recognition. Access is granted to only certain IP addresses. In a distance learning environment, though, most users will want to access licensed online resources from home or office, using Internet service from one of any number of ISPs (Internet service providers); therefore, the range of IP addresses for these computers is typically not known to the subscribing library. A solution to the remote access issue is use of a proxy server at the subscribing library, thus providing a known IP address. All users who want to access online materials subscribed to by the library must do so by going through the proxy server. Firewalls and other network security measures can prevent the proxy server from fulfilling its role, so users will have to be attentive to this (ibid.).

Other Web-based resources are freely available to users. For starters is the library's own Web site. The first step, in terms of distance learners, should be to acknowledge their existence. All services should be spelled out so that distance students can find information applicable to them as a group. Organizing all useful information in one place on a distance learning Web page—one-stop shopping—is particularly helpful to these students.

It is also good to create multiple access points to the same information. Users follow different paths to the same end. A distance learner looking for borrowing policies, for example, might not start with the Distance Learning page, but with the Circulation page. The challenge for libraries is "to provide useful, but not excessive, redundancy" (Linden, 2000: 101) and to avoid conflicting or out-of-date information. The site must be regularly checked to make its information current. If the library has a database-driven site, the information needs to be updated only once in the database (ibid.).

Government Resources

Government information is another source of freely accessible information. MedlinePlus (http://medlineplus.gov), maintained by our National Library of Medicine (NLM) located in Washington, D.C., is probably the best first choice as a source for quality consumer health information available and a great starting point for finding credible medical information. It includes an online medical encyclopedia, medical dictionary, drug information, interactive tutorials, and on and on. It is also available in Spanish as well as in English.

The NLM also maintains WISER: Wireless Information System for the Emergency Responder (http://wiser.nlm.nih.gov), a database that supports firefighters, emergency medical services (EMS) personnel, and so forth, in identifying unknown substances. A PDA or laptop may be used to access WISER. Once a substance is identified, WISER provides guidance on immediate actions necessary to save lives and protect the environment (Mashayekhi, 2005).

Other government sites, such as those for the Centers for Disease Control and Prevention in Atlanta (www.cdc.gov/), the U.S. Department of Health and Human Services (www.hhs.gov), the National Institutes of Health (NIH) (www.nih.gov), and the World Health Organization (WHO) (www.who.int/en/), are treasure troves of medical information. MedlinePlus frequently links users to these other sites. They are freely available and some of the best examples of our tax dollars being put to good use.

Universities and medical centers also offer quality information sites to the health information consumer and professional. One such example is that from the University of Texas School of Public Health at Houston, CHARTing Health Information for Texas: Providing Context and Instruction for Health and Vital Statistics, (www.sph.uth.tmc.edu/charting/), maintained by Helena Von Ville, librarian. One of her objectives is "to develop meaningful access to publicly available health outcomes, socio-demographic, and community data for Texas" (Von Ville, 2006). Another example is the World Lecture Hall from the University of Texas at Austin, http://web.austin.utexas.edu/wlh/index.cfm. Free online course material is available at this site, including notes and syllabi for certain nursing classes.

Medical Web Sites

For a comprehensive medical Web site, the Mayo Clinic online (www.mayo clinic.com) is hard to beat. Like the Mayo Clinic Web site, WebMD (www.webmd. com) offers a vast amount of information on numerous diseases. Texas A&M Health Science Center's Hometown Health site (http://tamhsc.edu/news/hometown/) covers a wide array of health-related topics. The Texas Cooperative Extension's Family and Consumer Sciences Web site (http://fcs.tamu.edu/) contains practical information on food, nutrition, and general health. For information on specific diseases, more specialized sites are useful: the American Cancer Society (http://www.cancer.org), the American Diabetes Association (www.diabetes.org), and the American Heart Association (www.americanheart.org) (*Texas A&M System News Online*, 2005).

Other "core Web medical reference" sites are noted in *The Kovacs Guide to Electronic Library Collection Development: Essential Core Subject Collections, Selection Criteria, and Guidelines* (Kovacs and Robinson, 2004). NOAH: New York Online Access to Health Home Page (www.noah-health.org) consists of consumer health information sponsored by the New York Academy of Medicine and the New York Public Library. Although specifically designed for residents of New York, this site includes a great deal of useful health resources that all consumers will find helpful. The National Library of Medicine Gateway (http://gateway.nlm.nih.gov) allows searching of multiple NLM databases, including MEDLINE, MedlinePlus, and others. Clinical Trials.gov (http://clinicaltrials.gov) is also offered through the NLM to provide the public with current information on clinical research trials, and Public Library of Science (PLoS) contains open-access (freely available) journal article material as well as other document types. PLoS (www.publiclibraryof-science.org) is "a nonprofit organization of scientists and physicians committed to making the world's scientific and medical literature a freely available public resource" (PLoS, 2006).

E-Books and Linking

E-books, such as those offered through netLibrary and ebrary, are other resources that should be considered for acquisition. Consortium arrangements typically enable libraries to get the most favorable pricing for e-books.

The OpenURL technology standard enables context-sensitive linking from within online resources. For example, a citation in a bibliographic database might have a link to the full-text online article or document if the library subscribes to the electronic journal in question. SFX is one such link-resolver (Distefano, Rudestam, and Silverman, 2004).

Online Special Collections

Libraries are using technology to put their own resources and special collections online. Photos, correspondence, and other types of material are scanned into digital format and made available through digital libraries. These libraries must provide ways for users to find relevant digital objects they contain. Information about the resources, metadata, is entered into a database or XML (extensible markup language) data format. The metadata are indexed for searching in an information retrieval (IR) system. If the text of some document is "marked up" with tags that describe physical and intellectual aspects of the document, this is a value-added service for the patron. The Text Encoding Initiative (TEI) has defined a set of markup tags for including these kinds of descriptions in electronic documents. The tag set now makes use of XML (ibid).

An increasing number of institutions are creating their own institutional repositories that typically offer free and readily available scholarly communications of their faculties to the public. Successful examples of such repositories include Stanford University Libraries HighWire Press (http://highwire.stanford.edu). This site hosts "the largest repository of free, full-text, peer-reviewed content, with 918 journals . . ." (Stanford University Libraries HighWire Press, 2006). According to the site, it produces seventy-three of the two hundred most frequently cited journals, many of those in the medical, physical, and biological sciences.

Another successful institutional repository is the eScholarship Repository of the California Digital Library (http://repositories.cdlib.org/scholarship/). It supports the full range of scholarly output from the University of California System, one of the most productive systems in the world.

The next challenge for libraries is to better integrate different collections and services with one another. Two technologies, in particular, have helped in this effort—federated, or distributed, searching and harvesting. Federated searching allows queries to be sent to multiple resources and the results combined for viewing by the patron. An alternative to federated searching is harvesting, in which the metadata for the virtual collection are gathered on a periodic basis from multiple resources. Searches can find relevant items and go only to the remote server to get the digital object. Performance is typically much faster than with federated searches (ibid.).

Both federated searching and harvesting require that metadata conform to common standards for interoperability. The Dublin Core metadata initiative is an example of such a standard. Standards such as MARC (machine-readable cataloging) and Dublin Core for metadata, XML for text encoding and Web services, and Web and IP protocols for information transmission provide a basis for the convergence of library and other academic services for distance education. These technologies are being used to provide access to library resources and services for remote students and faculty. The resources themselves are increasingly not on campus or in any one place. (ibid.).

SERVICES FOR DISTANCE LEARNERS

Key library services also must be delivered to distance learners. Reference and instruction are some of the most critical of these services. Most academic libraries offer e-mail reference service, at a minimum. This service should be monitored days, nights, and weekends, if at all possible. Distance learners often do their research during evening and weekend hours, so it is important for reference librarians to be available at these times. Virtual Reference (VR) has become a very hot topic in librarianship in recent years. Virtual reference services are now being offered so that students, no matter where they are located, can get help with their academic research. Virtual reference can mean one of a number of possibilities—responding to asynchronous e-mail requests or allowing simultaneous "chatting," instant messaging (IM), or searching of online resources. The latter is also called "live reference." Its advantage is that both the library user and the librarian simultaneously search in real time, look at the same pages together, and "talk," either by using voice or typing, about that shared experience, even though the user may be many miles away. This simultaneous searching is called "co-browsing." Big questions relating to VR include determining how many hours per day and days per week the service can and should be offered. VR software includes that offered by DocuTek, Tutor.com, QuestionPoint, and others. Librarians must spend time in training using this software, however, before they launch into virtual reference service delivery (ibid.).

Virtual Instruction

Planning and delivery of virtual instruction involves many of the same considerations as delivery of virtual reference service and can, to some extent, utilize the same software solutions as VR, only in a "one-to-many" mode, instead of a one-to-one framework. In distance learning, computer literacy is a pre-requisite to gaining information literacy (ibid.).

In the area of instruction, Web pages, including the library's own Web page, and Web-based tutorials and user guides are exceedingly important. Most libraries now have their customized pathfinders or subject guides available on their Web sites.

Web Tutorials

Web tutorials are particularly useful to distance learners the librarians will never see. Students can utilize these at their own pace and at times that are convenient to them. Information literacy tutorials such as the University of Texas TILT (http://tilt.lib.utsystem.edu/) have been released under Open Publication License (OPL). Many schools, including Indiana University–Purdue University at Indianapolis (IUPUI) have adapted TILT for their own use. IUPUI's customized version of TILT is named inflite (http://inflite.ulib.iupui.edu). Instructional designers were critical in the local adaptation of this software. It is always important to have qualified technological support when maintaining Web-based resources (Moline, March 2004).

An example of a well-developed CINAHL tutorial is one by Pamela Sherwill-Navarro and Beth Layton of the University of Florida Health Science Center Libraries (www.library.health.ufl.edu/help/CINAHL/index.htm). This tutorial was recently accepted into ACRL's Instruction Section, Emerging Technology in Instruction Committee's PRIMO: Peer-Reviewed Instructional Materials Online database (www.ala.org/ala/acrl/bucket/is/iscommittees/webpages/emergingtech/primo/index.htm) (*ACRL IS Newsletter*, fall 2005). Other mini-tutorials from the University of Florida Health Science Center Libraries are those on logging into EZproxy and a series of short catalog tutorials (www.library.health.ufl.edu/George/EZ/EZ.html and www.library.health.ufl.edu/help/UFCatalog/home.htm) (Mary Edwards to the OFFCAMP mailing list, July 15, 2005). Minitutorials done by Esther Grassian at UCLA on searching for articles can be found at www.sscnet.ucla.edu/library/rtr.phy?module=Find&section=Articles&page=01a (Allyson Washburn to the OFFCAMP mailing list, July 18, 2005). A well-developed Flash tutorial on the use of Boolean operators is one from Louisiana State University, at www.lib.lsu.edu/ref/flash/Boolean.html.

Multimedia creation software can give tutorial development quite a boost. Flash technology allows for the creation of dynamic, Web-based content. It creates small, easily streamed files. Flash files can be readily served from a Web server; that is, special software or hardware is not required to do this. Flash does require a Flash Player plug-in on the viewer's browser, but this has become almost ubiquitous. And if, by chance, the user doesn't have the plug-in, it can be easily downloaded and installed in a matter of minutes.

Flash-authoring Tools

Leading Flash-authoring tools, according to Ken Burhanna (August 2004), seem to be Robodemo (www.macromedia.com/software/robodemo) and Viewlet-Builder by Qarbon (www.qarbon.com). Another popular product, Camtasia Studio (www.techsmith.com/), is not really a Flash-authoring tool but is actually a desktop recording solution—one that is capable of exporting Flash files. Camtasia lacks much of the functionality for interactivity that Flash provides, but it does provide some of the best quality screen captures and recordings.

Robodemo was recently acquired by Macromedia. Since Macromedia is the creator of Flash technology, this acquisition can be seen as a positive development. While use of Flash requires specialized programming skills, RoboDemo, for those who feel fairly comfortable with computers, is less complicated to use. Robodemo can also produce what is called a "manifest file," which can communicate data to course management systems such as WebCT. This has implications for WebCT-based library instruction. It would allow an instructor to assign a Web-based learning module with quizzing capability to students. The module would then report via the manifest file that the student viewed the module and what the student's quiz results were (Burhanna, August 2004).

Samples of Burhanna's Flash-authoring work can be seen at www.ulib. csuohio.edu/help/hands-on. For quick animated tutorials, William Badke at Trinity Western University recommends a freeware product called Wink (www.debug mode.com/wink/). It creates flash tutorials without the creator having to learn Flash. Sample creations are available at www.acts.twu.ca/lbr/AcSePr.htm. Another suggestion from Marcia Keyser at Drake University is Swish (www.swishzone. com/), a utility that builds Flash animations (ACRL Instruction Section, Emerging Technologies in Instruction Committee, March 2004).

IMPORTANCE OF STUDENT LEARNING STYLES

In teaching it is important to remember that different people have different learning styles. Try to address all styles—visual, auditory, and kinesthetic—so that no one group of students is left at a disadvantage. Everyone uses all three styles, depending on the particular situation; however, most people have a preference, or favorite. About 60% of the population are visual learners, 30% are auditory, and 10% are kinesthetic. Only a very small percentage of the population (2–3%) can learn using any style at any time. Text, graphics, and animation are particularly useful to visual learners. Auditory learners learn best by hearing information, such as in recorded lectures. Kinesthetic learners learn best by doing, so hands-on activities, discussions, and so forth are important ways for this group to learn (Library Education at Desktop (LE@D) Tutorial, 2005).

COURSE MANAGEMENT SOFTWARE

More and more institutions are using course management software, such as Blackboard and WebCT, to deliver classes online. Blackboard has recently acquired WebCT. A recent announcement from a WebCT partner, SAGE, the Simulation and Advanced Gaming Environments for Learning Network, is "the development of collaborative, online, multimedia, problem-based simulations for nursing and medical students, as well as for practicing health professionals" (*WebCT Newsletter*, November 14, 2005). Fictional characters arrive at fictional clinics presenting symptoms and background narratives. Medical teams collaborate online to diagnose and treat the patients. SAGE will use WebCT Campus Edition 6 and the WebCT Vista PowerSite Kit module to help track learner activities within these courses. They will also analyze the effectiveness of gaming in the learning process and in the behavior of the students (*WebCT Newsletter*, November 14, 2005).

Another WebCT partner, WestNet Learning Technology, offers customers access to thousands of graphics and animations. A WestNet Learning Objects Flash demo is available at http://store.westnetlearning.com/mkt/WebCT_int.asp.

EMERGING TECHNOLOGIES

Podcasting is a rapidly growing form of communication and information delivery both in business and academia. The number of podcast listeners using iTunes alone grew from one million in July 2005 to six million in August 2005 (Gerry McKiernan e-mail to the Information Literacy Instruction mailing list, January 6, 2006). Apple has a great Web page titled "iPod in the Classroom" (www.apple.com/education/ipod/) (ibid.). Podcasting allows anywhere, anytime access to lectures, speeches, audio books, and so forth. Harvard University has joined the fast-growing ranks of institutions offering courses as podcasts (*The Chronicle: Wired Campus Blog*, November 28, 2005). The opportunities to use podcasting in the classroom are simply endless.

Instant messaging has been used as an additional way for students to reach reference librarians. The Library Success Wiki (www.libsuccess.org/index.php?title=Online_Reference,) contains articles about IM reference. *First Monday* also contains a recent article on the topic: "'IM Here' Reflections on Virtual Office Hours," by Shannon L. Roper and Jeannette Kindred (November, 2005), at http://firstmonday.org/issues/issue10_11/roper/.

Another recent announcement from Indiana University and the University of Michigan signals a project funded by the Mellon Foundation to develop online tools to make the "invisible Web," which includes resources such as subscription-based online journals and databases, more visible. This project will enable professors to link to thousands of online library resources from within the course management software. Currently, in order to access library resources from course management systems or other Web-based applications, students must often visit library Web sites separately. The project will use open-source software, so the good news is that other universities will benefit from the results of this project (www. dlib.indiana.edu/projects/sakai/) (*Library Journal Academic Newswire*, January 19, 2006).

OTHER ONLINE SERVICES

Today's online catalogs (OPACS) typically include online renewal and similar functions. Patrons can login to the online catalog, see what materials they have checked out, renew items and, in some cases, put "holds" on items others have checked out.

Users can also request needed material through interlibrary loan/document delivery. Often, materials can be obtained and delivered electronically. If the home library has the needed item in print or microform, that document can be scanned into digital format (usually PDF, or Portable Document Format, so multiple pages can be contained in one file), uploaded to a server, and delivered to the distance learner over the Internet. The Adobe Acrobat Reader is needed to view these files, but the viewer is free and easy to download. This kind of delivery is typically done when journal articles are needed. If books are required, these are usually mailed to students, via first class mail in the case of distance learners. Students may be asked to assume the cost of return postage.

E-reserves materials are commonly digitized into PDF format, as well. With electronic reserves, students can download needed materials from the Web for viewing or printing. Copyright laws limit access to the digital material. Access is typically password protected, so not just anyone is able to access the full text.

It is good for libraries to make arrangements with other libraries from which distance students can borrow books and other material. TexShare in the state of Texas (www.texshare.edu/generalinfo/about/programs.html) is an example of a resource-sharing agreement among different types of libraries throughout the state. Students must obtain a TexShare Card through their home institutions. This card may be used at other participating libraries for book checkout. Students need to understand what kind of identification is needed in order to borrow from other libraries, and they need to know how to obtain the ID. This kind of information should be included on a distance learning Web page, together with troubleshooting information and FAQs.

At Texas A&M University–Corpus Christi (TAMU–CC) and Del Mar Community College, the entire nursing program is available electronically through eLine (Electronic Learning in Nursing Education) at www.eline.tamucc.edu or at www. eline.delmar.edu. Classes are available anywhere, anytime via the Internet. Clinical experiences are close to home—this possibility is greatly appreciated by rural areas of the state, in particular, since they often experience severe nursing shortages. Administration, advisement, registration, and book purchase are available by way of the Internet. It is possible to choose an ADN (Associates Degree in Nursing) from Del Mar or a BSN (Bachelor of Science in Nursing) from TAMU-CC. eLine is funded, in part, by the U.S. Department of Education learning Anytime Anywhere partnerships of the Fund for the Improvement of Postsecondary Education (FIPSE).

CONCLUSION

Even as this chapter goes to press, Dr. Claudia Johnston, associate vice president of Academic Affairs-Special Projects, and her team at TAMU–CC are "building a learning platform in the virtual environment for clinical experiences for health care professions students at both the undergraduate and graduate levels" (Lois Barry, personal comment). The working title for this project is PULSE! It is an initiative of the U.S. Department of Defense through the Office of Naval Research. The possibilities for this project are endless. Truly, we are living in a "brave new world"—one that is also virtual.

WEB SITE REFERENCES

American Association of Colleges of Nursing—www.aacn.nche.edu/
American Cancer Society—www.cancer.org
American Diabetes Association—www.diabetes.org
American Heart Association—www.americanheart.org
Centers for Disease Control and Prevention in Atlanta—www.cdc.gov
CHARTing Health Information for Texas: Providing Context and Instruction for Health
    and Vital Statistics—www.sph.uth.tmc.edu/charting/
Clinical Trials.gov—http://clinicaltrials.gov
eLine (Electronic Learning in Nursing Education)—www.eline.tamucc.edu
eScholarship Repository of the California Digital Library—http://repositories.cdlib.org/
    scholarship
HighWire Press (Stanford University Libraries)—http://highwire.stanford.edu
inflite—http://inflite.ulib.iupui.edu
Library Education @ Desktop (LE@D) Tutorial, University of North Texas—http://web2.
    unt.edu/cmp_lead/
Mayo Clinic Online—www.mayoclinic.com
MedlinePlus—http://medlineplus.gov
National Institutes of Health—www.nih.gov
National Library of Medicine Gateway—http://gateway.nlm.nih.gov
NOAH: New York Online Access to Health—www.noah-health.org

OFFCAMP Mailing List—www.library.health.ufl.edu/help/UFCatalog/home.htm

PRIMO: Peer-Reviewed Instructional Materials Online—www.ala.org/ala/acrl/bucket/is/iscommittees/webpages/emerging- tech/primo/index.htm

Public Library of Science (PLoS)—www.publiclibraryofscience.org

Texas A&M Health Science Center's Hometown Health—http://tamhsc.edu/news/home town/

Texas Cooperative Extension's Family and Consumer Sciences—http://fcs.tamu.edu/

TexShare—www.texshare.edu/generalinfo/about/programs.html

TILT (Texas Information Literacy Tutorial)—http://tilt.lib.utsystem.edu/

U.S. Department of Health and Human Services—www.hhs.gov

WebMD—www.webmd.com

WISER: Wireless Information System for the Emergency Responder—http://wiser.nlm.nih. gov

World Health Organization—www.who.int/en/

World Lecture Hall—http://web.austin.utexas.edu/wlh/index.cfm

REFERENCES

ACRL Instruction Section Newsletter. Fall 2005. "PRIMO Database Accepts Four New Instruction Projects."

American Association of Colleges of Nursing. Nursing Shortage Fact Sheet. Available: www.aacn.nche.edu/Media/FactSheets/NursingShortage.htm (accessed January 5, 2006).

Burhanna, Ken. "InfoTech Tips and Trends, Survey of Multimedia Creation Software. ACRL Instruction Section Emerging Technologies in Instruction Committee." Available: www.ala.org/ala/acrl/bucket/is/iscommittees/webpages/emergingtech/techtips/ august 2004 (accessed January 5, 2006).

Chronicle: Wired Campus Blog. 2005. Crimson Coursecasts. Available: http://wiredcampus. chronicle.com/2005/11/crimson_coursesec.html (accessed November 28, 2005).

Distefano, Anna, Kjell Erik Rudestam, and Robert J. Silverman, eds. 2004. *Encyclopedia of Distributed Learning.* Thousand Oaks, CA: Sage Publications.

Kirschner, A. 2005. "The Future of the Liberal Arts, Alma Mater in the Time of TiVo Information Technology," *Chronicle of Higher Education.* Available: http://chronicle.com (accessed December 9, 2005).

Kovacs, Diane K., and Kara Robinson. 2004. *Kovacs Guide to Electronic Library Collection Development.* New York: Neal-Schuman.

Library Education at Desktop (LE@D) Tutorial, University of North Texas. Available: http://web2.unt.edu/cmp_lead/ (accessed January 5, 2006).

Library Journal Academic Newswire. 2006. "Indiana, Michigan Receive Grant for Invisible Web Project." Available: www.libraryjournal.com/clear/CA6300733.html (accessed Jaunary 19, 2006).

Linden, J. 2000. "The Library's Web Site Is the Library: Designing for Distance Learners." *College & Research Libraries News* 61, no. 2: 99–101.

Mashayekhi, Bijan. E-mail to the NLM–WISER List. June 6, 2005.

McKiernan, Gerry. E-mail to Information Literacy Instruction mailing list. January 6, 2006.

Moline, Julie. "InfoTech Tips and Trends, Use of Course Management Systems in Instruction." ACRL Instruction Section Emerging Technologies in Instruction Committee. Available: www.ala.org/ala/acrl/bucket/is/iscommittees/webpages/emergingtech/techtips/march2004 (accessed January 19, 2006).

PLoS. Public Library of Science. www.publiclibraryofscience.org (accessed January 19, 2006).

Roper, Shannon L., and Jeanette Kindred. 2005. "'IM here': Reflections on Virtual Office Hours." *First Monday*. Available: http://firstmonday.org/issues/issue10_11/ (accessed January 19, 2006).

Stanford University Libraries HighWire Press. 2006. Available: http://highwire.stanford.edu/lists/freeart.dtl (accessed January 5, 2006).

Texas A&M System News Online. 2005. "Internet Offers an Abundance of Wellness Resources. Available: http://amsnews.tamu.edu/use1.html (accessed January 19, 2006).

Von Ville, Helena M. 2006. "CHARTing Health Information for Texas: Providing Context and Instruction for Health and Vital Statistics." Available: www.sph.uth.tmc.edu/charting/ (accessed January 19, 2006).

WebCT Newsletter. November 14, 2005. www.webct.com (accessed December 21, 2005).

▶10

DESIGNING ONLINE INFORMATION LITERACY TUTORIALS

SUSAN J. CLAYTON

Overview: In this chapter two examples of online tutorials developed in the Black-board Course Management System are discussed. One of the tutorials was developed for a teacher-credential program for a school of education, and the other was developed for entering MBA students in a school of business. The planning, development, and implementation of the tutorials are the topic of this chapter.

◀

INTRODUCTION

"Librarians are creating interactive, self-paced tutorials, designed in segments, to introduce information-research concepts and techniques, and then to provide practice and reinforcement of them" (Grassian, 2004: 25). This chapter will focus on two examples of online information literacy tutorials: one for students pursuing their teaching credential in a school of education and the other for new MBA students in a school of business. The amount of information available in today's society is overwhelming to anyone and especially to those students who are returning to college after some work experience. The students in the two schools are composed of both off-campus students and evening students, which means that an online tutorial is a great benefit to the students in terms of time and convenience. These students often do not have the familiarity with online resources that many of the undergraduate students possess. An examination of the literature on online information literacy tutorials shows that articles have been written on the subject for first-year college students, but little has addressed subject-specific tutorials for students in professional schools, such as business and education. This chapter will explain the history and development of the tutorials as well as their content and method of delivery. To begin designing information literacy tutorials for any subject area, the support of the faculty as well as the information technology staff is necessary. Another important consideration is the time that must be allotted to such a project by the faculty, the librarian, and the technology staff. A number of useful articles on this topic are listed in the references at the end of this chapter.

DEVELOPING THE INFORMATION LITERACY TUTORIAL FOR EDUCATION

The three areas of education, information technology, and the library came together in a committee of three people. These three were a professor from the school of education, the manager of instructional technology, and the off-campus services librarian, who is the library liaison to the school of education. Several factors led to the development of the information literacy workshop. There had not been an off-campus services librarian for two years, and projects that the school of education had wanted to develop were deferred until the library position was filled. The instructional technology department was beginning to use the Blackboard Learning System for online courses and workshops. And for accreditation renewal, the teacher-preparation program in the school of education was required to include an information literacy module in its program. These three factors came together at a time, fall semester 2003, when these three committee members could work closely together to create the information literacy workshop. There were actually two workshops created: a beginning workshop and an advanced workshop; both will be covered in this chapter. In fall 2003 the committee met and began to work on the workshop titled "Information Literacy I: Beginning Workshop." The committee took the outline of the presentation that the librarian had created for in-class presentations and found information online from such sites as the California Technology Assistance Program (CTAP) Information Literacy site and the National Educational Technology Standards (NETS) site. The committee began to develop an online workshop in Blackboard from these resources. Throughout the fall semester the committee met to review the progress and add to the resources. The professor indicated the types of information needed in the workshop, such as a definition of information literacy, information on copyright, Web searching, plagiarism, and citing sources. These were the elements of the beginning workshop. The same elements are used in the advanced workshop, but in this workshop the teacher-credential students are presented with resources for teaching information literacy to their classes at all grade levels. By the end of the fall semester 2003, the beginning workshop was up and running and was used with students in January 2004. After the committee finished the beginning tutorial, it was used as a model for the advanced tutorial. By the middle of the spring semester, we were ready to use the "Information Literacy II: Advanced Workshop" with students in May 2004. During the 2003–2004 academic year we had completed both the beginning and advanced information literacy workshops and began presenting them to the students.

OVERVIEW OF THE EDUCATION TUTORIALS—BEGINNING AND ADVANCED

The first tutorial begins with an overview of the concept of information literacy and outlines the learning objectives. The learning objectives are: to synthesize information about information literacy by viewing several Web sites, to explore the concept of copyright and its guidelines as it relates to education, to develop strategies for effective Web searching, to understand what constitutes plagiarism, and to understand the correct method for citing resources in the APA (American Psychological Association) format. Each of these learning objectives corresponds to an activity that the students must complete in the workshop.

The first activity consists of an overview of information literacy from the California Technology Assistance Project, while the second explores copyright issues and presents several related Web sites. The third activity helps to develop better Internet searching skills using Google. Exploring various issues relating to plagiarism constitutes the fourth activity. The fifth activity explores citing sources in the APA format. A scored quiz takes place following all the activities.

The purpose of the advanced workshop is to prepare the teacher-education students to teach the concepts of information literacy to their classes at various grade levels. The students have already participated in the beginning workshop during their Educational Foundations course. For the advanced workshop, the students are enrolled in advanced teacher-education courses, and the advanced information literacy workshop is a module in these courses. The advanced workshop is designed to provide future educators with an overview of the importance of teaching information literacy skills by looking at national technology standards, exploring the Big6 theory for teaching information literacy skills, reviewing ways to evaluate Web site information, and by looking at various K–12 acceptable use policies. Learning about each of these topics is the objective of this workshop. While the beginning workshop included five activities for the students with a final quiz, the advanced workshop includes four activities with a final quiz.

The first activity is an overview of NETS, with the second introducing the students to the Big6 skills approach to information literacy. The Big6 Skills is an approach to teaching information and technology skills. These six steps are used in K–12, higher education, and corporate training programs. The third activity helps students to develop better Web site evaluation skills. An introduction to and definition of acceptable use policies takes place during the fourth activity. The final activity is a scored quiz.

It is a requirement for each course in "Educational Foundations" (EDUC 500) and "Single-" or "Multiple-Subject Content Area Literacy" (EDUC 508 or 509) that the students take and pass the online quiz for both the beginning and advanced workshops. There are ten questions in each quiz, and the students must pass with a score of 80% or higher.

DEVELOPING THE BUSINESS INFORMATION LITERACY TUTORIAL

Several of the faculty members in the school of business were interested in developing an information literacy tutorial for students beginning the MBA program. These faculty members had seen the tutorials developed for the school of education and requested a similar tutorial be developed for their school. The manager of instructional technology, the off-campus services librarian, and the director of the MBA program met from August through October 2004 to develop the business information literacy tutorial. It was first used during the fall 2004 new student MBA orientation in November. The basic model for the business tutorial was the same as was used for education, but the examples included were business resources. This tutorial is also in the Blackboard Course Management System.

OVERVIEW OF THE BUSINESS TUTORIAL

The business tutorial begins with an introduction to locating business information online. The second part presents an overview on how to locate information on industries and companies. Specific activities in this part of the tutorial involve locating and using industry SIC (Standard Industrial Classification) and NAICS (North American Industry Classification System) codes. Students then use the code to locate company information in the Lexis-Nexis database. The next activity in the tutorial involves locating economic data using the U.S. Census Bureau and the Federal Reserve System. This is followed by an activity searching for journal articles in databases and citing the articles in APA format. The final activity is an overview of plagiarism including some examples of plagiarized work. At the end of the tutorial is a quiz, which must be completed with a passing grade; the tutorial must be taken and passed to be able to complete the first course in the MBA program: "Preface to Leadership."

HOW THE TUTORIALS ARE DELIVERED

The tutorials are presented to the school of education and school of business students in different ways. A description of each method follows.

Education

The education information literacy tutorials are offered online and in face-to-face sessions. The students may choose the method they prefer. Face-to-face workshops are offered in the school of education computer lab during the hour before the evening education classes begin, usually from 4:00 PM to 5:15 PM. Each workshop (beginning and advanced) is offered Monday through Thursday during a week of the instructor's choosing. The off-campus services librarian conducts the face-to-face workshops throughout the specified week, and students sign up for the workshop date of their choice. If the students prefer, they may review the entire workshop online through the Blackboard Course Management System and complete the quiz. Completion of both the beginning and the advanced workshops and the accompanying quizzes is a course requirement. The Blackboard System retains each student's quiz results, which can be reviewed by the professor when grading the coursework. The two workshops are currently offered only to the students in the teacher-credential program. The beginning information literacy workshop is included in the course "Educational Foundations," and the advanced workshop is included in "Single-Subject Content Area Literacy" or "Multiple-Subject Content Area Literacy."

Business

The business information literacy tutorial is offered both online and in face-to face sessions, again based on the model for the education tutorials; however, the business tutorial is offered during the day-long orientation for new MBA students and is held on Saturdays during the fall, spring, and summer semesters. The librarian has time on orientation day to present the business information literacy to the new students. Students then take the tutorial and the quiz at any time during their two weeks of orientation. The tutorial grade is added into the grade for the introductory MBA course.

PROS AND CONS OF USING THE TUTORIAL

During the classes that the tutorials have been used, several favorable and unfavorable issues have become clear. For example, the face-to-face tutorial sessions with the librarian are preferred by both education and business students, according to reports from both of the professional schools. For the school of education, class time is not used for the information literacy tutorials; they are scheduled during the hour before evening classes begin. Some students who would like to attend face-to-face sessions are unable to attend at this time owing to other schedule constraints, such as work or family obligations. The face-to-face tutorials are particularly helpful to students who have difficulty negotiating the Blackboard System on their own. On the other hand, the online tutorials are available to all students at any time, which is helpful with regard to the scheduling issue.

With each new class session, both the education and business tutorials must be checked and Web site links must be updated. Both the school of education and school of business classes begin every six or eight weeks throughout the year. The manager of instructional technology and the off-campus services librarian update the tutorials. The librarian is responsible for requesting copyright permission for the use of various Web sites, as needed. At the school of education students sign up for each information literacy tutorial, while at the school of business the tutorial is included as a part of the MBA orientation day. All MBA students receive the information literacy tutorial at the same time, while at the school of education the tutorial is held four times during the designated week (Monday through Thursday before classes begin). For all the tutorials in both schools, the Blackboard System automatically records the online tutorial attendance through the final quiz. Overall, the quiz is a positive component of both tutorials. It is an assessment tool for the faculty, and it records attendance. In addition, it also makes the students take the tutorial sessions more seriously, since the quiz must be passed in order to complete the degree.

CONCLUSION AND FUTURE OF INFORMATION LITERACY TUTORIALS

It is difficult to say how long these tutorials will continue to be used before they are changed to reflect new approaches to the teacher-preparation courses and the MBA coursework. The trend seems to be that gradually more students are taking information literacy tutorials and the accompanying quizzes online, although many students prefer the personal touch of face-to-face tutorial presentation. Perhaps equally as positive as the reception of the tutorials by the students has been the close working relationship that has developed among the school of education, the school of business, the library, and the department of instructional technology. This cooperative effort has been the true success of the online tutorial project.

WEB SITES USED IN THE EDUCATION AND BUSINESS TUTORIALS

EDUCATION INFORMATION LITERACY: BEGINNING WORKSHOP

An overview of information literacy for teacher education:
www.ctap4.org/infolit/index.htm
An introduction to copyright issues and information:
www.copyright.com

EDUCATION INFORMATION LITERACY: ADVANCED WORKSHOP

An introduction to information literacy standards for K–12:
http://cnets.iste.org
An overview of how to evaluate Web sites:
http://liblearn.osu.edu/tutor/les1/

BUSINESS INFORMATION LITERACY WORKSHOP

A resource for locating business and economic statistics:
www.census.gov
A resource for locating U.S. economic information:
www.federalreserve.gov
An introduction to APA style for business students:
www.apastyle.org/aboutstyle.html
A resource to help students identify examples of plagiarism:
www.plagiarism.org

REFERENCES

American Psychological Association. "About APA Style." Available: www.apastyle.org/about style.html (accessed January 16, 2006).

Asselin, Marlene. "Guiding the Inclusion of Information Literacy." *Teacher Librarian* 31 (April 2004): 63–64. Available: http://proquest.umi.com (accessed January 9, 2006).

Asselin, Marlene M., and Elizabeth A. Lee "'I Wish Someone Had Taught Me': Information Literacy in a Teacher Education Program." *Teacher Librarian* 30 (December 2002): 10–17. Available: http://vnweb.hwwilsonweb.com (accessed January 9, 2006).

Board of Governors of the Federal Reserve System. "Federal Reserve Home Page." Available: www.federalreserve.gov (accessed January 16, 2006).

Boudreau, Signe, and Tracy Bicknell-Holmes. "A Model for Strategic Business Instruction." *Research Strategies* 19 (2003): 148–162.

Carr, Jo Ann. "Information Literacy and Teacher Education." *ERIC Digest* (November 1998) ED424231. Available: www.eric.ed.gov (accessed January 9, 2006).

"Copyright.com—Copyright Licensing and Compliance Solutions." Copyright Clearance Center. Available: www.copyright.com (accessed January 16, 2006).

Crouse, Warren F., and Kristine E. Kasbohm. "Information Literacy in Teacher Education: A Collaborative Model." *The Educational Forum* 69 (fall 2004): 44–52.

Eisenberg, Michael B. "Beyond the Bells and Whistles: Technology Skills for a Purpose." *Multimedia Schools* 8 (May/June 2001): 44–51. Available: http://vnweb.hwwilsonweb.com (accessed January 9, 2006).

"Evaluating Web Sites." Net.TUTOR. Ohio State University Libraries. Available http://lib learn.osu.edu/tutor/les1/ (accessed January 16, 2006).

Fiegen, Ann M., Bennett Cherry, and Kathleen Watson. "Reflections on Collaboration: Learning Outcomes and Information Literacy Assessment in the Business Curriculum." *Reference Services Review* 30 (2002): 307–318.

Germain, Carol A., and Deborah Bernnard. *Empowering Students II: Teaching Information Literacy Concepts with Hands-On and Minds-On.* Pittsburgh: Library Instruction Publications, 2004.

Grassian, Esther. "Do They Really Do That? Librarians Teaching Outside the Classroom." *Change* 36 (May/June 2004): 22–27.

Henderson, Martha V., and Anthony J Scheffler. "New Literacies, Standards and Teacher Education." *Education* 124 (winter 2003): 390–395.

"Information Literacy Resources." California Technology Assistance Project. Available: www.ctap4.org/infolit/index.htm (accessed January 16, 2006).

iParadigms, LLC. "Plagiarism.org Home Page." Available: www.plagiarism.org (accessed January 16, 2006).

Judd, Vaughn, et al. "Evaluation and Assessment of a Library Instruction Component of an Introduction to Business Course: A Continuous Process." *Reference Services Review* 32 (2004): 274–283.

Krueger, Karla, Lisa Hansen, and Sharon E. Smaldino. "Preservice Teacher Technology Competencies." *TechTrends* 44 (April 2000): 47–50. Available: http://vnweb.hwwilson web.com (accessed January 9, 2006).

Lenholt, Rob, Barbara Costello, and Judson Stryker. "Utilizing Blackboard to Provide Library Instruction: Unloading MS Word Handouts with Links to Course Specific Resources." *Reference Services Review* 31 (2003): 211–218.

Lombardo, Shawn V., and Cynthia Miree. "Caught in the Web: The Impact of Library Instruction on Business Students' Perceptions and Use of Print and Online Resources." *College & Research Libraries* 64 (January 2003): 6–22.

Luke, Carmen. "New Literacies in Teacher Education." *Journal of Adolescent & Adult Literacy* 43 (February 2000): 424–435. Available: http://proquest.umi.com (accessed January 9, 2006).

Mahoney, Patrick, ed. *Distance Learning Library Services: The Tenth Off-Campus Library Services Conference.* Binghamton, NY: Haworth Information Press, 2002.

"National Educational Technology Standards (NETS)." International Society for Technology in Education. Available: http://cnets.iste.org (accessed January 16, 2006).

Ratteray, Oswald M. T. "Information Literacy in Self-Study and Accreditation." *The Journal of Academic Librarianship* 28 (November 2002): 368–375.

Roldan, Malu, and Yuhfen D. Wu. "Building Context-Based Library Instruction." *Journal of Education for Business* 79 (July/August 2004): 323–327. Available: http://vnweb.hwwilson web.com (accessed January 9, 2006).

Rutledge, Daniel P., and Alicia Maehler. "An Assessment of Library Education Contributions to Business Student Learning: A Case Study." *Journal of Business & Finance Librarianship* 9 (2003): 3–19.

Shinew, Dawn M., and Scott Walter. *Information Literacy Instruction for Educators: Professional Knowledge for an Information Age.* Binghamton, NY: Haworth Information Press, 2003.

Tyner, Kathleen R. *Literacy in a Digital World: Teaching and Learning in the Age of Information.* Mahwah, NJ: Erlbaum Publishers, 1998.

U. S. Census Bureau. Home Page. Available: www.census.gov (accessed January 9, 2006).

▶11

COMPARING AN ONLINE AND A CD-ROM LIBRARY TUTORIAL

JOHN-BAUER GRAHAM
JODI POE

Overview: This chapter presents an intriguing look at the use of two library tutorials: one on CD-ROM and the other presented online in the Blackboard Course Management System. The chapter discusses how a survey was conducted to determine which format was preferred by the distance education students. The survey results and conclusions are presented.

INTRODUCTION

Jacksonville State University (JSU) is a medium-sized, public comprehensive university offering both undergraduate and graduate programs. It was founded in 1883 as Jacksonville State Normal School. Its purpose in 1883 was to provide a preparatory education for citizens of a rural Alabama county and the surrounding areas. The mission and the student population of the university have changed over time. The current enrollment is approximately nine thousand students, with the university hosting students from all over the United States and from almost every corner of the globe. Its institutional borders have expanded; it is no longer bound to the twelve acres of land it originally sat on, having grown beyond actual physical space.

The university, like almost all institutions of higher learning, has witnessed a boom in distance education. According to Yi, "Nearly half of the four thousand major colleges and universities offer courses over the Internet or use the Web to enhance campus classes" (2004: 47). Yi also notes that the National Center for Education Statistics estimates that in 1997–1998 over 54,000 distance education courses, over 1,200 degree programs, and over 300 certificate programs were offered. JSU's Distance Learning Mission Statement indicates that Jacksonville State University strives to meet the needs of all students. Distance education enhances this capability by utilizing the ever-expanding set of technological tools to reach students who may be unable to participate in the traditional university environment. With new tools such as videoconferencing and online courses, students from all walks of life can participate in a university environment while continuing with their employment schedules and family responsibilities. Distance education provides an outstanding level of education for everyone, not just select individuals at strictly delineated times of the day. From fall 2001 until spring 2005, the number of distance education courses and supplements rose from 34 to 384. A 300% increase! The number of students enrolled in distance education courses also rose during that period, from 957 in fall 2001 to 8,772 in spring 2005.

The growing distance education community has obviously had an impact on JSU's library. Library services at JSU are centralized in the Houston Cole Library (HCL). The library, which is staffed with fourteen professional and nineteen paraprofessional employees, has a collection of more than six hundred thousand titles. Because the number of students enrolling in distance education courses is increasing, library services and resources need to be as flexible as possible to ensure that "distant" students are afforded the same services and resources available to on-campus students. In this same vein, more and more of the library's resources are moving to the online environment. This has been a welcome event for faculty, staff, and students, but it has also led to growing problems of how to both disseminate information about library access and instruct individuals on using these resources. How do librarians better serve a population that they do not see day to day, semester to semester, or even once a year? Is it possible to create, implement, and maintain a level of service to an invisible library patron? What about existing services—how do librarians assure that the traditional library services such as reference and bibliographic or library instruction are afforded to the patron that does not walk through the front door for these services, but instead enters the library through a computer?

A major concern for HCL was how to "reach and teach" the distance education students. How does the library provide instruction for a student population that does not meet on campus? These were questions the library needed to address. In reviewing the various options (online tutorials, virtual reference/chats, CD-ROMs, and so forth), the library first decided to create a tutorial on a CD-ROM. Although reference and virtual chat services were available for purchase, the cost of virtual reference/chat services was beyond the budget. The use of CD-ROMs allowed the library to customize everything about the tutorial and provides easy access to the students, who could use the CD with any computer without having to be online. In addition, or rather as a bonus, the CD helped the library meet the requirement of the Southern Association of College and School (SACS) for providing equivalent services to distance education students. Additionally, having something to offer distance education students fulfilled an Association of College and Research Libraries (ACRL) guideline for services by offering a program that is: "designed to instill independent and effective information literacy skills while specifically meeting the learner-support needs of the distance learning community" (ACRL, 2004).

Once fully implemented, the CD-ROM tutorial/orientation extended the library's ability to address its students' information requirements and served the mission by enhancing the students' awareness of library services and resources, facilitating the development of information literacy, perpetuating lifelong learning skills, and improving the learning environment for distance education students. The library was receiving positive feedback from the initial CD-ROM tutorial; however, the increase in online courses changed the direction of the tutorial. At this time, the university as a whole began to strongly encourage its faculty to use an online course management system (namely, Blackboard) for every course taught by the university, in particular, for every course offered online or through another distance education medium.

Owing to an increasing number of faculty members using Blackboard for supplemental coursework, and the students using Blackboard more often, the library decided to use this system to deliver its instruction as well. To develop an online tutorial, the elements of the CD-ROM were added to a Web page. Since the CD-ROM tutorial was based on hypertext markup language (HTML) and JavaScript, it was simple to move the code to a Web page and present it in this fashion. Once the page was created, the library established links to these pages through the Blackboard course created for library instruction. A content area labeled "Faculty Information" also was included to provide information about the Instructional Services Coordinator and the Distance Education/Electronic Resources Manager. The standard "Announcements" area was included. An additional link was created for the survey. Thus, the Blackboard course consisted of four content areas: Library Tutorial, Survey, Faculty Information, and Announcements. This made it very simple for the students to find all of the required sections. The library soon realized that this medium would allow for greater flexibility in that changes, such as those with redesigned page and database interfaces, could be made quickly and presented immediately. In addition, no extra charge would be incurred such as with CDs, which would have to be re-created, copied, and distributed with each change. Because of the differences in these delivery methods, the library needed to determine which method would be best received by the students.

LITERATURE REVIEW

There is an abundance of literature related to providing instruction to distance education students. Unfortunately, most of it offers general information about instruction options or relates to a specific library's efforts in this endeavor; whether it created a CD-ROM, used a Web-based tutorial, and so forth. Unfortunately, no articles were found that directly compared the use of CD-ROM with Web-based delivery methods.

A number of writings provide general information about library instruction and distance education students. Goodson (2001) discusses a variety of issues related to library services and distance education students. She briefly introduces the various instruction options available to libraries, as well as furnishes a bibliography with URLs for instruction-related materials. Hricko (2001) details how Kent State University provides instruction to distance education students. Her article offers information about three common delivery methods: videoconferencing, computer-mediated, and Web-based. In addition, Hricko notes the problems that Kent State encountered with each delivery method and gives suggestions for solving these problems. She does not mention which method worked best for the library.

Of all of the articles concerning library instruction for distance education students, there is limited literature related to CD-ROM tutorials. Jones details one library's development of a CD-ROM tutorial and provides information about the "nine events of instruction" (Jones, 2004: 187) that should be included in tutorials. She also describes work-arounds for these elements and the applications her library used to create its tutorial.

The majority of the literature relates to Web-based tutorials. May (2003) describes how the library at the University of North Texas used the Texas Information Literacy Tutorial (TILT), the Web-based instructional tool created at the University of Texas at Austin, and the course management system, WebCT, in use at the university to provide instruction for its distance education students. She also specified how the librarians created and used subject guides and class-specific Web pages to enhance the instruction. A number of good ideas regarding creating Web-based tutorials can be found in this article. Behr (2004) details the process Western Michigan University's library staff used to create a Web-based instruction resource. She describes the limitations of using WMU's current service for distance education students, which is similar to the service provided by HCL.

The service currently in place at the HCL is face-to-face instruction sessions. At Western Michigan University, the librarians travel to the distance education sites and provide face-to-face sessions (ibid.). This is a major limitation in terms of those online students who do not meet at a specific location or time. The author provides possible solutions for these limitations and examples of what other types of instruction services were reviewed in Western Michigan's search for an equitable solution. Yi (2004) details the trend of moving library instruction online and some reasons to follow that trend. In addition to describing the trends, the author explains the experiences California State University at San Marcos encountered during its move to an online environment.

Finally, a new evolution in library instruction is using course management systems for delivery. Several articles detail how libraries can use a course management system to provide library instruction. Ladner et al. (2004) provide information about their experience with creating Web pages designed specifically for two courses and then linking the pages through WebCT for access. Lenholt, Costello, and Stryker (2003) detail their enhancement of face-to-face, hands-on instruction by adding the handouts from these sessions into Blackboard. These same authors later describe using the identical approach for providing instruction as detailed in their 2003 article, but augmenting it for generations X and Y students (Costello, Lenholt, and Stryker, 2004). Silver and Nickel (2003) furnish information about using Blackboard as a delivery method for instruction. Although the sessions were delivered through Blackboard, it was not necessarily geared toward distance education students. In addition to providing this service for the distance education students, the authors also use their Blackboard session as an optional format for those students who could not attend a face-to-face session.

STUDY AND SURVEY METHODS

After the library created the online tutorial, it was determined that one hundred students should be an ideal sample size for the study. The library polled thirty-four faculty members teaching an online course during the university's summer 2005 terms. Of those polled, the library received immediate feedback from eight faculty members regarding the request. Of the eight, the library contacted the first five who responded. The courses used in the study were Physical Education 109 ("Concepts of Wellness"), Nursing 400 ("Research and Outcome Management"), Political Science 100 ("Introduction to American Government"), Geology 256 ("Physical Geology"), and Public Safety Telecommunications 325 ("Management Principles in Public Safety Communications"). These selected classes provided a broad range of courses offered at JSU. The library was hoping for some upper-level courses, but there were limited graduate level courses being taught online during these terms. A class roster was obtained for each of these courses, and the students were assigned a unique number from 1 to 129. The authors used Research Randomizer (www.randomizer.org/form.htm) to create two sets of participants. Set 1 was to use the CD-ROM, while set 2 was to use the online tutorial. Of the randomly created sets, the first fifty in each set were selected to be the sample population of one hundred.

Once the students were selected, their e-mail addresses were gathered. Each student received an introductory e-mail message congratulating him or her on being selected for participation. The students receiving the CD-ROM tutorial were notified that their material had been mailed to their home address. Materials sent included the CD-ROM and a cover letter regarding the study. Those receiving the online tutorial were given the URL for Blackboard, along with the username and password to access the library tutorial course. Both sets of students were provided general information and instructions about the course and contact information in case there were problems. Reminder messages also were delivered to the students' e-mail addresses, noting the deadline for survey submissions.

The survey consisted of ten questions, the first of which asked the students to state their status (undergraduate or graduate). Question 2 asked them to identify how they were currently receiving their classes, that is, all online or some online, and whether they were currently taking their classes out of state or on campus. In question 3 they were asked to identify which tutorial they had received (either CD-ROM or online). Question 4 was asked to gather information about the students' past experiences with any formal library instruction prior to receiving the tutorial. Question 5 was a four-point Likert scale question asking the students to rank how helpful the tutorial had been. The following question again used a four-point Likert scale to discover how confident the students had felt after completing the survey. The survey asked (using a four-point Likert scale) how easy the tutorial had been in helping to determine which delivery method would be best for the students. The survey then asked whether or not the participants would be willing to recommend the tutorial to a classmate. Finally an open-ended question was asked in order to get feedback as to how the tutorial could be improved.

RESULTS

Out of the one hundred students surveyed, thirty responded. The majority of the respondents were undergraduates (87%). About 60% of the respondents were taking all of their courses online, with the remaining respondents indicating that they were at least taking some of their courses online. There was a fairly even distribution of how the respondents received their tutorial: sixteen received the tutorial via CD-ROM, while the remaining respondents (fourteen) received their tutorial through the online Blackboard course. There was also a similar distribution between the number of respondents who had received formal library instruction (51%) and those who had not (43%). Using a four-point Likert scale to measure how helpful the tutorial was to the participants (1=not helpful, 2=somewhat helpful, 3=helpful, 4=very helpful), the survey demonstrated that over 70% of the respondents reported that the tutorial was either very helpful or helpful (see Figure 11.1). Only

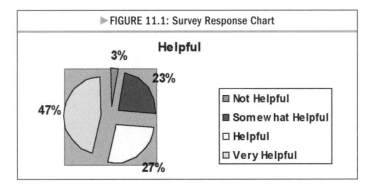

▶FIGURE 11.1: Survey Response Chart

Helpful

3%

23%

47%

27%

☐ Not Helpful
■ Somewhat Helpful
☐ Helpful
☐ Very Helpful

one respondent indicated that the tutorial was not helpful. This particular respondent had taken the tutorial online. Additionally, this respondent also indicated that he/she had received formal library instruction before taking the tutorial.

In addition to the tutorial being helpful, the library hoped that the tutorial would also increase the confidence of the user toward using the library's resources after completing the tutorial. Again, using a Likert scale from 1 to 4 (1=not confident, 2=somewhat confident, 3=confident, 4=very confident), the survey indicated that all (100%) of the respondents reported they were confident or very confident using the library's resources after completing the tutorial. Using a four-point Likert scale (1=very difficult, 2=difficult, 3=easy, 4=very easy), participants were asked to rank how easy or difficult their tutorial had been. When comparing two different ways of delivering a tutorial, this is perhaps one of the most important questions. Overall, eighteen of the respondents reported that the tutorial was very easy to use, eleven indicated that it was easy to use, and one indicated that it was difficult. Broken down into the different delivery methods of the tutorial, the ease of use seemed to be similar (see Figure 11.2). Of the sixteen respondents taking the tutorial via the CD-ROM, five reported the use as easy and eleven as very easy to use. Of the fourteen respondents who took the tutorial online, six reported the use as easy, seven reported it as very easy, and one reported it was actually difficult to use. None in either group reported that the tutorial was very difficult to use.

▶ FIGURE 11.2: Ease of Use

Delivery Type	Very Difficult	Difficult	Easy	Very Easy
CD-ROM	0	0	5	11
Online	0	1	6	7
Total: 30	0	1	11	18

The success of any program implemented in higher education often depends on the students' acceptance of said program and their willingness to share with fellow students their positive or productive experiences. Word of mouth, so to speak, was the impetus for the next survey question, and the library was happy to report that 93% of the respondents would recommend the tutorial to their friends. Only two respondents (one online tutorial taker and one CD-ROM tutorial taker) indicated that they would not recommend the tutorial to their friends.

CONCLUSIONS

The library was pleased with the results of the survey and was also pleased with the many positive comments received from the open-ended question about the tutorials at the end of the survey. Several respondents reported that the tutorial was indeed a great idea (in both formats) and that they only wished they had had such a tool sooner. The survey results indicated that students surveyed were just as satisfied and well served by receiving the tutorial in CD-ROM as compared with those who had received the tutorial online; however, because there was an equal number of students satisfied with the online version of the tutorial, it was determined that this was, in fact, the best route for the library to pursue. Online materials are less expensive because the library does not need to purchase, copy, and distribute individual CDs to students. If both tutorials were indeed "getting the job done," then the most cost-effective way to deliver the tutorial would be the one pursued and developed. Additionally, the library could not ignore the increasing number of university courses (not just distance education courses) that were migrating to an online environment. Librarians would be able to reach and teach a larger number of the student population by offering a Web-based tutorial; nevertheless, the tutorials on CD-ROM will still be produced but will be used on a "by request" basis or as promotional material to be handed out at student and library-related functions.

It was interesting to note that despite a strong instruction program offered in traditional form by the library, many of the participants indicated that they had not received any formal library instruction. This quietly illustrates the point that the library needed to do more to reach its distance education population. In conclusion, the library remains determined to provide the best possible service to all its patrons. Even though the university has grown beyond its acreage and includes students from every corner of the globe, the library remains well within their reach.

REFERENCES

ACRL "Guidelines for Distance Learning Library Services." 2004. Available: www.ala.org/ala/acrl/acrlstandards/guidelinesdistancelearning.htm (Accessed August 10, 2006).

Behr, Michele D. 2004. "On Ramp to Research: Creation of a Multimedia Library Instruction Presentation for Off-Campus Students." *Journal of Library Administration* 41, no. 1/2: 19–30.

Costello, Barbara, Rob Lenholt, and Judson Stryker. 2004. "Utilizing Blackboard in Library Instruction: Addressing the Learning Styles of Generations X and Y." *Journal of Academic Librarianship* 30, no. 6: 452–460.

Goodson, Carol F. 2001. *Providing Library Services for Distance Education Students: A How-to-Do-It Manual.* New York: Neal-Schuman.

Hricko, Mary. 2001. Developing Library Instruction for Distance Learning. Paper presented at the 6th Annual Mid-South Instructional Technology Conference, Tennessee.

Jones, Marie F. 2004. "Creating a Library CD for Off-Campus Students." *Journal of Library Administration* 41, no. 1/2: 185–202.

Ladner, Betty, et al. 2004. "Rethinking Online Instruction: From Content Transmission to Cognitive Immersion." *Reference & User Services Quarterly* 43, no. 4: 329–337.

Lenholt, Rob, Barbara Costello, and Judson Stryker. 2003. "Utilizing Blackboard to Provide Library Instruction: Uploading MS Word Handouts with Links to Course Specific Resources. *Reference Services Review* 31, no. 3: 211–218.

May, Frances A. 2003. "Library Services and Instruction for Online Distance Learners." In *Integrating Information Literacy into the College Experience: Papers presented at the 30th National LOEX Conference.* Ann Arbor, MI: Pierian Press.

Silver, Susan L., and Lisa T. Nickel. 2003. "Taking Library Instruction Online: Using the Campus Portal to Deliver a Web-based Tutorial for Psychology Students." *Internet Reference Services Quarterly* 8, no. 4: 1–9.

Yi, Hua. 2004. "Library Instruction Goes Online: An Inevitable Trend." *Library Review* 54, no. 1: 47–58.

▶12

CREATING AND USING AN INFORMATION LITERACY TOOLKIT FOR FACULTY

KATE MANUEL

Overview: Rather than from a student perspective, this chapter examines the faculty perspective on library instruction and distance learners. The chapter presents a modular toolkit for faculty to introduce library skills into their courses. The chapter also suggests alternatives to the traditional research paper. ◀

INTRODUCTION

Many college and university faculty members—whether teaching on-campus or by way of distance education (DE)—report feeling that there is "too much" course content for them to devote time to teaching library skills (Cannon, 1994; Feldman and Sciammarella, 2000; Thomas, 1994). DE faculty members feel these time constraints more keenly than other faculty members, however; and standard guides to teaching DE caution that it can take substantially longer to "cover" course content via DE than in a face-to-face classroom situation (Palloff and Pratt, 2001). Additionally, DE faculty often teach students who are geographically remote from the home campus and its library, and they may feel that the use of library resources or education about them are thus irrelevant impossibilities for their students; or they may believe that students who must use the Web to access course materials automatically will know how to use Web-based library and information resources.

Whatever reasons explain individual faculty members' decisions not to incorporate library assignments and instruction into their DE courses, the fact remains that DE students are much less likely than their on-campus counterparts to be formally introduced to information research skills. Statistical data both from the New Mexico State University (NMSU) Library Instruction Program and from national surveys confirm this. Only 122 of the 6,731 students receiving library instruction in the NMSU Library Instruction Program in academic year 2003–2004 were distance education students,[1] while nationally only 11% of libraries relied upon information literacy instruction programs to introduce students to library services and resources (Thompson, 2002). The under-representation of DE students among those receiving library instruction is particularly unfortunate, since DE students' physical distance from campus makes them less able to rely upon the information assistance services provided to on-campus students by librarians in the campus library. Moreover, demographic characteristics of DE students suggest they need library instruction at least as much as—if not more than—on-campus students. DE students are likely to be older and female (Hillesheim, 1998), demographic factors that can correlate with decreased effectiveness in technologically based information seeking and use (Horrigan, 2003).

This chapter describes an attempt by the NMSU Library Instruction Program to promote library instruction among DE faculty by developing a modular Web-based toolkit, which faculty could draw upon to more effectively integrate information literacy skills and concepts into their teaching. The toolkit approach was inspired by the work of Jerilyn Veldof and her colleagues at the University of Minnesota. They developed their toolkit in part to serve a large segment of distance and online learners and in part to provide "instructors and librarians with an efficient means to develop customized learning resources in a time of expanding availability of information resources and more complex information access" (Butler and Veldof, 2002). The NMSU toolkit resembled the University of Minnesota model in its orientation toward DE students and in its general goal of providing efficient means of developing learning resources. However, it also had the more specific goals of

▶ reminding DE faculty members that the purpose of information research assignments and instruction is not to teach students how to use a particular physical library but rather to develop the eighty-seven skills comprising information literacy;

▶ emphasizing that information research assignments need not be ten- or twenty-page research papers but can take other forms and

▶ encouraging DE faculty members to initiate or rethink partnerships with librarians in designing and providing library instruction.

Key to accomplishing all three of these goals was the modular nature of the resources comprising the toolkit: smaller, "chunked" units enabled faculty members to understand better the skills that could be fostered by library instruction, promoted alternatives to the research paper, and prompted even faculty members with histories of using library instruction with their in-person classes to reshape their partnerships with librarians.

MODULARITY AND ITS BENEFITS

In general, as an adjective, *modular* denotes something "composed of standardized units or sections for easy construction or flexible arrangements," or, as a noun, "a self-contained unit or item that can be combined or interchanged with others like it to create different shapes or designs" (*Random House*, 1991). This general use of the terms *modular* or *modules* maps in educational contexts to those items that are also known as "learning objects" or, in digitized form, "low-threshold applications/activities" (LTAs). A learning object is any grouping of materials structured in a meaningful way and tied to an educational objective. Learning objects can be thought of as LEGO building blocks or atoms because they are, respectively, "small units that can be fitted together any number of ways to produce customized learning experiences," or "made up of smaller pieces which by themselves are not as useful as the whole; they can be combined . . .; and they form compounds which can then be combined or deconstructed again" (Smith, 2004; Wiley, n.d.; Wiley, 2002). An LTA is basically a digital learning object, or an "educational use of information technology that is reliable, accessible, easy to learn, non-intimidating and (incrementally) inexpensive" (Gilbert, 2002).[2]

Such modules are important to information literacy instruction—particularly for DE students—for several reasons. First, they allow instructors to plan and implement instruction easily by drawing upon already created, or micro-learning, units, many of which yield student products other than research papers. Faculty members' gravitation toward the research paper as the "natural" result of the information research process is probably inevitable, given the production of dissertations as the requirement for the professoriate and the place of the scholarly journal article as the sine qua non of academic promotion. Nevertheless, ten- to twenty-page research papers are problematic vehicles for ensuring students' mastery of subject content or information research skills because of the disjunction between faculty and student views about the purposes and goals of research papers. That many students see research papers as "closed-ended exercise[s in] information gathering" that matter primarily for the grades earned, while many faculty see research papers as "open-ended process[es], involving critical thinking, inquiry, and discovery" that are intrinsically valuable (McMackin, 1994, 107; cf. Valentine, 2001), has lead many academics to speculate that research papers "may not be as valid an approach to the acquisition of either knowledge or of writing skills as is commonly believed" (Kloss, 1996: 3). Research papers are further problematic when the students and faculty are involved in DE, since many faculty are convinced both that research papers are the only possible product resulting from information research and that DE students do not have the time or resources to write research papers. Hence, these faculty conclude that since research papers are not an option for their DE students, library instruction is irrelevant to them. Given the problematic nature of research papers in general and faculty members' lack of knowledge of alternatives to research papers, it thus became vitally important for the toolkit to include numerous alternatives to research papers. These alternatives, some of which will be discussed in the next section, gave faculty members awareness of other products that could result from student research. Often these products were more easily graded than a traditional research paper, and the modular approach allowed faculty to "plug" one or more of these alternatives into their courses with minimal initial work.[3]

Second, the toolkit's modules help to make real to faculty members that the focus of library instruction is the development of information literacy competencies, not just skills in effectively using the academic library, particularly its article databases and scholarly journals. Too often, DE faculty members rely on "one-shot" instructional sessions for their students; these sessions either try to give the students everything they need to know about the library in fifty minutes or provide a first-you-click-here, then-you-click-there introduction to a database. Students cannot learn everything they need to know about the library, or effective information-seeking strategies, in fifty minutes, though. Even if they could, the library's services and collections are constantly changing, as are the workings of particular databases. The constancy of change in libraries and information resources, coupled with the frequency of change in disciplinary content knowledge and in individual workers' careers, makes it impossible for students to ever have all the content they would need to know to use libraries and information resources effectively forever thereafter. In reality, information becomes outdated so fast that "by the time a student studying engineering graduates [from college], half of his knowledge is already obsolete" (Tapscott, 1998: 145) and "twenty percent of the knowledge generated within a company becomes obsolete in less than a year" (Rifkin, 2000: 22). This realization has led to calls for "lifelong learning," for workers to keep learning new information and skills on their own after they graduate,[4] and recognizing this, educators, librarians, and business leaders developed the process-oriented (as opposed to content-oriented) approach to effective seeking and use of information known as "information literacy." The modular approach helps faculty members see that the range of information literacy skills their students need is much broader than they might have thought; the modular format per se helps to illustrate the incremental, cumulative nature of information literacy. It negates the facile equation of information literacy with traditional library use skills and begins to break the construct of information literacy down from the five broad standards into the twenty-two performance indicators and eighty-seven outcomes of the *Information Literacy Competency Standards for Higher Education* (ACRL, n.d.).

Moreover, because the modules are small and self-contained, their use presumes some plan for interconnections among them—a factor that greatly facilitates the development of a standardized and tiered approach to building skills among students, as well as the development of discipline-specific information competencies. Modular curricular integration can be a difficult concept because it requires each faculty member to think of his or her courses' curriculum within a broader context, rather than as his or her individual domain. It has, however, been done success-fully at other institutions, most notably in the College of Textiles and Engineering at North Carolina State University (Nerz and Weiner, 2001), and there is a rudi-mentary plan for doing so at NMSU (see Figure 12.1). Modular curricular integra-tion is the only way out of the current impasse in which motivated faculty take it upon themselves to introduce their students to everything they need to know about the library—with the result that some students get four or five such intro-ductions to the same material and are bored (a phenomenon recognized by John Lubans as early as 1974), while others get one introduction whose information they cannot begin to comprehend, and yet others get no introduction and must muddle through on their own. Modular curricular integration is also a must for at-taining discipline-specific library instruction. Faculty members often need to be re-minded that, even if they cannot get other faculty members in their departments to partner with them in developing a tiered, modular plan, they are still better off if they do not try to introduce their students to everything about the library and in-formation research all at once but rather build modules developing a few skills closely tied to course content.[5]

Finally, the modular approach facilitates good pedagogy. Information research assignments are best, and most easily, introduced to students as separate, short modules that prompt students to explore and force them to reflect upon their ex-periences. The information research process is overwhelmingly daunting for most students, especially when not explicitly broken down into its components of initia-tion, selection, exploration, formulation, information gathering, and presentation (Kuhlthau, 1997). Beyond making the information research process seem less overwhelming to students prone to "library anxiety," breaking down the process into discrete components also has the advantage of building on the strengths of a constructivist approach to learning. It helps each student to be "actively involved in building on what he or she already knows to come to a new understanding of the subject under study" (Kuhlthau, 1997: 710).

DEVELOPING THE TOOLKIT

The NMSU toolkit (http://lib.nmsu.edu/instruction/toolkit/toolkit.htm; see Figure 12.1) was developed largely by the instruction coordinator working in con-junction with the vice provost for distance education and five members of the stu-dent services subcommittee of the Distance Education Advisory Board. Planners intentionally used a "static" Web page to provide access to the toolkit's resources in order to reiterate the comprehensive nature of information literacy. Each of the five ACRL *Standards* has its own table that lists the performance indicators—al-though not the more detailed learning outcomes—associated with it, as well as rec-ommended readings addressing that topic, informational handouts, and suggested

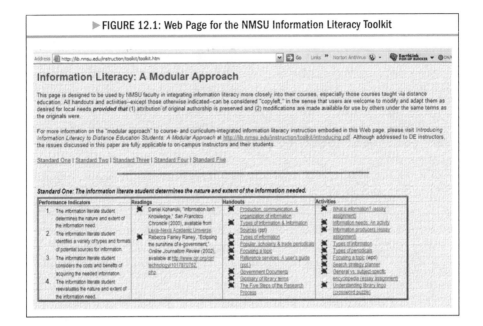

► FIGURE 12.1: Web Page for the NMSU Information Literacy Toolkit

activities. In selecting handouts and activities for inclusion, priority was given to locally produced instructional materials since these materials had already been used
successfully with faculty and students at this specific institution and since these materials could be made available to faculty members for their modification without
worries about copyright. However, links were made to selected items from such national repositories of learning objects as Merlot (www.merlot.org); Low Threshold
Applications: An Evolving Program with Growing Resources (www.tltgroup.org/re-
sources/rltas.html); Cloe Stories (http://learnware.uwaterloo.ca/projects/
CCCO/cloe_stories.html); and PRIMO: Peer-Reviewed Instructional Materials
Online (http://cooley.colgate.edu/dbs/acrlprimo/showrec.html). Often the creators of the learning modules listed in such repositories will grant permission for
instructors to modify these materials for local use, especially since learning objects
are commonly touted for their flexibility in allowing their "expansion, contraction,
or adaptation to meet the needs of many specific class situations" (Ladner et al.,
2004: 331).

All of the activities listed are alternatives to the traditional ten- or twenty-page research paper.[6] Examples include:

► Jigsaw exercises that might, for example, involve a faculty member's dividing
the class into four to six (or even more) groups (depending upon the number
of students and the number of types of sources instructors would like students
to examine) and then making each group responsible for presenting on the
type of source it examined, including (1) the titles of specific examples of this

source type that they examined, (2) descriptions of the type(s) of information they provide, (3) discussion of how current the information provided by this type of source is, (4) ideas on how a professional in the field could use the information in this type of source, and (5) descriptions of any limitations to or problems with this type of source (cf. Ragains, 1995).

▶ Brief writing assignments (one-page papers) prompting students to compare and contrast information on a topic found in popular or scholarly periodicals; on the Internet and in a commercial, "library" database; or via subject or keyword searching.

▶ Searching problems, which confront students with a "problematic" set of search results—such as the retrieval of no (0) results for a given search in a particular database—and ask them to propose, justify, and test other strategies for finding information on that topic (cf. Cooperstein and Kocevar-Weidinger, 2004). (See Figure 12.2.)

▶ Presenting students with an example of a failed information search or failed use of information taken from real life and asking them to "correct" the problems. For example, engineering faculty have used the PowerPoint slides prepared by Boeing as part of the debris-assessment report for NASA's *Columbia* space shuttle launch to prompt students to find important documentation missing from the slides or to correct the misrepresentations of technical information contained in them.

▶ FIGURE 12.2: Example of a Fix-a-Search Activity

Search Strategies:
An Activity
(Combining Your Knowledge of Database with Your Knowledge of Searching Techniques)

Directions: Below are 7 real-life search "problems," taken from situations NMSU students have recently encountered and discussed with reference librarians. Read the description of the search situation, look at the results given, and come up with a strategy for how you could fix this search using the same database described in the situation.

Scenario I
Database Used: NMSU Library Catalog (available at http://libcat.nmsu.edu/)

Search Terms/Syntax: Did a quick search – using the keyword option – for **world trade center**.

Results: Got 10000 results, the first three of which are pictured below

▶ Research logs, asking students to track how they looked for information and why they selected particular sources, when researching for an oral report. (For a sample log, see www.library.umass.edu/subject/anthro/database-log.html.)
▶ Creation of pathfinders, resource guides, or annotated bibliographies on a topic. (For examples, see www.library.csi.cuny.edu/dept/history/lavender/researchlogging.html or www.potamusplace.net/pathfinder.html.)

Yet other non-research-paper assignments require students to conduct a class debate based on the information found (for example, recommending whether or not a given Fortune 500 company should be taken over, or what would be the best location for the site of a particular business). They ask students to nominate someone for a Nobel Prize or some other discipline-specific award, to develop interview questions for a specific person, or to prepare for a visit from—or to—someone from another culture (cf. *Sample Library Assignments*, n.d.). Students create a "term bank," or thesaurus of terms for researching a broad topic area; they find sources to document a response to a provocative theory or editorial; they compare literature on a topic from two different time periods; they compare the bibliographies of two (or more) published works on a topic; they create a policy to address a social problem; they create a library on a topic (for example, if you had $500 to spend on key resources on this topic, what would you get and why?); they create a teaching handout; they update the bibliography of an article that is three or more years old; they give the prognosis for a specified medical condition and treatment; they write about what is not known on a topic; they compare the views of three experts on a topic; they write a sample grant proposal; they research who makes reference to a particular primary source (cf. Saines, 2002); or they create a reading packet or list on a topic (cf. Tacoma Community College, n.d.).

WORKING WITH FACULTY AND MEASURING SUCCESS

The Library Instruction Program unveiled the toolkit at the 2004 annual NMSU distance education conference in the fall semester. This unveiling involved a presentation about the toolkit to an audience of some forty DE faculty members, as well as publication of a paper based on the presentation in the conference proceedings and on the Web (http://lib.nmsu.edu/instruction/toolkit/introducing.pdf). The toolkit was also heavily promoted in other venues—such as in the campus DE newsletter, in the library newsletter, and in Library Instruction Program correspondence with DE faculty—but the primary audience for testing its success consisted of the faculty members in the audience at the 2004 annual New Mexico State University DE conference. Seven faculty members committed to work with the instruction coordinator in introducing or modifying library instruction components in their DE courses based on the toolkit modules. The faculty members were, of course, self-selected and are unrepresentative of NMSU faculty as a whole. Four faculty members came from the college of education and three came from health and human services. They used a total of thirty-four modular components in their courses during the remainder of annual year 2004–2005. The most popular components were interviews uncovering information needs in a particular field, interviews with information producers, activities on general search techniques, activities in general and subject-specific databases, activities on evaluating sources, activities on citing sources, activities on identifying plagiarism, and case studies on plagiarism.

CONCLUSION

Changes in Library Instruction Program personnel precluded more formal assessment of the student learning outcomes from the inclusion of or change to modular library instruction components in DE courses. However, anecdotal comments from faculty members and usage statistics on the toolkit suggest that its pilot had a positive impact—and that other libraries could benefit from providing DE faculty with incremental modular instructional units to be integrated into their courses. Between October 2004 and May 2005, there were 7,950 "hits" on toolkit pages—and most of these hits represent uses by NMSU faculty members and their students. Implementing such a program does, however, possess one additional challenge that should not be underestimated: librarians may need to assert themselves in establishing the appropriate scope and sequence of instructional programming with faculty. It can be tempting, for many librarians, to give the faculty member exactly what he or she has requested—even when they know that the same cohort of students got an identical lecture to the one now being proposed on library services for DE students. Negotiating with faculty members to reshape the nature of their request, or even declining to furnish inappropriate instruction, can be difficult, but DE students and faculty alike are better served when librarians assert themselves as equal partners in the educational enterprise.

ENDNOTES

[1] This despite the fact that there are over one thousand students enrolled in fifteen technology-based DE programs at NMSU.

[2] Modular approaches, particularly learning objects, are not without controversy, however. Some skeptics claim that "knowledge is the subjective experience of a community of learners, not an object that can be transported from its disciplinary setting." See Acker, Pearl, and Rissing for a summary of and reply to some views of "opponents" of learning objects.

[3] Given the disjunctions between faculty and students' views of information-based research papers, it should not be surprising to find that certain types of research paper assignments correlate with heightened incidences of plagiarism. Asking students to pick a topic tied to

the course content and research it over the course of a semester, and then turn in a paper at the end of the term—especially without viewing drafts of the paper—can sometimes be the practical equivalent to asking students to buy a paper from a paper mill or to cut and paste one from the Web (Harris, 2002).

[4] Coverage of all "important" or "necessary" disciplinary content knowledge is further complicated by the expansion of this knowledge. Steven Rissing, an evolutionary biologist, "estimates that only 27 percent of his introductory biology text is covered in any one quarter" (Acker, Pearl, and Rissing, 2003).

[5] Faculty who are resistant to addressing information literacy competencies in general can often be persuaded by the close correspondences that have been noted between the *Information Literacy Competency Standards for Higher Education* and other skills that educators seek to develop in their courses (cf. Laherty, 2000; Manuel, 2005). Close correlations have been noted, for example, between the *Information Literacy Competency Standards for Higher Education* and the National Science Education Content Standards and the National Standards for History. See, for example, the standards for Chemical Information Retrieval, available at www.chemistry.org/portal/a/c/s/1/acsdisplay.html?DOC=education%5Ccpt%5Cts_chem info.html, or those proposed by the Information Literacy in the Sciences Task Force, available at http://sciencelibrarian.tripod.com/ILTaskForce/ILIndex.htm#SYNOPSIS.

[6] A most creative term paper alternative is described by Ken Peterson, professor of economics at Furman University, in *The Economics of "The Perfect Storm": A Novel Approach to Economic Concepts* (http://alpha.furman.edu/~kpeterso/peterson/perfectstorm.htm). Peterson has students read the novel *The Perfect Storm* to introduce them to both key economics concepts (such as total revenue, explicit cost, variable cost, shut down point, tragedy of the commons, and so forth) and to sources for researching economic information (for example, using the *Occupational Outlook Handbook* and the *Statistical Abstract of the United States* as well as the Bureau of Economic Analysis home page and library databases to document, for example, the answer to the question Which form of market organization best describes the swordfish market circa the 1970s through the 1990s?).

▶ FIGURE 12.3: IL Competencies for NMSU Students at Various Levels

First-Year Students
Introduction to library research

Skills	Courses (Current or Potential)
▶ Locations of library materials and service points ▶ How to read call numbers ▶ Awareness of basic library services (reference, reserves, etc.) and policies (circulation period, renewals, etc.) ▶ Keyword searching in the OPAC and a general article database ▶ Differences between full-text library resources and the Web ▶ Use of APA or MLA to cite sources in a reference list/works cited ▶ Knowledge of strategies for limiting a search (use of AND, searching in title only, date, publication type, etc.)	LSC 111 (8 or 16 weeks); ENGL 111; UNIV 150; 100-level courses in various departments; workshops and tours

(Cont'd.)

▶ FIGURE 12.3: IL Competencies for NMSU Students at Various Levels *(Continued)*

Second-Year Students
Transition to research in the major

Skills	Courses (Current or Potential)
▶ Locating subject headings/descriptors from the results of keyword searches and using these subject headings/descriptors to construct new searches ▶ Awareness of discipline-specific databases related to students' majors (e.g., General Science Abstracts, Social Science Abstracts) ▶ Awareness of subject-specific encyclopedias ▶ Knowledge of strategies for limiting a search (use of AND, searching in title only, date, publication type, etc.) ▶ Awareness of the differences between scholarly, popular, and trade periodicals ▶ Awareness of interlibrary loan services ▶ Independent ability to check for electronic availability of articles cited	LSC 211 (8 weeks); ENGL 203, ENGL 211, ENGL 218; other 200-level courses in various departments; workshops

Third-Year Students
Transition to research in the major

Skills	Courses (Current or Potential)
▶ Awareness of subject-specific databases related to students' majors (e.g., PsycINFO); ability to perform basic searches in these databases ▶ Awareness of appropriate subject-specific reference sources ▶ Knowledge of strategies for limiting a search (use of AND, searching in title only, date, publication type, etc.) ▶ Knowledge of what constitutes primary, secondary, and tertiary information in their field ▶ Effective use of interlibrary loan services ▶ Independent ability to check for electronic availability of articles cited ▶ Awareness of subject-specific citation styles (Chicago, ACS, etc.)	LSC 311; PSY 310; other 300-level courses in various departments; workshops

Fourth-Year Students
Research in the major

Skills	Courses (Current or Potential)
▶ Ability to implement more sophisticated searches in subject-specific databases related to students' majors (e.g., PsycINFO); knowledge of subject-specific search strategies (e.g., structure searching in chemistry) ▶ Ability to find references to information resources using non-database tools (as appropriate to students' majors—e.g., archival finding aids) ▶ Knowledge of strategies for ensuring the comprehensiveness of a search (OR, truncation, wildcards, etc.) ▶ Knowledge of the publication processes in their discipline and how they relate to finding information ▶ Knowledge of what constitutes primary, secondary, and tertiary information in their field ▶ Ability to use subject-specific citation styles (Chicago, ACS, etc.)	LSC 311; 300-and 400-level courses in various departments; workshops

(Cont'd.)

▶ FIGURE 12.3: IL Competencies for NMSU Students at Various Levels *(Continued)*

Graduate and Professional Students

Skills	Courses (Current or Potential)
▶ Ability to implement more sophisticated searches in subject-specific databases related to students' majors (e.g., PsycINFO); knowledge of subject-specific search strategies (e.g., structure searching in chemistry) ▶ Ability to cite sources in accordance with the norms for publication in the discipline (journal-specific citation styles) ▶ Ability to find references to information resources using non-database tools (as appropriate to students' majors—e.g., archival finding aids) ▶ Knowledge of strategies for ensuring the comprehensiveness of a search (OR, truncation, wildcards, etc.) ▶ Knowledge of the publication processes in their discipline and how they relate to finding information ▶ Ability to tap into communication processes/invisible colleges within their discipline ▶ Willingness to look for nonlibrary and non-Web sources—interlibrary loan; historical societies; personal interviews; independent data collection; etc. ▶ Basic knowledge of the research processes of undergraduates and characteristics for effective library assignments (for teaching-track graduate students); ability to apply effective information finding and use strategies in the field (professional students and non-teaching-track graduate students)	LSC 511; graduate courses; workshops

REFERENCES

Acker, Stephen R., Dennis Pearl, and Steven Rissing. 2003. "Is the Academy Ready for Learning Objects? *Syllabus*. Available: www.syllabus.com/article.asp?id=7886 (accessed August 30, 2004).

Association of College and Research Libraries. n.d. *Information Literacy Competency Standards for Higher Education*. Available: www.ala.org/ala/acrl/acrlstandards/informationliteracycompetency.htm (accessed August 30, 2004).

Butler, John T., and Jerilyn R. Veldof. 2002. "Information Literacy Toolkit: Meeting the Challenges of a Large Research University." *Academic Exchange Quarterly* 6(4): 34–41.

Cannon, Anita. 1994. "Faculty Survey on Library Research Instruction." *RQ* 33(4): 524–541.

Cooperstein, Susan E., and Elizabeth Kocevar-Weidinger. 2004. "Beyond Active Learning: A Constructivist Approach to Learning." *Reference Services Review* 32(2): 141–148.

Feldman, Devin, and Susan Sciammarella. 2000. "Both Sides of the Looking Glass: Librarian and Teaching Faculty Perceptions of Librarianship at Six Community Colleges." *College & Research Libraries* 61(6): 491–498.

Gilbert, Steve. April 15, 2002. "Librarians Help with LTAs?" Posting to the TLT-SWG Listserv (accessed August 30, 2004).

Harris, Robert. 2002. *Anti-Plagiarism Strategies for Research Papers*. Available: www.virtualsalt.com/antiplag.htm (accessed August 30, 2004).

Hillesheim, Gwen. 1998. "Distance Learning: Barriers and Strategies for Students and Faculty." *The Internet and Higher Education* 1(1): 31–44.

Horrigan, John. 2003. *Tech-Savvy Americans Are Increasingly Attached to Their Computers, the Internet and Cell Phones.* Pew Internet and American Life Project. Available: www.pewinternet.org/reports/ pdfs/PIP_Info_Consumption.pdf (accessed August 30, 2004).

Kloss, Robert J. 1996. "Writing Things Down vs. Writing Things Up: Are Research Papers Valid?" *College Teaching* 44(1): 3–7.

Kuhlthau, Carol Collier. 1997. "Learning in Digital Libraries: An Information Search Process Approach." *Library Trends* 45(4): 708–724.

Ladner, Betty, Donald Beagle, James R. Steele, and Linda Steele. 2004. "Rethinking Online Instruction: From Content Transmission to Cognitive Immersion." *Reference and User Services Quarterly* 43(4): 329–337.

Laherty, Jennifer. 2000. "Promoting Information Literacy for Science Education Programs: Correlating the National Science Education Content Standards with the Association of College and Research Libraries Information Competency Standards for Higher Education. *Issues in Science and Technology Librarianship.* Available: www.library.ucsb.edu/ istl/00-fall/article3.html (accessed August 30, 2004).

Lubans, John. 1974. Objectives for Library-use Instruction in Educational Curricula. In *Educating the Library User.* Edited by John Lubans. New York: R. R. Bowker.

Manuel, Kate. 2005. "National History Day: An Opportunity for K–16 Collaboration." *Reference Services Review* 33(4): 459–486.

McMackin, Mary C. November 1994. "How Teachers and Students View the Task of Report Writing." *The Clearinghouse* 107–110.

Nerz, Honora F., and Suzanne T. Weiner. 2001. Information Competencies: A Strategic Approach. *Proceedings of the 2001 American Society for Civil Engineering Annual Conference and Exposition.* Available: www.lib.ucdavis.edu/eld/fulltext/00510_2001.pdf (accessed August 30, 2004).

Palloff, Rena M., and Keith Pratt. 2001. *Lessons from the Cyberspace Classroom: The Realities of Teaching Online.* San Francisco: Jossey-Bass.

Ragains, Patrick. 1995. "Four Variations on Drueke's Active Learning Paradigm." *Research Strategies* 13(1): 40–50.

Random House Webster's College Dictionary. 1991. New York: Random House.

Rifkin, Jeremy. 2000. *The Age of Access: The New Culture of Hypercapitalism, Where All of Life Is a Paid-for Experience.* New York: J.P. Tarcher/Putnam.

Saines, Sherri. 2002. *Creative Assignments Using Information Competency and Writing.* Available: www.library.ohiou.edu/libinfo/depts/refdept/bi/alternatives.htm (accessed August 30, 2004).

Sample Library Assignments. Available: www.sunysccc.edu/library/services/sampleassn.html (accessed August 30, 2004).

Smith, Rachel S. 2004. *Guidelines for Authors of Learning Objects.* Available: www.nmc.org/guidelines (accessed August 30, 2004).

Tacoma Community College Library. n.d. *Sample Library Research Assignments.* Available: www.tacoma.ctc.edu/library/sampleass.shtml (accessed August 30, 2004).

Tapscott, Don. 1998. *Growing Up Digital: The Rise of the Net Generation.* New York: McGraw-Hill.

Thomas, Joy. 1994. "Faculty Attitudes and Habits concerning Library Instruction: How Much Has Changed since 1982." *Research Strategies* 12(4): 209–223.

Thompson, Hugh. 2002. "The Library's Role in Distance Education: Survey Results from ACRL's 2000 Academic Library Trends and Statistics." *College & Research Libraries News* 63, 5. Available: www.ala.org/ala/acrl/acrlpubs/crlnews/backissues2002/may/librarys role.htm (accessed August 30, 2004).

Valentine, Barbara. 2001. "Legitimate Effort in Research Papers: Student Commitment versus Faculty Expectations." *Journal of Academic Librarianship* 27(2): 107–115.

Wiley, David A. n.d. *Connecting Learning Objects to Instructional Design Theory: A Definition, a Metaphor, and a Taxonomy.* Available: www.reusability.org/read/chapters/wiley.doc (accessed August 30, 2004).

Wiley, David A., ed. 2002. *The Instructional Use of Learning Objects.* Available: www.reusability.org/read/ (accessed August 30, 2004).

▶13

USING VIRTUAL CLASSROOM SOFTWARE FOR LIBRARY INSTRUCTION

NAOMI EICHENLAUB
DANA MCFARLAND

Overview: This chapter describes in detail one Canadian university library's experiment with using virtual classroom software for distance library instruction. While the concept has many positive inducements, such as the librarian not needing to travel to a distant site for library instruction, the authors found that the technical aspects of using the equipment and software outweighed the advantages. They hope in the future to be able to use a virtual classroom as part of their online delivery of library instruction.

INTRODUCTION

Royal Roads University (RRU), situated in Victoria, British Columbia, and founded in 1995 after the closure of Royal Roads Military College, is distinguished by a government mandate to provide applied professional online degree programs. Programs are offered at the graduate level and are delivered using a distributed learning model. This model combines an on-campus residency of two to four weeks with online distance courses. Given the programming and model of the university, it has been essential for the library to develop online collections and services wherever possible.

Royal Roads University Library became involved in a pilot distance continuing education short course, "Interprofessional Practice and Clinical Informatics," early in the course development process in 2003. From the beginning it was clear that the pilot course, with its health information science emphasis and distributed online delivery, presented new challenges to the achievement of library outcomes that would have to be met by developing a new model. Owing to the focus on health information science, mastering information literacy and fluency outcomes would be more critical than ever to learner success. Also, while certain learner objectives might be met through independent, asynchronous study, an element of real time, "high touch" interaction would be highly desirable to bring the synergy of a group to learning in the moment.

In his article in the *Hedgehog Review* theme issue "What's the University For?" Jackson Lears wrote, "Distance learning is to learning as phone sex is to sex: it may be better than no learning at all, but you wouldn't want to confuse it with the real thing" (2000: 18). While librarians at Royal Roads University did not view distance learning quite so negatively, we recognized that to be effective, to achieve the same outcomes as the "real thing," the online-only mode would require different design strategies and tools for instruction than those used in face-to-face instruction.

In fact, several months before this project, we had begun to investigate means of enriching existing asynchronous service offerings with the capacity to interact with learners online in real time. Motivated by two distinct purposes, we found ourselves exploring synchronous tools in two different categories:

▶ *Virtual reference*—synchronous online support for the individual distance learner at point of need in the research process. Typical characteristics of virtual reference applications include page pushing, chat, co-browsing, session transcripts, and application sharing.

▶ *Virtual classroom*—synchronous online learning environment for groups. Typical virtual classroom functionality includes application sharing, question management features, audience polling, whiteboard sharing, session archiving and exporting, and chat.

By fall 2002 we were encouraged by early indications that there was at least one library-oriented product available, LSSI Virtual Reference software, which offered functionality for both virtual reference and virtual classroom. We combined our background research with a product trial, site visit, and conversations with other librarians who had started using this software. We concluded that the product might fulfill the virtual reference imperative for users on the same local area network but was not sufficiently robust for remote access users. Also, we were never able to see the virtual classroom function in operation.

While this product had been favorably received at some libraries, we later learned that at least one early adopter library moved to a stand-alone instant messaging product, citing as a cause a high percentage of bad transactions, ranging from impaired functionality of the software to dropped connections. It may be that some libraries draw a high proportion of their traffic through their internal network, which would be the best performance environment for this application. The expectation at Royal Roads could not be the same, because 80% of the learner population is working from a distance at any given time. Subsequent development of LSSI Virtual Reference and other similar applications may have resulted in greater stability, although this remains a topic of discussion in professional forums such as the DIGREF listserv and in the professional literature (Coffman, 2004).

Our investigations helped to refine our requirements for a synchronous tool and the features best suited to our client needs. In our circumstances, then and now, virtual reference does not offer sufficient value for money over our present synchronous and asynchronous tools—e-mail and telephone. As most of our learners are graduate students, their questions tend to be complex. Librarians who use online synchronous applications have told us that they are more effective for finite transactions than for extended research support. Accordingly, we concluded that we would gain the most from a virtual classroom application that would allow us both to support program offerings in a distributed, online-only mode and to address in a tutorial setting some of the shared research support needs of graduate learner teams. Consequently, in late autumn 2002 we began examining virtual classroom applications that did not have a specific library orientation. In taking this direction we recognized that the library was only one potential user of such an application at the university. Moreover, some product trials had already been conducted by other departments on campus, thereby providing the potential for internal partnerships.

Early in 2003 the pilot course entered the scene and provided a focal point and a timeline for our efforts. One objective of the pilot was to assess the relative effectiveness of various synchronous and asynchronous tools in facilitating learning for health professionals in a distributed continuing education setting. Because of our evolving related interest, the library volunteered to fulfill part of this objective by delivering content through the medium of a synchronous online tool. We subsequently continued our review of such tools together with representatives from other stakeholder groups in the pilot delivery, including instructional design and the technical trainers, who were to provide both content for the course technical training outcomes and end user support for the technologies used in the course.

EVALUATION AND SELECTION OF SYNCHRONOUS TOOLS

Synchronous online learning products were evaluated on the basis of software features as well as issues surrounding their implementation, delivery, and use by learners and instructors. Based on our previous research into virtual reference software and collaborative online tools, the list of features that we hoped to find in our virtual classroom product included whiteboard functionality, audio enabling, application and document sharing, breakout spaces, instant messaging, archiving, and session playback functionality, as well as the ability to export the saved session.

In addition, all stakeholders involved in the software evaluation determined that the tool selected must be accessible through a minimum of a 56K modem, Macintosh and Windows compatible, scalable, relatively easy to support (from a technical support standpoint), easy to configure, and capable of application and document sharing (particularly important to the library to enable co-browsing of library online databases). We were also interested in being able to save transcripts of synchronous sessions in order to build a knowledge base. Other features identified as useful included participant polling and question queuing.

Our primary concern was that the product be as easy to use. For this reason, one of the most important considerations was whether learners would be required to download and install software on their end. We did not want installation and configuration to present an obstacle to the content, especially since the library activity would occur early in the context of the course. In addition, we anticipated that some participants would not use their own computers and therefore might not have the requisite permissions to download software or clients. Postcourse feedback confirmed that this was the case with 50% of the learners.

Based on our initial research and on system requirements and features, we narrowed down the preferred synchronous products to HorizonLive and PlaceWare. At the time, both PlaceWare and HorizonLive required plug-ins for their sharing features, but these were small downloads and required only for presenters rather than participants. The attendee configuration for HorizonLive required the presence of common plug-ins for audio and video, but verification of these features could be facilitated by an online wizard prior to attending a session.

While both HorizonLive and PlaceWare offered the ability to play back prerecorded sessions (archiving), PlaceWare did not offer voice-over-IP to distribute one-way audio over the Internet. PlaceWare's only solution for audio delivery over the Internet was to record the session with audio conferencing, which would then require playback from the Internet at a later date. Since HorizonLive did offer one-way voice-over on the Internet as part of its package, it was possible to have people listen over their computer speakers and/or through a telephone audio bridge. To enable this audio broadcasting, the presenter had to download and install a special plug-in from HorizonLive and have his or her telephone and computer connected. Without this device, the voice-over-IP portion would not function when using a telephone bridge. This scenario provided a solution for people who needed to listen over their computer (using speakers, microphones, or headsets) rather than through a telephone. It would also be useful for single dial-up connections.

Trial access to PlaceWare and HorizonLive allowed the software evaluation group to test the products as both participants and presenters. Both products offered the choice between using a collaborative mode or an auditorium mode for the delivery of synchronous instruction. Collaborative mode allows for audience participation and control over tools equal to that of the presenter, whereas auditorium restricts participants' ability to co-browse, co-share, or coauthor on the whiteboard, and so forth.

The test scenario involved delivering mock library and help desk instruction in a simulated virtual classroom environment. Initial demonstrations using the collaborative mode revealed that synchronous sessions delivered in this environment might quickly become chaotic. This can be acceptable or even desirable in a workshop or team collaboration setting, but it clearly would not be viable to facilitate an instructor-led session in this mode. In order to ensure a more controlled and effective delivery, we decided that the auditorium setting would be the best mode for delivering our sessions.

In the end we selected HorizonLive as the preferred product for the delivery of the pilot project instruction. HorizonLive offered a participant software and interface that was both user-friendly and intuitive. This fit well with the earlier identified need of finding a tool that would be relatively easy to support from a help desk perspective.

In testing both HorizonLive and PlaceWare, we came to a new appreciation for the level of resources, both human and technical, required to effectively deliver synchronous online instruction. In terms of human resources, it appeared to be necessary to have one person manage the content delivery, with an additional person to field audience questions. We reflected that it would even be helpful to have a third person who could assist the other two presenters with troubleshooting or in the event of heavy question volume.

CONTENT DEVELOPMENT FOR VIRTUAL CLASSROOM DELIVERY

Our initial plan was to derive content for the pilot course from our face-to-face instruction sessions. It quickly became apparent, however, that the content was not unaffected by the medium of delivery. Because this course was designed as an exploration of health information sources, the students could be expected to have more interest in the mechanics of how to search and how information is structured than in the results of searches themselves. This expectation was confirmed in meetings and e-mail exchanges with the course instructor, who was interested in presenting diverse online information databases more for interface variety than for the content they might contain. Accordingly, we decided to structure the content in three parts:

1. Introduction to library services and overview of library instruction objectives;
2. Defining the research question, search strategies and techniques, and the role of controlled vocabulary; and
3. A sample search in one online licensed health database using the skills introduced above.

This strategy for organizing the content was in large part adopted to respond to the features and constraints of the online synchronous tool. To begin with, it would have been very time consuming to script and record a perfect session of more than twenty minutes duration. HorizonLive archiving does not allow any pauses or edits. Because we expected to use the tool synchronously, this did not strike us as a liability until we began to consider asynchronous delivery. In subsequent content development for asynchronous use, we have employed a screen capture application with Flash output that offers greater flexibility in editing, including sound. There are a number of applications of this kind, but the tool we have used for this is the Qarbon Viewlet product.

In creating archived sessions in HorizonLive, and later in Viewlet, we conjectured that the students would neither want nor have time to listen to one lengthy tutorial. We also wanted to keep files to a size that a learner could successfully download to a remote computer. Creating a series of shorter tutorials rather than one lengthy tutorial would allow us to distribute responsibility for content development among a number of librarians, thereby giving us all experience in using the tool while sharing the workload equitably.

A challenge in using HorizonLive to archive sessions was how to integrate other software applications into the tutorial. The first two parts of the tutorial captured a voice-narrated PowerPoint presentation, but in HorizonLive the imported PowerPoint slides become a series of GIF (Graphics Interchange Format) images, with the consequence that you can no longer navigate in and out of slides by clicking on embedded URLs. This created a need to import screen captures into the PowerPoint demonstration. Moreover, there was a slight time delay between the audio recording and the software navigation, so that when we were narrating, particularly the demonstration of the database searching, we had to take care to pace carefully in order to ensure that the demonstration remained as synchronized with the audio as possible.

Although important, HorizonLive was just one tool in the online delivery of this tutorial. We also developed a Web page to give context to and direction for the HorizonLive sessions and to provide a gateway to library resources for this course. Later we used the Web page to present alternate Flash versions of the HorizonLive sessions. The HorizonLive sessions took a disproportionate amount of time to create, partly because of our inexperience with the software but also because of the complexities of using the software in the way that we did, since we tried to anticipate and obviate difficulties in delivery.

The amount of time required to develop the online tutorial sessions for this course far surpassed the amount of time that we require to prepare for equivalent face-to-face encounters. Again, that is partly because of our lack of experience with the synchronous tool. Even assuming familiarity with the tool, however, the level of planning, scripting, rehearsal, and coordination of effort needed to develop the content for the online synchronous session was much greater than that required to produce a well-planned face-to-face session.

INVESTMENT IN TRAINING AND INSTRUCTIONAL DESIGN

As we began to develop content, librarians conducted further testing. This included experimenting with local and remote connections and trying various software features and instruction scenarios. Ultimately, we concluded that the complexities of live application sharing using HorizonLive posed too great a risk of compromise to the learning event in this case and with this group of learners.

Hours of training and exploration were required to learn how to create and deliver content for what was to be a relatively short online session. Although we could foresee picking up speed as we developed our expertise, we felt that at least two librarians (and at least two computers) would always be necessary to do a synchronous online demonstration: to work through the content, to answer questions, and to verify that the tool was working from the user perspective. Furthermore, we would have to hold multiple sessions both to accommodate diverse shift schedules among the learners and to restrict online group size to facilitate coherent participation. In addition, it became clear that training users in the synchronous tool was not a good investment in the unique circumstances of this course. We would have little prior knowledge of users' technical abilities, level of information fluency, platforms, or connection speed. Also, the duration of the course was quite short, and, since this tool was to be used only at the very beginning of the course for relatively small segments, the training for live interaction would take as much or more time than the actual session that the tool was meant to facilitate.

For the reasons described above, librarians decided to create "archived" demonstrations using the HorizonLive tool, together with PowerPoint presentations that the students could view independently at the beginning of the precourse week. Synchronous question-and-answer (Q&A) sessions using HorizonLive would be scheduled for the latter half of the week. This altered approach would give the students an introduction to the synchronous tool, exposing them to the look and feel of the software without requiring interaction or much navigation. We felt that having had this experience, together with their other technical training, the students would be prepared for a library Q&A HorizonLive session. The inclusion of co-browsing, if it worked, would be good but not essential in a Q&A situation. Using the features of the auditorium mode, we knew that we could create archived sessions with HorizonLive relatively easily. The archived sessions would include a mixture of PowerPoint introductory material and a demonstration of a search within one of the online databases. We would also include audio, and the archived sessions would be no more than one hour in total length.

We also planned for three one-hour Q&A sessions scheduled at various times to accommodate health professionals. These sessions were intended to allow participants to give feedback on the archived sessions and to ask questions about the archived material or about library research generally. They would also allow the library to test HorizonLive in a live setting. The content for the archived sessions was identified, scripted, and created. It was then submitted to the instructor for review.

Shortly before the course went live, the university stakeholders involved in the pilot held a meeting where it was decided that HorizonLive would not be used as a live tool for either the technical training or for the library Q&A sessions. This decision was reached partly because of growing concern about the technical literacy levels of the learners based on their early contacts with technical trainers and partly because of bandwidth problems that we had begun to encounter in testing the product for remote access.

The bandwidth concern resulted mainly from the co-location of all instructors at one site with the users widely distributed, with all attempting to use a third party–hosted Web application. Each individual user competes for bandwidth within his or her system and institutional frameworks. This scenario could occur at any institution, and there were a few, not unexpected, problems as a consequence. Any bandwidth-consuming process on the university network could lead to a situation wherein learners are able to reach the common external server with ease while the instructors, co-located at the university, have difficulty reaching both the same server and the learners owing to delays getting outside the university. In that scenario all external users would see excellent response while those inside would experience unacceptable delays. The problem can be controlled through the use of bandwidth management software to prevent any one or two processes from consuming the entire off-campus bandwidth capacity. In this instance there was insufficient time to implement the solution prior to course start-up.

The decision to not use the synchronous tool in a live interactive form was a difficult one. Despite the considerable investment in development, there was general concern that learners might gain a negative impression about the course as a whole if early on they were inappropriately challenged to use a new learning technology or if for any reason the tool did not work well from the trainer end.

We decided to proceed with the archived HorizonLive library sessions as an introduction to library research, as well as providing similar information in other more accessible formats in case the students had problems viewing the archived files. Q&A was handled using the asynchronous discussion group tool already available on the RRU learning platform. Discussion groups were monitored over the course of three days. Students were requested to participate, but participation was not mandatory. Synchronous contacts between librarians and learners occurred one-on-one over the telephone.

As the course went live, some students had difficulties viewing the HorizonLive archived sessions because they either lacked the commonly available plug-ins required for audio and video or had difficulties installing plug-ins on local computers. The considerable interest in the library sessions led us to explore various options for improving the accessibility of the content on the fly. The most effective solution was to make the sessions available using Camtasia, a screen capture software that makes a compressed Flash file. The output has a movielike quality but does not require any plug-ins. The university technical trainers did not use HorizonLive for their presentations, but they did create documentation to lead the learners to access the archived library sessions. Their Q&A was handled using teleconferencing as a synchronous tool.

LESSONS LEARNED

Once we chose an application and began work on a project with a deadline, the learning points came quickly. We learned the importance of:

▶ **Granularized content:** Smaller is better, in both production and delivery; designing and producing content at a very granular level makes it easier to record, update, and download. A segment of twenty minutes is suddenly not so small!

▶ **Time required planning and delivering:** The HorizonLive sessions took a disproportionate amount of time to create, partly because of our inexperience with the software but also because of the complexities of using the software in the way that we did. The time required to develop the online tutorial sessions for this course far surpassed the time that we require to prepare for equivalent face-to-face encounters.

▶ **Staff and technology resources:** Even assuming familiarity with the tool, the level of planning, scripting, rehearsal, and coordination of effort needed to develop the content for the online synchronous session is greater than that required to produce a well-planned face-to-face session. We also learned that a minimum of at least two, preferably three, librarians and corresponding equipment would be required to effectively deliver an online session using synchronous technology: one person to facilitate and navigate, one person to monitor and manage questions from the audience, and a third person to monitor the audience view of the presentation to ensure that everything runs smoothly.

▶ **Adequate bandwidth:** Our bandwidth issues resulted mainly from the co-location of all instructors at one location with the users widely distributed, and all attempting to use a third party–hosted Web application. Each individual user competes for bandwidth within his or her system and institutional frameworks. Some mitigation is possible through the use of bandwidth management software that prevents any one or two processes (for example, streaming MP3s, from consuming the entire off-campus bandwidth capacity. Unfortunately, we did not have bandwidth management in place until shortly after the course start-up. There are many home users who are still constrained to 56K.

▶ **Minimizing end user configuration/installation:** As the course went "live," some students had difficulties viewing the HorizonLive archived sessions because they either lacked the commonly available plug-ins required for audio and video or had difficulties installing these plug-ins on computers locally. Troubleshooting these issues consumed instructional time.

▶ **Alternative delivery strategies:** We learned that a backup plan is essential. The considerable interest in the library sessions led us to explore various options for improving the accessibility of the content on the fly. The most rapid and effective solution was to make the sessions available using Camtasia, a screen capture software that makes a compressed Flash file. The output has a movielike quality but does not require any plug-ins.

Both the library and the instructional design group are considering future use of synchronous online applications, but there are no current deployments at Royal Roads University. Considerations for a successful future deployment include the ease of support of the tool (plug-ins, customizability, authentication issues, and so forth all need to be in the background), the investment in learning (will learners use the tool for multiple activities?), the affordability of the tool, and ensuring there is adequate bandwidth for participants using the software.

It is also important to consider if synchronicity is appropriate and useful when your students are working on diverse schedules or are located in multiple time zones. For example, it would be a challenge to find a reasonable time to hold a session for learners who are twelve hours ahead. Bandwidth and other technical challenges also are considerations in using virtual classroom software to support students across time zones. While awaiting new developments in synchronous applications, we have been actively working to improve our asynchronous services.

CONCLUSIONS

In conclusion, all university stakeholders agree that the experiment with content development and delivery using a synchronous tool provided a valuable learning opportunity, with many of the learning points unanticipated. In the library, our experiences have been applied in subsequent content development for online delivery in an asynchronous mode and have influenced our thinking about how we might use a synchronous application in the future.

Our pilot online synchronous efforts did not demonstrate efficiencies over face-to-face, e-mail, or telephone, largely owing to the time required for set up of synchronous tools on the presenter end, the learning curve for using the software, the number of people required to deliver instruction, and so forth. Nevertheless, we are encouraged that while remote instruction has required travel on the part of a librarian or other instructor, online content can be delivered effectively using various strategies and tools, perhaps in the future including an online synchronous learning tool.

REFERENCES

Coffman, Steve. 2004. "To Chat or Not to Chat—Taking Another Look at Virtual Reference." *Searcher* 12, no. 7: 38–46.

Lears, Jackson. 2000. "The Radicalism of Tradition: Teaching the Liberal Arts in a Managerial Age." *The Hedgehog Review* 2, no. 3: 7–23.

▶Part III

COLLABORATING FOR DISTANCE INSTRUCTION

▶14

COLLABORATING WITH FACULTY AND INSTRUCTIONAL TECHNOLOGY STAFF

LISA T. NICKEL

Overview: This chapter presents an exploration of faculty, instructional technology staff, and librarian collaboration. It suggests ways to find faculty and IT staff who are interested in collaborating. The chapter also recommends ways for librarians to become involved as participants in online courses. The author presents a thoughtful and practical approach to productive collaboration.

◀

INTRODUCTION

Throughout this book, there is much discussion about the importance of library instruction for distance learners, frequently focusing on their specific needs and circumstances. As a result we can see that distance learners, especially, need to be taught the information literacy skills they need in an environment in which those skills are directly applicable. As librarians we need to work with teaching faculty and instructional designers in order to secure a prominent (or at least visible) position on students' radar screens.

Collaboration and cooperation between teaching faculty and librarians in information literacy instruction is not just a good idea—it is a necessity. We live in a world where information is rapidly created, constantly changing, and readily accessed. The library's role in the digital age continues to evolve as more and more information is available outside of our domain. Boundaries are blurring all across campus as we realize that blending content, technology, and information makes for a better overall educational experience. The problems occur for our students when the information that they access is not appropriate, or complete; when they do not know the primary research resources for their field; when their literature reviews turn up only articles found via Google or another search engine. Librarians and faculty must collaborate in order to integrate information literacy skills into the curriculum and work together to promote learning and increase student success.

METHODS

Finding a partner in collaboration can be the most difficult part of your enterprise. If you do not currently have a teaching faculty member to work with, think about approaching someone with whom you have worked before, possibly teaching a library research class for their students or even serving on a committee together. You can also approach new faculty members, who are just planning their courses and therefore may be open to exploring options for collaboration. Explain the benefits of incorporating a library component to their courses: information-literate students produce better work, learn skills that they can transfer to their other classes, and contribute higher quality research to the college or university as a whole. Another way to get buy-in from faculty is to cultivate "champions" in each department and have them spread the word about your successful past partnerships. Department faculty tend to pay attention to colleagues in their own area who have success stories to share. Finally, creating a sample course in WebCT, Blackboard, or whichever course management system your institution uses, that has embedded library resources in it may encourage faculty to get involved in a partnership with you—this way, they can see firsthand the value that can be added to a course through cooperation with the library.

COMMUNICATION

Communication is the key to most successful endeavors, and collaborating for information literacy is no different. True collaboration is based on uniting the strengths of each partner to create an environment where the content, information, and technology blend to create a cohesive learning situation for our students. It also involves working together to achieve the same goals. Discussing the goals for the course and finding a shared vision ensures that your hard work will pay off with a meaningful end product. Some steps towards good communication include discussing ground rules and defining the scope of involvement for everyone.

Carefully defined roles can eliminate confusion and structure the workflow. Issues for librarians to consider are: Will you be an actual partner in the class? Is it possible for you to team teach some sections or even create your own content? Or does the teaching faculty member envision you as a cooperative ally, supporting the needs of the class, but not as an independent facilitator? If your role is that of a guest in the class, you need to delineate which activities are appropriate for you to conduct within the course or course management system. For instance, can you create a distinct library section and control all of the content in there? Can you start discussions or contribute to discussion topics? What about assignments and quizzes? They can be very helpful when assessing the success of your collaboration, but they have larger implications. A quiz or graded assignment will affect the students' overall grade and needs to be factored in before the class begins.

Many of the same issues will apply to the instructional designers with whom you work. Are they partners, helping to plan the course and delivery, or will they function more as translators, facilitating the move from in-person to online class? Often, instructional designers are simply seen as the "gatekeepers" to course management systems, but they are so much more than that. In many ways, librarians and instructional designers have the same issues with regard to their status on campus. Many faculty members do not fully understand either our training or our expertise. Admittedly, librarians do not always understand what it is that instructional designers do, either. Depending on their educational background, instructional designers can be technology specialists, have pedagogical expertise, and add great value to online learning.

> Good pedagogy implies that the instructor can develop targeted learning objectives. Online instruction is more than a series of readings posted to a Web site; it requires deliberate instructional design that hinges on linking learning objectives to specific learning activities and measurable outcomes. Few faculty members have had formal education or training in instructional design or learning theory. To expect them to master the instructional design needed to put a well-designed course online is probably unrealistic. A more effective model is to pair a faculty member with an instructional designer so that each brings unique skills to the course-creation process. (Oblinger and Hawkins, 2005)

And since librarians can contribute their own unique skill set, a collaboration including all three is a recipe for success.

PLANNING

Planning is essential for success when collaborating with faculty and instructional designers. Getting involved in planning the learning objectives for a particular course as early as possible is always recommended. If that is not possible, try to become involved soon after the course is designed. If your institution has defined information literacy outcomes and objectives, your job can be easier. If it does not, you can still use and refer your partners to the ACRL *Information Literacy Competency Standards for Higher Education* and work together to integrate your learning objectives with theirs. Once the objectives have been decided, there are many decisions that need to be made, among them: What content is going to be included? Who is responsible for completing each of the different sections? Which delivery method is appropriate to each concept? And how will the material be integrated into the course or assignment? Instructional designers can be especially helpful here. If they are experienced, they will be able to draw upon previous work to relate which methods have proven successful for them in the past. They will also be able to educate you about which formats lend themselves well to certain topics/objectives. Use this opportunity to try out new and different technologies or methods that they recommend. Innovation comes from trial and error.

Another important part of the planning is the give and take in finding out what library experiences the instructor has been pleased with in the past and what the problem areas were for their previous students or classes. Share the methods that you have found to be successful and explain how these methods could apply or be used to assist their current students. Discuss which strategies you will implement in order to reinforce your key concepts and create assignments that require students to use library research skills to enhance their work. Brainstorm ways to address all of the aforementioned issues and include everyone involved in the discussion.

CHALLENGES

When working on your project with the faculty and instructional designers, be especially aware of using library jargon. Oftentimes, despite our best efforts, we tend to use terminology that is confusing or misunderstood by others. Refer to John Kupersmith's *"Library Terms that Users Understand,"* where he suggests not using acronyms and using natural language equivalents. For instance, instead of "interlibrary loan" try "borrowing from other libraries" or instead of referring to your OPAC with a nickname, or saying "periodical indexes," use target words in your descriptions, like "find books" or "search for articles" (Kupersmith, 2006). Once your content is complete, it is often helpful to have the instructional designer look over your written/posted documents and identify problem terminology. Remember to ensure consistency by checking all of the library terminology against the assignment directions from the teaching faculty member and any by the instructional designer. At the same time, make sure that you understand the terms that the designer and instructor use; speak up to clarify that which you find unclear. Summarizing all of your meetings via e-mail is always a good idea and lessens confusion as you move ahead.

EXAMPLES

Depending on the mode of instruction for the distance learners that you assist, there are many options for successful collaboration. The specific "classroom" examples in this chapter will deal primarily with *online* distance learning, using various course management systems, such as Blackboard, WebCT, ANGEL, Desire2Learn, Moodle, and so forth. Most of the practices, however, are applicable to any type of library instruction for distance learners.

Working in most course management systems requires you to have access to individual courses with a login name and password. There are different account designations that grant you the ability to view grades, add or change content, post announcements, begin or contribute to discussion boards, create quizzes, and so forth. Some of the various designations are: developer, designer, and teaching assistant (TA). You may be limited to a particular designation depending on the policies of your institution or the instructional technology department and, of course, based on the agreement between you and the teaching faculty member. If you are not granted a login or permission to create course content within the course management system, start small. Create the materials and have the faculty member or instructional designer add them to the course. Some seemingly small contributions, such as adding a link to the library or electronic course readings or including library research guides into the course, can be a very big step to some faculty members. You can also gain experience to build upon and work for change, gradually building up the trust between you and your faculty partner. The more successful collaborations you have can provide you with arguments to change some minds and policies.

Instructional designers often create and hold classes where they instruct the teaching faculty in creating and designing their online courses. Initiate collaboration with the designers for you to add a library component to the training: showcase different options for librarian–faculty–instructional designer collaboration in their courses. Try creating a repository of learning objects that faculty members can incorporate into their online courses a la carte. Include items such as remote access instructions, subject-specific research guides, online streaming tutorials, and sample library research assignments. Allowing the instructors to pick and choose and customize the library resources that they want to add to their course can create a feeling of self-efficacy for them.

If you are able to work directly with the teaching faculty and designers in creating content for the course, some examples of activities used to enhance and incorporate library instruction into the curriculum are:

▶ *Student Research Logs:* Students detail what research activities they engaged in for research assignments. Include detailed questions for students to respond to, such as: What is the resource name? What is the student's evaluation of the resource? What, if any information gathered from that resource is useful? What is the student's rating of the usefulness of the resource for his or her work? Provide feedback to the student by suggesting alternative sources or commenting on the appropriateness of the information gathered to the assignment.

▶ *Bibliographies:* Students create a bibliography of sources used for their research. Librarian checks or "signs off" on the sources, ensuring that they are acceptable according to what has been agreed upon by the instructor and librarian for the assignment.

▶ *Online Discussion Boards:* Create a library or research discussion board where students can ask library-related questions or get advice from the librarian on research strategies.

▶ *Virtual Reference Service:* Offer online reference service, via synchronous chat, instant messenger (IM), or e-mail.

▶ *Online "Office Hours":* Librarians post times that they will be available live (online) to answer student inquiries, via either discussion boards, chat, or possibly video conferencing.

CONCLUSION

The collaborative opportunities possible among teaching faculty members, librarians, and instructional designers are as abundant as your imagination and creativity. Remember to be flexible, respect your partners' expertise, and embrace all opportunities for collaboration.

REFERENCES

Association of College and Research Libraries (ACRL). 2000. *Information Literacy Competency Standards for Higher Education.* Chicago: ACRL. Available: www.ala.org/ala/acrl/acrl standards/informationliteracycompetency.htm (accessed January 30, 2006).

Kupersmith, John. 2006. "Library Terms that Users Understand." Available: www.jkup.net/ terms.html (accessed January 30, 2006).

Oblinger, D., and Brian L. Hawkins. 2005. "The Myth about E-Learning: We Don't Need to Worry about E-Learning Anymore." *EDUCAUSE Review* 40, no. 4 (July/August 2005): 14–15. Available: www.educause.edu/apps/er/erm05/erm05411.asp (accessed January 30, 2006).

▶15

MARKETING LIBRARY INSTRUCTION TO OFF-CAMPUS FACULTY AND STUDENTS

JILL MARKGRAF

Overview: This chapter presents a number of excellent ways to market library instruction to off-campus students and faculty. It includes suggestions for creating a marketing plan, determining the target markets, and selecting the best marketing strategies. For the librarian who is not familiar with marketing techniques, this chapter is a great introduction.

◀

INTRODUCTION

"If we build it, will they come?" is a question that appears repeatedly in the literature on off-campus library services. If libraries develop services for off-campus students, such as remote access to library resources, document delivery, online tutorials, and virtual reference, will students use them? If libraries offer instruction for their off-campus students, will the students take advantage of it? Experience suggests that maybe they will but usually not without some encouragement. Most off-campus students do not expect—and therefore do not seek out—library services designed for them (Summey, 2004). Those who are aware of the resources and services may not be motivated to use them unless they have a clear need to do so. It is not enough for libraries to provide access to information for off-campus students; libraries should ensure that students are aware of resources and services available to them and that they know how to use them. Furthermore, libraries need to gather information about and feedback from these students in order to improve services and respond to their needs. This is where marketing comes into play. Marketing is often thought of synonymously with promotion, but promotion is just one ingredient in the marketing mix.

Marketing off-campus library instruction, not unlike the marketing of any library service, should begin with a marketing plan. The thought of developing a marketing plan may seem daunting, but it need not be. While it is unlikely that most libraries have the resources to develop and conduct in-depth and formal marketing plans for off-campus library instruction services, it is possible even with limited resources to develop a simple and effective plan. A marketing plan should include at a minimum an analysis of the current situation (an assessment of existing services, resources, and target markets), a statement of goals and objectives, marketing strategies, and an evaluation component.

SITUATION ANALYSIS

In assessing the current situation, consider the forms of instruction your library provides for off-campus students. For whom are these services available? Who is currently using them, and who might benefit from them but may not currently be using them? What do you know about your existing and potential markets?

When assessing current services, it is useful to step back and define what is meant by *library instruction* and to consider what activities and services fall under that umbrella. Library instruction for off-campus students manifests itself in a variety of formats beyond those that might be considered part of an on-campus instruction program. Anything from real-time instruction (such as sessions presented to off-campus students attending an on-campus orientation, or instruction delivered via video or online conferencing) to on-demand instructional products (such as videos, CDs, online tutorials, or learning objects) may compose the instruction program. Beyond formal presentations and instructional products, instruction for off-campus students often requires a one-on-one, personalized approach that includes phone conversations, online chat, discussions embedded in online course management systems, and e-mail. It may take the form of an in-depth written "guest lecture" in an online classroom or a concise user guide posted on a Web page. The format that instruction takes will depend on the needs and characteristics of the students and faculty, as well as the resources and initiative of the library.

TARGET MARKETS

Identifying the target audiences, as well as their needs and characteristics, is an essential step in successfully marketing off-campus library instruction programs.

Students

Students are an obvious target market for off-campus library instruction services, but within this population are smaller more narrowly defined segments. For example, off-campus students may include nursing students all working at the same hospital two hours away with access to a hospital library collection as well as graduate students enrolled in an online international MBA program and scattered around the globe. Students may be in a class that meets synchronously (at the same time) via videoconferencing technology, or they may be in an online class that is asynchronous, meaning that the instructor and students never meet at the same time. The library instructional opportunities for working with these populations will vary considerably.

In gathering information about the off-campus student market, it may be useful to find out how many off-campus students there are, where they are, what they are studying, what access to other information sources they have, how they typically go about seeking information, and what technology skills they possess. It will also be useful to know the delivery modes of the courses offered, the duration of courses, and faculty expectations for research.

Gathering such information may sound like an overwhelming task, suggesting the need for exhaustive surveys and research, but much information is already available. As Kotler and Armstrong (2001) suggest, a wealth of marketing information can be obtained by simply observing. Librarians already do that routinely in the course of working at the reference desk; in responding to e-mail, phone, and chat inquiries; and in tallying statistics on document delivery requests or hits on a Web page, for instance. Other simple methods for gathering information about student needs and preferences might include simple surveys. Online surveys accompanying online tutorials or other online library instruction modules can be effective in gathering information (especially if the instructor requires completion of the survey). Distance education students are often asked to complete a survey prior to commencing an online course to assess their computer literacy skills and access to technology. Likewise, most students complete course evaluations at the end of a term. Embedding a few questions about information literacy skills and library access into existing survey instruments such as these is a relatively simple way to get desired information.

Using existing data is an effective and affordable way to obtain information about your students. Inquire with your registrar's office or institutional planning office to see what data is available. They may have demographic information on off-campus students that you can access. If your library has conducted surveys or other user studies, mine what you can from that data. Do what comes naturally to librarians. Look to the literature for existing studies and reports on student characteristics and behavior, distance education students, generational learning styles, and the like. From these goldmines of data you can extrapolate to your own target market. A report such as the OCLC's *Perceptions of Libraries and Information Resources* (De Rosa et al., 2005) is an example of a rich data source that can assist in understanding student needs, behaviors, and attitudes toward library services.

Faculty

Students are not the only population to be considered in marketing off-campus library instruction services. Because we know that most off-campus students, like on-campus students, are unlikely to avail themselves of library resources and services unless their instructors expect or require them to do so (Davis, 2003; Valentine, 2001), faculty constitute a target market as important as students and arguably even more so. Successful collaboration with faculty in incorporating and promoting information literacy and library instruction into the classroom is often cited as a significant determinant of fruitful library instruction programs.

Students and faculty constitute the primary audience for library instruction marketing efforts, but it is important to mention other often-overlooked target markets that can play leading roles in the success of off-campus library instruction programs.

Technology Support Staff

Instructional design and technical support staff can be important allies in incorporating library instruction in off-campus courses. Whereas traditional on-campus faculty often work quite independently in the planning and provision of instruction, faculty in distance learning environments often rely heavily on technical support and design staff in the development and delivery of their courses. Librarian collaboration with course development support staff can be an effective strategy for incorporating and promoting library instruction services (Markgraf, 2002).

Administrators

The success of an institution's distance learning programs hinges not only on the quality of instruction but also on the quality of the entire experience, which includes support services. To garner administrative support for library programs, in terms of funding, staffing, and other resources, it is imperative that librarians emphasize the integral role that library instruction plays in the quality of distance learning offered by the institution. Administrators often pay attention when accrediting requirements are invoked, and most accrediting agencies stress the importance of information literacy skills. Similarly, administrators must always be cognizant of retention issues that affect an institution's bottom line and reputation. Librarians should ensure that administrators are aware of the value of high quality support services, such as library instruction and assistance, in student satisfaction and retention. "When geographic boundaries are removed, distance students have more choices in where to receive their education," writes Dermody (2005: 42), and "the support services that students receive can also affect whether or not they remain in a distance course or program."

If an institution has a central distance learning administrative body, it often serves as a contact point for distance students. Making sure that distance learning administrative staff are aware of library services will not only provide them with additional perks they can use to lure potential students, but it will also help them to better advise and refer existing off-campus students to available library services. Often a centralized office will be responsible for disseminating information to off-campus students and may be willing to include a brochure or other information about library instruction in its mailings. If the office maintains a distance education Web site, its personnel may be willing to link to a library services Web site for off-campus students. As Lippincott (2005: 37) writes, "Libraries must actively request placement of links to their homepages from resources where they think members of their constituency are likely to be in cyberspace."

Library Staff

"Successful service companies focus their attention on both their customers and their employees," write Kotler and Armstrong (2001: 319) in discussing the importance of internal marketing. Library staff make up an important internal target market, and it is imperative that they are aware and supportive of library instruction issues related to off-campus students. Public service staff should know how to respond to off-campus student questions and potential technical problems. Access services and library technical support staff often deal with unique problems and circumstances when assisting off-campus students. A commitment to flexible and responsive customer service in these interactions can influence students' overall impressions of the library and the likelihood that they will make use of other library services in the future. When the commodity is an intangible service, such as library instruction, rather than a product, the quality of the interaction when obtaining the service is paramount (Kotler and Armstrong, 2001).

GOALS AND OBJECTIVES

Goals and objectives for off-campus library instructional efforts may be derived from library and institution mission statements and strategic plans. They may also be directed by accrediting agency information literacy requirements or professional guidelines. The ACRL *Guidelines for Distance Learning Library Services*, for example, advocate "a program of library user instruction designed to instill independent and effective information literacy skills while specifically meeting the learner-support needs of the distance learning community" (ACRL). Clearly stating goals and objectives of your instruction services for off-campus students will assist you in developing strategies for attaining them and in evaluating outcomes to determine what worked and what did not. For example, is an objective of instructional efforts to have more off-campus students use library resources? Do you want off-campus students to cite more scholarly resources in their research papers? Do you want off-campus students to critically evaluate and select Web resources? Consider how you might be able to measure these outcomes. Perhaps you are considering assessment as structured as a bibliometric study of student research papers, or perhaps your resources allow simply for an informal discussion with a faculty member regarding the quality of the papers at the end of the semester. Measuring outcomes may be achieved through observation. For example, perhaps as a result of library instruction marketing efforts, the library observes a decrease in questions from students confused about how to access databases from off-campus or an increase in books and articles requested by off-campus students.

MARKETING STRATEGIES

Once objectives have been established, strategies for achieving them must be developed. The marketing mix is a combination of strategies often called the "4 Ps," product, price, place of distribution, and promotion. Evolving from the 4 Ps are the 4 Cs, an alternative marketing mix paradigm that reflects a more customer-centered orientation. The 4 Cs describe marketing strategies in terms of customer value, cost to consumer, convenience, and communication (Kotler and Armstrong, 2001). This latter formula lends itself more readily to the service orientation of library instruction services.

Customer Value

"If students see the direct value of the library to their academic success they will be more likely to make use of the library" (Ault, 2002: 32). Some students immediately recognize the value of library services, but many do not, and libraries cannot assume that the value they represent is self-evident. Because students are increasingly content with the information they find via Internet search engines and quite confident in their ability to critically evaluate what they find (De Rosa et al., 2005), they may not be likely to intrinsically value library instruction. Faculty, however, often have quite different assessments of student research abilities. Because faculty are often frustrated with the quality of research performed by their students, librarians must demonstrate how providing library instruction for their students can help faculty solve this identified problem. Libraries may not be able to sell the value of their services directly to students until they have sold it to the instructors. Once students are aware of their professors' expectations, they will come to value how libraries can assist them in meeting those expectations. "By inviting us into their classrooms professors are validating the usefulness of the library, the expertise of librarians, and the relevance of this information to the class" (Ardis, 2005).

Cost

The cost to students in using library services is closely related to convenience because the cost is not as often a monetary one as it is one of time and effort. However, in considering the cost of library instruction services in the marketing mix, it is important to consider the cost to the user as well as the cost to satisfy the user. How best can a library maximize limited resources in meeting user needs and expectations? Libraries need to take into account what level of service they can afford to provide and to whom. Are there economies of scale that will make instruction for distance education students more manageable? One-on-one interactions with distance students, while providing a high level of personalized support, can be extremely time consuming. Are there common questions to which librarians devote a great deal of time answering one-on-one? If so, is there a way to improve service that would result in fewer questions? Is there a way to disseminate the answer to more than one student at a time? Librarian participation in online discussion threads, where all students can benefit from a response to one student's question, is one example of using economies of scale to provide library instruction. Sometimes a concept that is easily understood when demonstrated can require an enormous amount of time when it has to be explained via telephone or e-mail. Investing in screen capture software to create short visual demonstrations of common procedures can ultimately be a cost-saving strategy, freeing up a librarian's time for other activities, which ultimately benefits the student.

Convenience to Customer

Often a marketing plan will include a discussion of an organization's competitors or threats. For libraries, the undeniable convenience of searching the Internet is perhaps the most formidable competitor. When emphasis is placed on quality, credibility, and accuracy of information, however, libraries have an edge (De Rosa et al., 2005). But that is not enough. Libraries must do all they can to make finding and using quality information as convenient as possible for students. Galvin (2005) emphasizes the importance of providing user guides that address specific needs, are placed where students need them, and are labeled so that students understand immediately what purpose they serve. Strategies such as providing library instruction from within the course management system can be useful. Such instruction might include direct links to user guides, learning objects embedded into the online classroom, or a course librarian monitoring discussion threads within the online course. Studies show that whereas students in a library will typically go to a librarian for help with resources, most students do not ask for help in using online resources (De Rosa et al., 2005,). Because off-campus students are especially reliant on online resources, it is imperative that libraries provide assistance where students are most likely to use it, rather than expect that students will contact the library with questions. Inserting user instruction at the point-of-need whenever possible, such as context-sensitive help screens within a database or online catalog, will elevate a library's convenience factor. "Students are more likely to use information skills," Galvin writes, "when they learn these skills at the point of need" (Galvin, 2005: 354).

Several institutions are experimenting with methods of integrating library services into online courses. Rochester Institute of Technology Libraries, for example, has made "myLibrary" links a standardized part of the navigation bar in every online D2L course. Any experience students have in using the library will influence their perceptions of convenience, so efforts to simplify library functions in addition to instruction will contribute to a more favorable impression of the library. For example, federated searching promises one-stop searching, which may appeal to students who use Internet search engines. Seamless off-campus access to proprietary databases, simplified procedures for requesting books and articles, and personalized service and flexibility in accommodating off-campus students can all contribute to perceptions of convenience.

Library instruction offers convenience to faculty in several ways. Faculty are often the only contact off-campus students have with a campus and, as a result, often find themselves in the position of fielding questions that go well beyond the content of the course. Whereas an on-campus student may go to a computer help desk with technical questions, to a librarian with research questions, or to other students with questions about almost anything, in the online classroom many of these questions are directed to the professor. By offering to participate in an online classroom to field library-related questions and provide instructive comments, the librarian is offering convenience to the faculty member. Badke (2005) discusses another manner in which librarians can offer convenience to faculty. Librarians have the expertise to assist faculty in using the increasingly complex information systems they need to do their research. "If the eyes of faculty are opened to what we can do for them," he writes, "we have a much better chance of convincing them that their students need to benefit from our expertise as well" (Badke, 2005: 71).

Communication

The fourth C in the marketing mix is communication, which includes promotion but goes beyond it by emphasizing a two-way conversation. Libraries want to promote their services but also want feedback on what works and what would work better. Communication of library instruction services works best when aimed at faculty and others who may have a direct connection with off-campus students. As mentioned, administrative units such as a centralized distance learning office, if there is one, the registrar's office, or a continuing education office can be valuable conduits to students. Perhaps they would consider placing a testimonial from a satisfied off-campus student about the value of library support on their Web page promoting distance learning programs, or maybe a blurb about library support can be placed in the course catalog near the listing of distance learning courses.

Ultimately, however, faculty endorsement is what will encourage students to take advantage of library services, which will in turn drive the need for instruction in how to use and access those services. Faculty, like students, often do not assume that library support is available for off-campus students. The library must let them know through all means available. Strategies might include writing articles for campus newsletters; offering workshops or informational sessions highlighting available library services and successful collaboration with other distance learning professors; attending meetings or getting involved in committees that are likely to put the librarian in contact with distance learning faculty, thereby providing an opportunity to network and promote library services; and communicating directly with distance learning faculty via e-mail or campus mail, phone, or personal visits with faculty. Communication is most effective when the librarian is able to find out what faculty need, what they want, and what frustrates them—and then offer them services to address those issues. Some librarians have found success in carving out niche areas of expertise likely to catch the attention of faculty, such as plagiarism, citation styles, copyright, assignment design, assessment, and Web evaluation. These "hooks" can be useful in getting to know faculty, establishing credibility with faculty, and eventually building collaborative relationships through which faculty become stronger allies of and advocates for the library.

EVALUATION AND CONCLUSION

The final step of the marketing plan is to evaluate the results of the marketing efforts. Did the library achieve its objectives? If not, what were the obstacles, and what can be done to overcome them? What did the library learn along the way about its users and their needs? What can be done to address those needs? Once changes in service are made based on what was learned about and from the customers, how will those enhancements be promoted?

If the questions asked in evaluating the marketing efforts sound strikingly similar to those asked during other steps of the marketing process, it is intentional. Marketing is an ongoing, cyclical process of asking and attempting to answer questions. The result is an ever-evolving, ever-improving off-campus library instruction program.

REFERENCES

Ardis, Susan B. (2005). "Viewpoints: Instruction: Teaching or Marketing." *Issues in Science and Technology Librarianship*. (Spring). Available: www.istl.org/05-spring/viewpoints. html (accessed February 6, 2006.)

Association of College and Research Libraries. *Guidelines for Distance Learning Library Services.* Available: www.ala.org/ala/acrl/acrlstandards/guidelinesdistancelearning.htm (accessed February 6, 2006).

Ault, Meredith. 2002. "Thinking Outside the Library: How to Develop, Implement and Promote Library Services for Distance Learners." In *10th Off-Campus Library Services Conference Proceedings.* Edited by Patrick Mahoney. Mount Pleasant, MI: Central Michigan University.

Badke, William. 2005. "Can't Get No Respect: Helping Faculty to Understand the Educational Power of Information Literacy." *Reference Librarian* no. 89/90: 63–80.

Davis, Philip M. 2003. "Effect of the Web on Undergraduate Citation Behavior: Guiding Student Scholarship in a Networked Age." *portal: Libraries and the Academy* 3, no. 1: 41–51. Available: http://muse.hju.edu (accessed February 6, 2006).

Dermody, Melinda. 2005. "We Cannot See Them, but They Are There: Marketing Library Services to Distance Learners." *Journal of Library & Information Services in Distance Learning* 2, no. 1: 41–50.

De Rosa, Cathy, et al. 2005. *Perceptions of Libraries and Information Resources: A Report to the OCLC Membership.* Dublin, OH: OCLC.

Galvin, Jeanne. 2005. "Alternative Strategies for Promoting Information Literacy." *Journal of Academic Librarianship* 31, no. 4: 352–357.

Kotler, Philip, and Gary Armstrong. 2001. *Principles of Marketing.* 9th ed. Upper Saddle River, NJ: Prentice Hall.

Lippincott, Joan K. 2005. "Where Learners Go: How to Strengthen the Library Role in Online Learning." *Library Journal* (October 1, 2005): 35–37.

Markgraf, Jill S. 2002. "Collaboration between Distance Education Faculty and the Library: One Size Does Not Fit All." *Journal of Library Administration* 37, no. 3/4: 451–464.

Rochester Institute of Technology Libraries. *RIT Library's Desire2Learn Integration Project.* Available: http://library.rit.edu/desire2learn/ (accessed February 6, 2006).

Summey, Terri Pederson. 2004. "If You Build It, Will They Come?: Creating a Marketing Plan for Distance Learning Library Services." In *11th Off-Campus Library Services Conference Proceedings.* Edited by Patrick Mahoney. Mount Pleasant, MI: Central Michigan University.

Valentine, Barbara. 2001. "The Legitimate Effort in Research Papers: Student Commitment versus Faculty Expectations." *Journal of Academic Librarianship* 27, no. 2: 107–115.

▶Part IV

ASSESSING DISTANCE INSTRUCTION

▶16

DEVELOPING AND ASSESSING AN ONLINE LIBRARY INSTRUCTION COURSE

SANDRA ROTENBERG

Overview: In this chapter the author discusses the transition of a traditional "face-to-face library instruction course to an online course. She presents the various changes and revisions to the course to make it a successful online course and includes student comments.

INTRODUCTION

This chapter chronicles the life of a specific online library information course, from conception through middle age. I will give a brief description of my specific circumstances, a description of my evolution into an online teacher, and a general discussion of the issues I think are associated with developing any class of this kind that purports to teach students to use the Internet and master information competencies. Then, and perhaps most importantly, I will show examples of how the tools I used to assess my students changed through the assessment process: the genesis of a midterm from a "contact sport" to a student learning outcomes (SLO) assessment and of a "take home" assignment from general annotated bibliography to a demonstration of specific and relevant Web evaluation skills. Finally, I will quickly mention some of the things I am planning for future development.

BACKGROUND

I teach in a small community college library where I also work as a full-time access services librarian. While there are many differences between two- and four-year schools, for our purposes two things set community colleges apart from most four-year colleges. One is that we must accept all who apply, which means that our students run the gamut from high school students to senior citizens, with every possible level of preparation for college. The other is that librarians are considered faculty on an equal footing with our colleagues in the classrooms; we all have the same level of education required for our jobs.

At my college, librarians take on teaching assignments as overload—meaning they are paid overload (or overtime) hours, which for online instructors corresponds to the hours they would be lecturing in a traditional classroom, plus the final. Any work on the class needs to be done outside the librarian's thirty-five-hour workweek. To get started, new librarian instructors are given a two-page description of the course; we call it a Section K, which contains a brief outline of the course objectives. The rest of the content is up to each instructor to provide. This is true for both traditional and online courses.

TEACHING IN A CLASSROOM

I began working as a librarian at Solano Community College in August 2001. A few weeks after that I was teaching my first course, in a traditional classroom; and a year later I was teaching online for the first time. The first two times I taught the course, in the traditional classroom, at the beginning of the course's development I was focused on creating outlines for the material I would need to cover, putting them into PowerPoint presentations to keep myself on track during the two-hour session; creating homework assignments, quizzes, examinations; choosing a textbook; grading; and honing my delivery and classroom presentation skills.

Three things converged to inform both my teaching and my learning during the period I was teaching in a traditional classroom. I mention them here to give some context to what follows. Everyone has a different path and story, and mine might affect how useful the rest of the article will be to the reader.

The first thing that influenced me was the excitement/anticipation/cold reality of teaching. When I agreed to do it, I had never taught a course. I imagined I would be teaching and using already developed materials, since the class was starting in a few weeks. But instead, I was told that to use anyone else's materials would be a form of plagiarism. What I did not anticipate was that there would be very little time to learn to teach before I actually began teaching. So, my assignment was to very quickly create a whole course from a very short course outline (an average of four sentences per two-hour lecture).

Secondly, at about this same time, I attended a "flex-cal" (*flexible calendar* is our term for professional development) seminar that was recruiting online teachers— I thought my course would be a natural for that environment, and so I signed up. I was committed before I really understood what it meant, but I was in good company, since the online program was in a very early stage of development at that time: that fall, when I signed up, there were 7 instructors and 17 courses teaching 976 students (enrollments); the next year, when I began teaching online, there were 17 instructors and 34 courses; last year we had 57 instructors offering 122 courses to 5,630 students (enrollments). This seminar got me thinking about transferring my "classroom" course into an online course.

The third influence during that period was a community college convocation at the University of California at Berkeley, where Barbara Beno (president of Western Association of Schools and Colleges [WASC], our accrediting association) gave a talk about student learning outcomes and how they were going to change the way we approched education in this country. Since I was new to teaching, it seemed like a good idea for me to just start using this pedagogical approach. Another term for it is *backward design*. Begin at the end: where do you want your students to be when they walk out of your class?

I also read everything I could get my hands on about teaching online, teaching information literacy, and student learning outcomes. I joined our campuswide committee on Student Learning Outcomes and the Online Committee and the eTeachers group. I developed more detailed outlines and notes for lectures. I studied Web sites and handouts. Finally, I took an ACRL course, "Assessing Student Learning Outcomes," the upshot of which was the development of these interlinked student learning outcomes for my online course LR51, "Web Searching":

▶ Students will demonstrate knowledge of major search tools including engines, directories, virtual libraries, and proprietary databases by choosing the appropriate tool for assigned research projects.

▶ Students will demonstrate ability to develop an appropriate search statement using Boolean operators and wildcards, advanced search pages, etc.

▶ Students will know when to go for help with their research projects and where to find help online.

▶ Students will understand the economic forces that drive development online and how these forces affect what the student will find online from commercial search engines, subject directories, not-for-profit organizations, the government, public libraries, and educational institutions.

All of this got me to the pretty obvious, but now well-informed conclusion that developing a course for delivery in the online learning environment is different from developing a traditional course. There have been a lot of articles written about developing an online course, so I will limit my comments to my specific area of expertise and experience: teaching information competency and library skills.

I should warn you, both as a reader of this chapter and as a potential developer of an online course, that what happened for me in the development of this course was the process never really ended. I would write an assignment or a lecture, see how it worked or did not work, and then develop it further. Over the five years I have been teaching this course, the process has not stopped, although the pace has changed. The first two years I taught the course I was not very happy with it or proud of it; I reworked everything constantly and was barely keeping one week ahead of my students during the semester. Now I am generally very content with the basic course, but I am still always thinking of ways to improve it. I think it was the restlessness that came of not being happy that drove me immediately into the cycle of develop and assess and develop again, although the talk by Barbara Beno and other speakers at that convocation had given me an idea of what the SLO process looked like. Once you begin that cycle, it is hard to break.

TEACHING ONLINE

Teaching information literacy online is a great way to introduce our students to libraries, instead of waiting for them to wander into one; and it is one way to meet them where they are—online. It is an opportunity to reach some of the students who need these skills the most. These students are frequently taking online courses because time is at a premium; perhaps they are juggling children and work, and making time for regularly scheduled classes does not seem possible. When they are offered the option of taking the course online, they leap at it. These students are frequently comfortable with virtual relationships and turn first to the Internet for just about everything. A course like this is our chance to educate these online citizens about the value of librarians and to demonstrate that the value of libraries does not diminish because we are "virtual." Even if our methods and techniques change with the new technologies and the new environment, what remains true is that libraries are in this world to facilitate the retrieval of information for the student/citizen.

When I started to transform my course from real to virtual, my overarching concern about teaching online was the potential lifelessness and facelessness of an online course. But I quickly came to realize that teaching online is not about erasing your personality or turning your course into a generic series of interactive tutorials. Just like in teaching face-to-face, teaching online is about forging a living and breathing connection with your students that involves dialogue and teaching and learning; and just as using PowerPoint and computer displays does not necessarily create that connection in person, neither does using Flash and Java necessarily create it online. I fought this battle to connect in the online environment in two ways: first, I made the content as relevant and useful as possible for students in the real world, and second, I tried to somehow foster the kind of the student-student and student-teacher communication that occurs in successful traditional classrooms.

Goal 1

In trying to reach my first goal—relevance—I found that although the ACRL standards I had read and learned about were helpful, and the work done on those standards was helpful, what information literacy boiled down to for me, informally, in the context of my own course was: what our students need to know to find and use information for school and life in the online environment. My course focuses on online resources, while another course we teach focuses on learning about more traditional library resources (although because many of those are electronic now and accessed via the Internet, the lines are blurring). In LR51, I have to keep reminding myself that my goal is not to turn students into librarians who have a deep understanding of the way it all works and interrelates (although I make no secret of the fact that I love my work); but I can easily get them to understand the value of wasting fewer hours surfing fruitlessly for the information they need to do their papers. And all of them quickly come to understand that learning a bit of the girder of the Internet infrastructure and finding efficient ways to create queries help them do all their online work better. I portray the library and librarians as tools they can use. I talk about not reinventing the wheel. I talk about getting other people to do the work for them. I appeal to their need to save time and their lack of interest in "why" and "how." I tell them they do not have to memorize exactly how everything works; they just need to know that someone (the librarian) knows how everything works and to know how to find that someone (or the tools created by that someone). This works well to get them into virtual libraries, subject directories, advanced search pages, and proprietary databases. I try to make what I teach relevant to their lives.

Goal 2

My second goal was to deal with one of the classic problems of being in an asynchronous environment: that one never actually "talks" to anyone else in that environment, and for most humans it is difficult to make a connection without some form of conversation. A very useful tool for creating a more interactive conversational environment, in my experience, is a required chat room session. In the case of the course I teach, I need to forge an almost immediate connection with my students because I have access to them for only eight weeks. So I begin the course by putting up a discussion thread asking them to sign up for one of two or three sessions offered the following week (the number depends on my schedule and the number of students in the class). The sign-up sheet is there not because I need to know who will show up when, but to encourage students to put it on their calendars, their list of things to do. Since most of my students are working people, not full-time students, I try to schedule evening and weekend times; this increases the likelihood of their attendance. They get a point just for signing up and then up to nine points for attending and participating. When they get to the chat room, we chat. Usually we chat about the course, but not always. This is the kind of message that begins the chat: "There is no set agenda this evening—I just want to use this time to hear from all of you about what you are doing, what concerns you might have, questions, answers, and so forth." Then the conversation might be about the quizzes and course materials, or it might become a chance for the students to check their perceptions with one another, or maybe a philosophical debate about the role textbooks play, or anything, from the weather to a wedding to an experience with another class, and then back to a question about whether the class should be worth more than one unit. It is a great way for the students to get to know one another and me. This in turn facilitates future communication. They have a better idea of who they are e-mailing/calling, and it seems to make them more comfortable in their new classroom.

CONCERNS

So these were my main preliminary concerns, but as I began to actually teach the course online, I ran into other problems. For example, I realized that teaching in the online environment exaggerates some things, makes them stand out more, and puts them in stark relief. For me this might be truer because I grew up in a time (not that long ago) where seeing something in print meant it had been published—it was important and should be free of errors. Yet, online, everything is in print. Errors that you can correct immediately by lecturing in person become huge problems "lecturing" online in that you do not know how many students have read and taken notes on your mistakes. They feel like a very big deal. You have to correct them and then send an e-mail and post a notification announcing that the teacher is fallible. This fallibility is not always comfortable for the teacher or for the students. My answer to this is to use humor and encourage them to find my mistakes. If I can be confident that most of what I teach, and most of what they learn, is valuable, and I am, then a few mistakes cannot change that, and there will always be mistakes. I try to use my fallibility as a teaching moment, by pointing out that even their classroom requires their critical evaluation.

Another problem I encountered as I started to teach the course was more specifically relevant to teaching an information literacy course and had to do with student expectations about content. Most students take my course either because they need an extra unit to maintain eligibility for insurance or financial aid or something like that, or because they think "I know how to use Yahoo—what else can there possibly be?" and they want an easy A. (Many students think that because they are masters of MySpace.com, they are experts at everything relating to the Internet. But as I know from Pew and other sources, as well as from my own experience, MySpace and academic research have nothing to do with each other.) But I have found that student expectations change during the course. Here is a comment from one student that is echoed by others every semester:

> I have a confession to make. . . . I took this class because I thought it was going to be a breeze. I do research all the time online for the many different papers us college students have to write, so I thought I knew pretty much everything I needed to know, so therefore this class would be pretty simple. I was wrong. I realized I knew NOTHING about researching online, and I have learned that there is so much more out there to use. I've been sharing everything I've learned in this class with others, and they also had no idea. This is actually a class where I am going to be using the information I learn on a daily basis.

Because it is one unit, students expect to breeze to an easy A. I also have an added issue because the course is compressed into eight weeks instead of the usual sixteen, and many students forget that compressed courses are not abridged courses—they are the same course in a shorter time. Here is another student comment that is, I think, also representative of student reactions to my course and, probably by extension, to other information competency classes at other institutions.

> I have to admit, when first signing up for this class I was NOT looking forward to it AT ALL. I needed one more unit to make 12 so I started searching for a 1–2 unit class. I didn't search as early as I should have, so my first picks for classes were already full. The only class that would fit my schedule was this one. Although I knew I wasn't the best with computers and the Internet, this class was still of no interest to me. My attitude changed pretty quick though. After the second week, I loved it! One of my friends made fun of me all the time and thought I was completely insane because a lot of times I would spend more time with this class than some of my other ones, and this one is only 1 unit.

Another issue about student expectations that comes up when you are teaching a class like this is computer literacy versus information literacy: which are you teaching, and where do you draw the line? I put in my Welcome message the following: "The focus of this class is learning how to do academic research online. You should already know how to use a computer. Here are some of the things I will assume you know how to do: download files from the Internet; open and navigate with a browser; and use a word processor."

I also ask the students to take the tutorial produced by our course management software company and offer extra credit in the first week if they pass the quiz at the end with at least 80% correct answers. They usually do this, and it gives them good information about how to get around in the courseware. This frees me from the necessity of teaching the environment as well as the content.

Finally, as I started teaching online, I realized that the simple fact of not being able to see my students presented problems. In a traditional classroom most teachers can just look at the students while lecturing and tell whether they are snoring, confused, excited, and so forth—not true in an online class. There is no way really to tell (despite some technological advances) whether your students are reading the lectures—no way to take roll. To make up for that, online instructors develop myriad other "contact sports" (my name for all the games I play to engage my students and find out if they are "getting" the class). Quizzes, threaded discussion sections, "coffeehouses," online synchronous chatting for credit, e-mails, extra credit for finding errors, extra credit for reading additional articles and news stories (picked by me) and writing a short essay on the article and how it relates to the course and to real life, course evaluations—these are all ways of staying in contact with students. Some of these tools result in metrics; scores can be kept, for instance. But for others the only value is in feedback to me so that I can do what teachers in traditional classrooms do: go over something again that seems to be puzzling people, reinforce another point that no one seems to realize is important, fish for signs of dawning comprehension.

CHANGES AND REVISIONS

Some changes I made in the process of developing/assessing/developing were basically cosmetic: the paragraphs in my lectures got shorter; the lectures themselves went from being one long page to several pages with a "next" at the bottom of each page linking to the next page; there is more space around the text in every page; I incorporate audio and video by linking to outside Web sites such as NPR; I include a biography and a picture of myself in the syllabus; I put pictures in most of the weekly introductions, and they change according to the season and my mood; I require participation in two discussion threads each week, one much less formal than the other. However, some of the biggest and most far-reaching changes I made during the first couple of years involved restructuring two of the major assessment tools: the midterm and one of the "take home" assignments.

Midterm Exam

The first tool I changed was the midterm. Originally, the goal for all of the exams (quizzes, midterm, and the final) was to test students' comprehension of the course material. My goal was not to get them to memorize the details but to be able to put their hands on the answer and know that answers to this type of problem exist. To achieve this, I asked questions that fit into the multiple-choice true/false category. They were essentially some of the "contact sports" that I mentioned as my way of checking in with students to be sure they are doing the readings and getting familiar with the tools being introduced in the course. But I realized that I wanted at least one of the tests to assess the critical thinking process that was key to being information literate. I chose the midterm because I wanted to test the students in an exam environment.

The first revision to the midterm added five essay questions asking students to describe how they would solve different research problems. I asked them to think each one through and write it down—not to actually go online and test their answers. In the case of the midterm essay question, the student learning outcomes I assess are:

▶ Students will demonstrate knowledge of major search tools including engines, directories, virtual libraries, and proprietary databases by choosing the appropriate tool for assigned research projects.

▶ Students will demonstrate ability to develop an appropriate search statement using Boolean operators and wildcards, advanced search pages, etc.

I asked for complete search statements and a written explanation of where they would start (which search engine, database, or directory) and why. I think it took me close to twenty hours to grade the eighteen exams. It was an exhausting process, and it seemed that most of the students had completely missed the point. In the first revision, this was the introduction I gave them:

For the following question, describe your best search for the information requested—name the first place you would go to start your search and type in the specific search words/phrase you would use for that tool. Be sure to describe your reasoning. Be aware that if you tell me you are going to *Encyclopedia Britannica* and you don't put AND between your search phrases, I will assume you don't know that *Encyclopedia Britannica* defaults to an OR, and you will get the question wrong. Each of these questions is worth 5 points, for a total of 25 points—half the midterm—so take your time and get it right! All of the information you need is in your readings.

And here is the series of research problems they were to solve:
1. You need to research the increase in the occurrence of obesity in children for a paper for my Human Development class.
2. You are looking for information about Kurt Cobain for a paper you are writing in your psychology class.
3. You need to explore alternative medicine treatments for cancer.
4. You just got an e-mail asking for help in moving this Nigerian guy's money over to this country so he doesn't lose it, and you want to help. What do you do?
5. You are studying the Great Depression, and you need to explore the subject a bit to find the exact topic for your paper.

Here are a few excerpts from their responses:
▶ *"I would use Vivisimo because of its meta-search capabilities to get the most results."*
▶ *"I would go to the old Yahoo, then History button on the page, then I would browse until I found something."*
▶ *"I wasn't really sure where to start, so I figured Google would be a good starting point."*
▶ *"After reading this question, I would actually begin my search with the History Channel."*

▶ *"After reading this question I would start my search with the Web site Health Central. The actual Web site is: http://www.healthcentral.com. I chose this Web site, because my Mom frequents this Web site for many things, and has only given me good reviews and feedback."*

▶ *"To learn about the situation in the Middle East, I would search www.cnn.com."*

▶ *"I wasn't too sure about this question and wasn't sure where to begin, so I used one of the search engines I frequent most."*

Having this new midterm fail so dramatically both from my perspective and from the students' (only one student passed the midterm the first semester) was a good lesson. What I learned was that teaching, at least for me, was going to be a process of trying something, assessing its efficacy for both the students and the instructor (because it needs to work for both of us if it is going to work in the long term), revising it based on the results of the assessment, and starting the cycle over again. The other lesson I learned with this failure was that students could be partners in the educational process. When I finished grading the exams and realized that only one student had passed (and the class had a pretty typical bell curve on other assignments), I took the problem to the students. I explained that the exam failed. I explained that this had created a problem we would need to solve together. We had some discussion about the options, and the upshot was that they all read over the notes I wrote on their midterms, and then I opened the test for another three days and offered them the opportunity to redo the essays. The results required another over-the-top time commitment from me (and from them), but the students performed much better on the exam.

This experience taught me several other lessons. One was that the students were not making any connection between the questions on the test and what they were learning in the course (assuming of course that learning was taking place, which I would have been hard put to prove at that point). Another was that the students were not reading the paragraph of instructions, or if they were reading it, they did not understand what I was asking for. Also, I found that detailed individual feedback for five essay questions for twenty students was way more work than I could handle.

Finally, I saw with this type of midterm question how difficult it was for students to leave the comfort of their favorite search engines, especially in a stressful situation like an exam. They needed more encouragement and practice in the rest of the course to feel comfortable with the task in the examination. This exam altered almost every one of the discussions for the following semester because I changed them from things the students could just talk about to things that they needed to go out and experience and then come back and discuss.

This comfort issue popped up in many places throughout the course. Because the Web is a tool that most people already use before they arrive in my "classroom," many have developed their own patterns and comfort zones; it is sort of like trying to coax a child to try a new food. I learned to tell my students that their tests and discussions are specifically designed to test what they are learning in class, not what they already know.

As a result of all of this, the following semester I cut the number of questions down to three, and it is now just one. I kept the number of points for this section of the midterm at one-third of the total, to indicate that it is a very important part of their midterm grade, but I get enough information about the student and his or her learning from just the one research problem.

The introduction to the single short essay question on the midterm now reads:

PLEASE READ THE INSTRUCTIONS VERY CAREFULLY:

For the following short essay question:
DO NOT actually do the search!!!!

Pretend that you have been given the assignment below and are going to need to do some research so you can write a paper on it.

Your answer to this question should be your first SEARCH STRATEGY. Describe how you would begin to explore this topic. Without actually doing it, describe how you would theoretically tackle the problem.

You will need to discuss what search tool you will start with and why. You will need to discuss what keywords you will use and why. Will you use nesting? Boolean? Or just keywords? In what combination and most importantly WHY?

HINT: Do not say that you are going to Yahoo because "you always go there" or "you like it." **This is a test of what you are learning in the course, not what you knew before you started.**

This question is worth 10 points—one third of the points for the midterm, so take your time and answer it completely! I would suggest you actually go write it in a word processor, then copy and paste your answer in the box below. All of the information you need is in your readings.

"Take-Home" Assignment

The other assignment I will use for an example of the develop-assess-develop-again cycle is one of the major "take home" assignments. This assignment started as an annotated bibliography on a topic of the students' choosing, but that did not end up demonstrating critical thinking and Web evaluation skills—it just showed that they could surf the Web and get a little information.

I realized that in its original form, while this was a good assignment in some ways—it worked for students who were already doing well in the course, and who were taking classes where they needed to do research—the others did not seem to pick up on the idea, and there were complaints that it was too "English 1." The other issue was that, again, many of the students were not challenged to go beyond their ruts, the same "comfort issue" I had experienced with the midterm.

Since I was still reading all of the articles I could find about teaching information competency, I decided to change the assignment to one suggested by many instructors—using hoax sites to teach evaluation. I thought that the idea had merit; hoaxes were exaggerations of things you want students to learn in evaluations that are sometimes more difficult to teach with real pages. I thought a site of this sort would be a good testing ground for assessing evaluation skills. I looked at several Web sites before settling on the Male Pregnancy page on the RYT hospital Web sites. (The Librarians' Internet Index has a number of good resources for teachers of information literacy. It can be found at http://lii.org/pub/subtopic/2664.)

The site for this assignment is www.malepregnancy.com. I chose this site from among the many mentioned by teaching librarians because it looked so right, and yet it just had to be wrong. I thought that most students would see it and automatically know it was a hoax of some kind. The site is very easy to pick apart because there are some obvious issues. The "hospital" does not have a phone number or street address. The only way to contact it is via an e-mail form. The other pages also are implausible: Genochoice offers visitors the ability to choose the genetic makeup of their child through a tool that accesses their thumbprint from their monitor; there are nanobots, small robots in the bloodstream; and Clyven the talking mouse. There is a link to Credits on the Genochoice page that does explain the purpose of the site. There are links to external media that seem right, until you realize that the USA Today story is three years old, making this one very long gestation period! If you "Google" it, you get information that identifies the site as an art installation and hoax. In short, there are lots of places on the Web site a student could point to and say, "obviously not a sign of authoritative and reliable information."

This hoax assignment comes in the week after we discuss the importance of evaluating Web sites with a critical mind. The reading that week includes two articles on Internet evaluation (Harris, 1997; Barker, 2005). The assignment then gives students one Web site and asks eight questions. Questions point them to places that should set off alarms. The hoax site contains many potential "aha" moments, places where the students can find something amiss or suspicious. What I found, though, was that, despite the previous week's lecture topic, the reading assignments, the pointed questions, and all the credibility issues on the Web site itself, semester after semester approximately 50% of my students believed the information on this site was true, despite all the clues. I realized that for these students, most of their problem is that they do not actually read, they just copy and paste.

Usually when these students get their graded papers back, they get a bit of a shock. This exercise becomes a fun opportunity for me to encourage critical thinking. Most of these students do not make the same mistake a few weeks later, when I give them a discussion thread on evaluating sites and slip in a few other hoax sites or questionable sites. They learn to read before copying and pasting. It also works beautifully for the students who do get it; they know it cannot be true, so they go looking for the evidence. It has a lot of rewards for the students who carefully examine; they take up the challenge and bring back lots of evidence. I even had one student who found a very interesting interview from a Canadian radio station with the author of the site. So, by changing the assignment from an annotated bibliography to a Web site evaluation, I managed to create an assignment that was rewarding and effective for all of my students, not just the ones who "got it" immediately.

FUTURE DEVELOPMENTS

In the future I would like to develop some group projects for the students. I want to add in some of my own video/audio pieces. I would like to explore using a social networking tool like del.icio.us to create a place where students can put up sites they find useful to share with the rest of the class or even the larger school community. One of the ideas I have seen discussed involves an academic portal of this sort where students could use social networking to advise one another; perhaps with a librarian or faculty team setting up the rules and adding comments to the sites chosen, we might end up with tools that the whole school could use to find good information, without all the labor involved when it is a one-person creation. I hope to become much more proficient with some of the tools I use now: Adobe Professional, HTML, XHTMLXML, CSS, Camtasia, and SnagIt. I would like to find a way to market the course better to both faculty and students. Finally, I would like to learn Macromedia Flash and Java and JavaScript.

CONCLUSION

The biggest lesson I learned over the past few years as an online instructor of library instruction is that the instruction is never over. Developing and assessing any course, but particularly one where the subject matter is dynamic and changes frequently, requires constant engagement. Many factors come into play while developing such a course. Instructors must deal with student expectations and basic computer literacy. Librarians must keep in mind that part of the task is to bring these online students into the library, making the connection that will help them in the future because while the technology may change, the essential role of the librarian—to facilitate access to information—will not. Assessment is also a multifaceted process; it applies to assessing not only the students and their learning but also the course and the quality and quantity of instruction and then the changes and improvements as they happen. These things require a balancing act to prevent student detachment or instructor burnout. Even while not teaching, I am always thinking about my course: keeping up with the literature by way of listservs such as

ILI, Web4Lib, and CJC-L and subscriptions to ACRL publications, the *Chronicle for Higher Education*, EDUCAUSE, League for Innovation in the Community College, Blended Librarian, and so forth; analyzing the results from the last semester; comparing data; tweaking lectures; updating readings; and learning new technologies.

Teaching online has mostly been a joyous experience. I have come to accept, at least with my teaching, that it is a journey and not a destination, and enjoy what I do. The students are by and large responsive and excited about what they are learning, and I feel that I have contributed skills that will be of benefit to them in the future. One of the other instructors at the college told me he had a group of students taking one of his computer forensics courses who had formed an impromptu group and called themselves "surf ninjas." They were taking my course. He said the difference between the quality of the work they turned in and the quality of work turned in by others who had not taken my course was startling and impressive. Of course, this is not objective, but it was great feedback.

REFERENCES

Barker, Joe. "Evaluating Web Pages: Techniques to Apply and Questions to Ask." Available: www.lib.berkeley.edu/TeachingLib/Guides/Internet/Evaluate.html (accessed March 22, 2005).

Harris, Robert. "Evaluating Internet Research Sources." VirtualSalt. Available: www.virtual salt.com/evalu8it.htm (accessed March 22, 2005).

▶17

REVIEWING ASSESSMENT TOOLS FOR LIBRARY INSTRUCTION

SANDRA LEE HAWES

Overview: In this chapter the author gives a thorough review of the many resources, online and in print, that are available on the assessment of distance learning library instruction. Alternative assessments to accommodate diversity also are
included.

INTRODUCTION

Distance education, like its traditional campus-centric counterpart, is subject to accountability measures requiring assessment of student learning. Distance learning
librarians, although well versed in library science, may lack a sufficient depth of
content knowledge to develop appropriate assessments of their varied instructional activities. A number of books are available on the subject, along with sup-
plementary Web sites, all of which provide assistance in developing and teaching
distance education courses. Although some of these resources discuss ways to
assess learning outcomes in distance education courses, few provide concrete examples from which distance learning librarians can develop individual in-house assessments. Distance learning librarians would do well to begin with the Association
of College and Research Libraries' Web site on information literacy, which offers
librarians assistance in the form of a bibliography of research articles comprising
a solid foundation on the theory and practice of assessments in libraries (ACRL).
More specifically, the Distance Learning Section establishes five criteria to use as a
guide in developing assessments for distance learning library instruction in its
online paper "Criteria for Successful Assessment Programs for Distance Learning
Library Instruction" (DLS). Additionally, librarians should consult the American
Association for Higher Education Web site for its nine principles of good practice
for assessing student learning (Astin).

The distance learning librarian, therefore, must be willing to adapt and adopt various resources, strategies, and assessment examples from the general library and educational communities, making use of distance education materials whenever possible (Pausch and Popp, 1997). Fortunately, several university and commercial Web sites offer quality help. Included here is a representative selection, all containing open-access materials, although some do include subscription-only portions of the Web site.

CONTENT AREA AND INSTRUCTIONAL PEDAGOGY

Librarians cannot be subject specialists in every discipline, yet they are called upon to address the needs of students across the curriculum. In addition to reference books that provide subject overviews, many Web sites are designed to quickly impart learning strategies appropriate to various disciplines and learning communities. One such resource of value to distance learning librarians is "Kathy Schrock's Guide for Educators" found at the Discovery Channel's Discovery Education Web site. Distance learning librarians developing in-house assessments will enjoy Schrock's easy access to Web page rubrics, rubric templates, activity builders, alternative assessments, e-portfolios, and graphic organizers (Schrock). The ACRL Instruction Section provides "Library Instruction Annotated Bibliography for Distance Education and Library Instruction," an overview of the literature on developing, delivering, and assessing distance library instruction" (ACRL-IS). Consult the National Education Association's Web site for "Online Teaching and Learning Resources" to build your site, review educational psychology, and borrow templates for assessment and evaluation (NEA).

Numerous colleges, universities, and professional organizations offer online assistance that distance learning librarians can consult, such as the Muskingum College Center for Advancement of Learning's "Learning Strategies Database," which arranges subjects in a hyperlinked grid for quick reference when developing lessons and selecting assessment strategies appropriate to different subjects and disciplines (Muskingum College). The Office of Institutional Effectiveness and Analysis of Florida Atlantic University offers "Assessment Resources" on its Web site, which provides links to resources on assessing student skills, knowledge, and values; as well as general resources on assessing student learning and resources for colleges and departments (Pusateri).

North Carolina State University maintains a comprehensive hyperlinked list, "Internet Resources for Higher Education Outcomes Assessment," touching on everything from e-portfolios, to assessing distance education and sample project and grading rubrics for use in higher education (NCSU). Of specific interest to distance learning librarians is the section of links to resources to help develop assessments for distance learning instruction, including links to Project ADEPT

(Assessment of Distance Education Pedagogy and Technology), which supplies sample assessments; the Distance Education Clearinghouse at the University of Wisconsin–Extension, which provides specialized resources and instructors' tools; and the University of Texas, Austin Center for Instructional Technologies' "Assessment Resources for On-line Courses," which links to furthers lists of online assessment resources suitable for distance learning applications (ibid.).

The e-Learning Centre in the United Kingdom provides an annotated, hyperlinked bibliography titled "Library Testing and Assessment Online" to help librarians develop good assessment instruments to use with online instruction (e-Learning Centre). The Centre has compiled annotated links to resources on topics such as security for online testing and how to develop simulation-like questions. It contains both open-access and subscription resources and services.

The University of Melbourne, Australia, offers assessment and evaluation resources on its Web site and provides access to printable worksheets that librarians can use to assess student learning with an emphasis on teaching students how to conduct literature searches (University of Melbourne). Yale University Library developed an assessment toolkit with many useful links to research and resources on the subject, including sample assessment instruments, such as a faculty survey to use following library instruction (Yale University Library).

IMPORTANCE OF ASSESSING PRIOR LEARNING

Assessing students' prior learning is an essential aspect of developing suitable assignments and assessments, particularly when working with adult learners in an online environment dominated by constructivist pedagogies, such as active learning assignments, peer feedback, and formative self-evaluations. Distance learning librarians would do well to adapt pretests so as to capture information about the prior learning of their students. It is wasteful of students' time to reteach them what they already know.

Kathleen Dunn, a librarian at Cal Poly Pomona University Library, developed an information competency assessment that provides students and librarians with a quick thumbnail sketch of what is known and what needs to be learned. Dr. Dunn's online resource can be adapted for specific online library instruction scenarios (Dunn). Another example of an assessment that can be used either as a pretest or as a test of prior learning was developed at Lexington Community College, in Kentucky, part of the Bluegrass Community and Technical College District. Its library assessment is designed to take advantage of Web interaction while revealing what students already know and what they have yet to learn (Lexington Community College).

The Web format, with its highly interactive aspect, can be adapted to accommodate specific distance learning library instructional requirements (Fusco and

Ketcham, 2002). In particular, telecommunications technologies, including the World Wide Web, allow for synchronous communication in online courses, so that traditional, informal question-and-answer (Q&A) assessment can be used in real-time sessions (Groen and Li, 2005).

ASSESSING ONLINE LIBRARY INSTRUCTION

Assessment of online library instruction takes various forms, many of which mimic those used in traditional classroom settings. These include both formal and informal assessment techniques, such as Q&A by videophone; writing students' comments on the class whiteboard or bulletin board; conducting virtual office hours to accommodate students who are having difficulty with the material or who missed the class session online; administering written pre- and posttests to measure gains from instruction; electronic journaling; electronic portfolios; online real-time chat and co-browsing; class Weblogs; opinion and attitude surveys; and formative skills assessments.

The commercial site Flashlight offers resources and services to institutional subscribers to facilitate development of in-house online assessments for distance learning. Its open-access pages provide links to other evaluation Web sites "useful for studies of teaching, learning, and technology," including examples of computer-aided assessment, student work, and methods and tools for evaluating courseware (TLT Group).

Perhaps the most common form of assessment in online library instruction are the traditional pre- and posttests. By using the assessment tools embedded in the course software, distance learning librarians can develop pre- and posttests for individual lessons (Farmer, 2005). When developing in-house tutorials on subject-specific databases, librarians should try incorporating formative assessment activities to supplement pre- and posttests, such as having students use an online catalog to find a book and then post the book's citation on the course bulletin board (Persson and Washington-Hoagland, 2004). The University of Maryland–University College's online information literacy and writing assessment project offers free tutorial materials to use as templates (UMUC). Distance learning librarians will find Section 4, "Designing Assignments That Contain Writing and Research," useful in developing online content and accompanying assessments. An illustrative set of sample questions with interactive answers teaches how to incorporate high-quality information literacy elements into course assessments. The site also includes characteristics of effective library assignments and an information literacy checklist.

Electronic journaling moves reflective writing from traditional classrooms to the online environment. This assessment tool provides the instructor insight into the students' learning process and focuses on specific learning activities or events

(Farmer, 2004). Electronic journaling, accompanied by student posts to class bulletin boards, fosters a sense of community in the online course environment. Electronic journaling, classroom chats, and bulletin board posts are a few simple ways librarians can provide online students with the same opportunities to become better writers and researchers as their face-to-face counterparts experience (Anson, 2002). Such informal writing assessments reveal information with which the astute distance learning librarian can assess individual students' information literacy skill levels and content knowledge. A class Weblog is another informal assessment method available to distance learning librarians (Martindale and Wiley, 2005). By analyzing the students' comments and questions, lesson plans can be improved, learning activities extended, and students directed to further reading material to expand and clarify lesson content.

An electronic version of traditional portfolio assessments, referred to as e-portfolios, is being used successfully with online courses and content delivery and is growing in popularity in the distance learning community. Some ideas and examples of e-portfolio use at "selected higher education institutions" can be found on the EDUCAUSE Web site (Lorenzo and Ittelson). The material is clear and easy to translate to library assessment efforts, particularly those presented as part of an online tutorial or as one-session library instruction within a content-area online course.

ASSESSING THE LIBRARY INSTRUCTOR

This topic is covered at some length in the general literature of academic assessment, so it is only briefly addressed in this chapter. Satisfaction surveys are an easy way for distance learning librarians to assess the utility of library instruction, either as a culminating activity or in a follow-up e-mail. Additionally, distance learning librarians can partner with colleagues in the institutional research department to have questions added onto the institution's exit survey for the course in which the library instruction was taught. Forms appropriate for peer review have been published and can be adapted for use by distance learning librarians delivering instruction online (Hutchings, 1995; Richlin and Manning, 1995).

ACCOMMODATING DIVERSITY (ALTERNATIVE ASSESSMENT)

Because the online classroom environment is populated by a diverse student group, many of whom are older students returning to college part-time while attending to families and jobs full-time, it is important to remember the following five essential principles of adult-oriented assessment practice.

1. Adult-oriented assessment recognizes multiple sources of knowing, that is, learning that occurs from interaction with a wide variety of informal and informal knowledge sources.

2. Adult-oriented assessment recognizes and reinforces the cognitive, conative [sic], and affective domains of learning.
3. Adult-oriented assessment focuses on adults' active involvement in learning and assessment processes, including active engage in self-assessment.
4. Adult-oriented assessment embraces adult learners' involvement in and impact on the broader world of work, family, and community.
5. Adult-oriented assessment accommodates adults' increasing differentiation from one another given varied life experiences and education

(Kasworm and Marienau, 1997: 8–13)

Additionally, online students may need special accommodations for language difficulties, learning disabilities, physical impairments, and other special needs, just as students in traditional, face-to-face classrooms do. Indiana University has assembled an array of "Alternative Assessment Techniques in the Language Arts" on its Web site, many of which are applicable to assessment of online library instruction, particularly those developed as part of a college or university "writing across the curriculum" initiative (Hsieh). The Indiana University site includes citations to ERIC articles, as well as links to articles on authentic assessment, alternative assessment for ESL (English as a second language) and other non-native English-speaking students, e-portfolio information, and alternative assessment strategies. This is particularly important for distance learning librarians to consider when developing content and assessment in an online environment because "[i]ndividuals who must learn at a distance have ongoing obligations . . . physical handicaps, or . . . live in geographically isolated areas" (Feasley, 1983). Information about adaptive technologies, access guidelines, principles and best practices for students with disabilities, and sample language can be found in the print literature (Goodson, 2001; Johnson, 2003).

The Council on Competitiveness has put together a Web site for K–12 students, teachers, and parents, where participants can compete against one another worldwide in the subjects of mathematics and science using its "GetSmarter.org" highly visual, interactive testing software. GetSmarter.org is an intriguing and challenging example of interactive assessments constructed in a style that would be appreciated by NetGen students at the college level (Council on Competitiveness). It could be used to generate ideas for similar assessments embedded in online library instruction sessions and courses requiring self-correcting Web-based interaction, although the distance learning librarian would need to possess Web-authoring skills to do so.

CONCLUSION

Library instruction program evaluations and surveys are available in print (Yang, March 2005; Smith and Khan, November–December 2005), and some program evaluations in the literature include accompanying statistical analyses (Nicholas and Tomeo, Summer 2005).

As assessment of student learning becomes the norm in library instruction, sufficient data will be available upon which to base program evaluation. Steve Hiller, Martha Kyrillidou, and Jim Self presented a paper, "Assessment in North American Research Libraries: A Preliminary Report Card," at the 6th Northumbria International Conference on Performance Measurement in Libraries and Information Services. Hiller et al. report on Phase I of a two-year project sponsored by the Association of Research Libraries, concluding that "organizational positioning of assessment is maturing rapidly" (Hiller, Kyrillidou, and Self, 2005: 9), and its application will move "library assessment from a project-based approach to a more programmatic, integrated, and sustainable operation within libraries" (Hiller, Kyrillidou, and Self, 2005: 1).

Researcher Michael Simonson set out alternative evaluation philosophies, including six categories of distance education evaluation still in common practice.

1. Measures of activity (how many students? how many classes? etc.)
2. Measures of efficiency (how many students completed the course? how much did the course cost to produce? etc.)
3. Measures of outcomes (exit interviews, student course surveys, interlibrary loan figures for the class, etc.)
4. Measures of program aims (student satisfaction surveys, etc.)
5. Measures of policy (market research, needs assessments, etc.)
6. Measures of organization (monitoring course development, on-site visits, interviews, etc.)

(Simonson, 1997: 88–90)

REFERENCES

ACRL. "Information Literacy Bibliography." Association of College and Research Libraries. Available: www.ala.org/acrlbucket/infolit/bibliographies1/assessmentbibliography. html (accessed March 20, 2006).

ACRL-IS. "Library Instruction Annotated Bibliography for Distance Education and Library Instruction." Association of College and Research Libraries, Instruction Section. Available: www.ala.org/ala/acrlbucket/is/iscommittees/webpages/educationa/distance. htm (accessed March 20, 2006).

Angelo, T. A., and K. P. Cross. 1993. *Classroom Assessment Techniques: A Handbook for College Teachers.* San Francisco: Jossey-Bass.

Anson, Chris M. 2002. *The WAC Casebook: Scenes for Faculty Reflection Program Development.* New York: Oxford University Press.

Ariew, S. Fall 2005. "If It's Worth Assessing, It's Worth Finding Out Whether They Learned It: Assessment Tools and Techniques for Library Instruction—Suggested Reading." Available: http://uweb.cas.usf.edu/%7Esariew/assmt.html (accessed February 6, 2006).

Astin, W. A. "9 Principles of Good Practice for Assessing Student Learning." American Association for Higher Education. Available: www.aahe.org/principl.htm (accessed March 20, 2006).

Banta, T. W., et al. 1996. *Assessment in Practice.* San Francisco: Jossey-Bass.

California State University Monterey Bay Library. 2005. *Student and Instructor Information Literacy Instruction Evaluation Forms.* Available: http://library.scumb.edu/instruction/ assess/samples/ (accessed February 6, 2006).

Council on Competitiveness. "GetSmarter.org." Available: www.getsmarter.org (accessed March 20, 2006).

DLS. "Criteria for Successful Assessment Programs for Distance Learning Library Instruction." Association of College and Research Libraries, Distance Learning Section. Available: http://caspian.switchinc.org/~distlearn/committees/instructional/critforasses. pdf (accessed March 20, 2006).

Dunn, Kathleen. "Information Competency Assessment." Cal Poly Pomona University Library. Available: www.csupomona.edu/~library/InfoComp/instrument.htm (accessed March 20, 2006).

e-Learning Centre. "Guide to e-Learning: Library—Testing and Assessment Online." Available: www.e-learningcentre.co.uk/eclipse/Resources/testing.htm (accessed February 6, 2006).

Farmer, Lesley S. J. Fall 2004. "Narrative Inquiry as Assessment Tool: A Course Case Study." *Journal of Education for Library and Information Science* 45, 1: 340–351.

Farmer, Lesley S. J. February 2005. "Using Technology to Facilitate Assessment of Library Education." *Teacher Librarian* 32, 3: 12–15.

Feasley, Charles E. 1983. "Serving Learners at a Distance: A Guide to Program Practices." ASHE-ERIC Higher Education Research Report No. 5. Washington, DC: Association for the Study of Higher Education.

Fusco, Marjorie, and S. E. Ketcham. 2002. *Distance Learning for Higher Education: An Annotated Bibliography.* Greenville, CO: Libraries Unlimited.

Goodson, Carol F. 2001. *Providing Library Services for Distance Education Students: A How-to-Do-It Manual.* New York: Neal-Schuman.

Gratch-Lindauer, Bonnie. "Assessment Methods by Learning Domains with Examples." California Association of Research Libraries. Available: http://fog.ccsf.cc.ca.us/~bgratch/ CARLhandouts.html (accessed March 20, 2006).

Groen, Janet, and Qing Li. November–December 2005. "Achieving the Benefits of Blended Learning within a Fully Online Learning Environment: A Focus on Synchronous Communication." *Educational Technology* vol. 45, no. 6, pp. 31–37. Nov./Dec. 2005.

Hiller, Steve, Martha Kyrillidou, and Jim Self. "Assessment in North American Research Libraries: A Preliminary Report Card." LibQUAL. Available: www.libqual.org/documents/admin/Hiller_Kyrillidou_Self_PM6.doc (accessed March 20, 2006).

Hsieh, M. "Alternative Assessment Techniques in the Language Arts." Indiana University. Available: www.indiana.edu/~reading/ (accessed March 20, 2006).

Hutchings, P., ed. 1995. *From Idea to Prototype: The Peer Review of Teaching.* Washington, DC: American Association for Higher Education.

Jacobson, T. 2004. *Motivating Students in Information Literacy Classes.* New York: Neal-Schuman.

Johnson, J. L. 2003. *Distance Education: The Complete Guide to Design, Delivery, and Improvement.* New York: Teachers College Press.

Kasworm, Carol E., and C. A. Marienau. 1997. "Principles for Assessment of Adult Learning." In *Assessing Adult Learning in Diverse Settings: Current Issues and Approaches.* Edited by A. D. Rose and M. A. Leahy. San Francisco: Jossey-Bass.

Lexington Community College. "Skills Test Example: Library Assessment." Bluegrass Community & Technical College District. Available: www.bluegrass.kctcs.edu/LCC/LIB/tutorial/skills.htm (accessed March 20, 2006).

Lorenzo, George, and J. Ittelson. "Demonstrating and Assessing Student Learning with E-Portfolios." EDUCAUSE. Available: www.educause.edu/LibraryDetailPage/666?ID=ELI3003 (accessed March 20, 2006).

Martindale, Trey, and D. A. Wiley. 2005. "Using Weblogs in Scholarship and Teaching. *TechTrends* 49, 2: 55–61.

Merz, L. H., and B. L. Mark. 2002. *Assessment in College Library Instruction Programs.* Chicago: American Library Association.

Muskingum College. "Learning Strategies Database." Muskingum College. Available: www.muskingum.edu/~cal/database/ (accessed March 20, 2006).

NCSU. "University Planning and Analysis." North Carolina State University. Available: www2.acs.ncsu.edu/UPA/assmt/resource.htm (accessed March 20, 2006).

NEA. "Higher Education: Online Teaching and Learning Resources." National Education Association. Available: www2.nea.org/he/abouthe/techip.html (accessed March 20, 2006).

Nicholas, Martina, and Melba Tomeo. Summer 2005. "Can You Hear Me Now? Communicating Library Services to Distance Education Students and Faculty. *Online Journal of Distance Learning Administration* 8, 2: 11 pp.

Pausch, Lois M., and Mary P. Popp. "Assessment of Information Literacy: Lessons from the Higher Education Assessment Movement." American Library Association. Available: www.ala.org/ala/acrlbucket/nashville1997/pap/pauschpopp.htm (accessed March 20, 2006).

Persson, Dorothy, and C. Washington-Hoagland. Fall 2004. "PsycINFO Tutorial: A Viable Instructional Alternative." *Reference & User Services Quarterly* 44, 1: 67–77.

Pusateri, Thomas. "Assessment Resources." Florida Atlantic University, Institutional Effectiveness & Analysis. Available: http://iea.fau.edu/pusateri/assess/index.htm (accessed March 20, 2006).

Ragains, P. 2000. *Assessment in Library and Information Literacy Instruction.* Available: www.unr.edu/~ragains/assess.html (accessed February 6, 2006).

Richlin, L., and B. Manning. 1995. *Improving a College or University Teaching Evaluation System.* Pittsburgh: Alliance.

Schrock, Kathy. "Kathy Schrock's Guide for Educators: Assessment and Rubric Information." Discovery Education Web site. Available: http://school.discovery.com/schrock guide/assess.html (accessed March 20, 2006).

Shonrock, D., et al. 1996. *Evaluating Library Instruction: Sample Questions, Forms, and Strategies for Practical Use.* Chicago: American Library Association.

Simonson, Michael R. 1997. "Evaluating Teaching and Learning at a Distance." In *Teaching and Learning at a Distance: What It Takes to Effectively Design, Deliver, and Evaluate Programs.* Edited by T. E. Cyrs. San Francisco: Jossey-Bass.

Smith, Henry L., and B. H. Khan. November–December 2005. "Evaluation of an Online Learning Program: What We Are Hearing from Adult Students." *Educational Technology* vol. 45 no. 6, pp. 56–57. Nov./Dec. 2005.

Summey, Tern. ACRL Instruction Section Education Committee. "Library Instruction Annotated Bibliography for Distance Education and Library Instruction." Available: www.ala.org/ala/acrlbucket/is/iscommittees/webpages/educationa/distance (accessed March 20, 2006).

TLT Group. "Articles: Flashlight and Other Relevant Assessment and Evaluation." Available: www.tltgroup.org/resources/farticles.html (accessed March 20, 2006).

UMUC. "Information Literacy and Writing Assessment Project: Tutorial for Developing and Evaluating Assignments." University of Maryland University College. Available: www. umuc.edu/library/tutorials/information_literacy/toc.html (accessed March, 20, 2006).

University of Melbourne. "Assessment and Evaluation@library: Beginning Research in Assessment and Evaluation." University of Melbourne. Information Division. Available: http://dozer.indofiv.unimelb.edu.au/SuRe/ (accessed March 20, 2006).

University of Puget Sound. 2005. Assessment Culture: *Annotated Bibliography.* Available: http://library.ups.edu/kfischer/AssessCul.htm (accessed January 19, 2006).

Walter, S. n.d. "Instructional Improvement in Academic Libraries." Available: http://people.ku.edu/~slwalter/instruction/index.html (accessed January 19, 2006).

Yale University Library. "Assessment Toolkit." Yale University. Available: www.library.yale.edu/assessment/toolkit/resources.html (accessed March 20, 2006).

Yang, Zheng Y. March 2005. "Distance Education Librarians in the U.S. ARL Libraries and Library Services Provided to Their Distance Users." *Journal of Academic Librarianship* 31, 2: 92–97.

▶18

RECOGNIZING THE IMPORTANCE OF ASSESSMENT IN LIBRARY INSTRUCTION

STEFANIE BUCK

Overview: In this final chapter in the collection, the author presents a history of distance library instruction and of library instruction assessment, and she stresses the importance of assessment in the accreditation process. The conclusion to this chapter suggests that the area of assessment is one that distance librarians must develop, improve, and realize its importance.

◀

INTRODUCTION

Librarians have been aware of the instruction needs of distance learners since universities first began offering correspondence courses in the 1930s; bibliographic or library instruction for distance education students was until recently relatively limited (Niemi, Ehrhard, and Neeley, 1998). This is not to say that librarians serving distance populations did not view library instruction as a significant service but simply that providing access to resources often took precedence (DeWald, et al., 2000; Niemi, Ehrhard, and Neeley, 1998; Riedel, 2002).[1]

Methods of providing bibliographic instruction, where it did exist, ranged from offering simple bibliographies to providing comprehensive library instruction manuals. Some librarians traveled to the sites to greet students at orientation or give a library instruction lecture in a class; some had the classes come to the parent institution. Some libraries experimented with video and satellite technology to overcome the hurdle of time and distance. Libraries in predominantly rural locations, such as in Alaska, Wyoming, and Canada, often led the way. The University of Alaska, for example, offered a training program that consisted of "a course designated as 'LIS 101-Library Skills.' A large resource kit accompanies the course and is left in the center's or village's library for the students' continuing reference." But examples like these are rare, and all in all, most librarians involved in library services for distance learners expressed a certain level of dissatisfaction and frustration with their instructional offerings.

Bibliographic instruction has been a "hot topic" since the early 1970s (Kirk, 1999). The first formal discussions of bibliographic instruction specifically for distance education students begin to appear in the literature in the early- to mid-1980s, when the Association of College and Research Libraries (ACRL) founded its Extended Campus Library Services discussion group (Viggiano, 2004). Librarians also began to see the value of working together to overcome the challenges of distance library services and organized conferences. In 1983 an Articulation Conference was held in Casper, Wyo. to discuss how different institutions—primarily university, college, and public libraries—could work together to provide services to remote users. The creation of LOEX (Library Orientation Exchange) founded in 1971 as a way to exchange ideas about bibliographic instruction (BI) and the first Off-Campus Library Services Conference (OCLS), organized by Central Michigan University and held in St. Louis in 1984, are more indications that the topic was gaining in national importance (Kascus and Aguilar, 1988; Kirk, 1999). At this first OCLS conference, BI was definitely a topic of discussion, with several librarians contributing articles specifically on bibliographic instruction to distance learners, but none dealt with assessment.[2]

In the late 1980s and early 1990s, the need for off-campus library instruction continued to be an important discussion topic (Dewald et al., 2002). But until the advent of the technology that allowed for more online access to resources and better interlibrary loan connections, for most of the librarians serving distance populations, the problem of how to provide physical access to books, articles, and other resources students needed to complete their coursework (as well as the lack of funding for additional services) was often overriding. In another early article about providing library support of off-campus programs, Kascus and Aguilar wrote that "the first and most critical problem is to provide access to bibliographic tools, collections and trained staff" (1988: 33).

Little is said about assessment in these early years, except to acknowledge its importance.[3] Bernard Lessin reviewed five model programs in 1991 that provided off-campus library services. Of these, only Central Michigan University, an acknowledged leader in library services to extended education users, mentioned assessment of library services as a whole, though not specifically instruction. All of the institutions, however, acknowledged the need to integrate library instruction or "appropriate information competencies" into the classroom (Lessin, 1991: 412). Some libraries did perform programmatic (library services to distance education students) assessment, often in the form of surveys concerned either with student knowledge and use of library services or with quantitative studies on book circulation to distance users and the number of interlibrary loan requests filled.

ASSESSMENT

In a broad, general sense assessment is a mechanism that improves both accountability and learning (Frederikson, 2002). For library instruction specifically, assessment "may have a variety of meanings: evaluation of the instruction session, evaluation of the librarian, evaluation of student learning, or evaluation of the library instruction program" (Colburn and Cordell, 1998: 125).

While the terms are often used interchangeably, there is a difference between *assessment* and *evaluation*. According to Grassian and Kaplowitz, assessment covers the gathering and analysis of data, while evaluation occurs "when the data is examined to see if identified objectives have been achieved and that information about the adequacy and effectiveness of an instructional endeavor is provided (2001: 267). Some authors distinguish between evaluation and assessment at different levels.

> In discussing assessment, it may be useful to distinguish between assessment and evaluation. According to Moran (1997), evaluation is used to make a judgment about how well an individual or group has done in reaching a particular goal. Assessment, conversely, describes learner achievement. Yet despite this seemingly clear distinction, the terms easily overlap and in fact are often used interchangeably. In effect, learner achievement is often a key aspect of the evaluation process, and so the two are inextricably related. As program planners have reconceptualized the learning experience, they have reconfigured the assessment process as well. Whereas once assessment was perceived as a fairly mundane effort, there is now fairly widespread recognition of the complexities involved. Assessment is not a static process but one of fundamental change and innovation. (Rose and Leahy, 1997: 97)

For the purpose of this chapter, the authors will use the term as defined by Moran.

Regardless of if it is done at the institutional, program, or learner level, assessment has two major goals. The first is to measure the quality of a program based on its stated goals and objectives. The second is to provide a mechanism for the improvement of the program or activity (Dalrymple, 2001). In library instruction "We assess, evaluate, and revise because we want to find out if our instruction has been effective" (Gratch-Lindauer, 2001: 365). In other words, we need to find out how well our goals and objectives have been met. Furthermore, we want to highlight areas where our efforts might be improved for the future.

Over the years, different factors have driven how and why institutions, and consequentially libraries, have performed assessment (Frederikson, 2002). These include the need "to provide statistical information to administrators, to compare delivery systems, to determine cost-effectiveness, to judge the performance of an individual learner, and to measure and provide feedback on overall learning in a course or course component" (DeWald et al., 2000). Today, the goal for many libraries is developing a "culture of assessment" or "culture of evidence" (Blixrud and Doles, 2005: 273), or, "a shift from 'How am I doing?' to 'How are you doing?'" (Kapoun, 2004: Lit Review Para. 5). The "ideal definition of program assessment would be the analysis of the library's effect on students' learning of information literacy skills" (Colburn and Cordell, 1998: 126).

Bonnie Gratch-Lindauer, who has written extensively on accreditation and its impact on library assessment, lists three major factors that account for the increased interest in assessment of library instruction programs.

1. Higher educational regional accrediting agencies, which have made student learning outcomes much more important
2. The *Information Literacy Competency Standards for Higher Education*, which have been widely endorsed and applied and have spawned many initiatives and local collaborations
3. Divisions of the American Library Association, such as ACRL and the American Association of School Librarians (AASL), along with the Association for Research Libraries (ARL), which have made information literacy and assessment of outcomes a priority

(Gratch-Lindauer, 2004: 122)

As Frederickson points out, "Teaching, learning and research remain major functions of academia. What has changed is how the results or outcomes of these activities will be measured and demonstrated" (2002: 336). For libraries this is especially significant because "assessment lends not only credibility to the program, but to the library as well, especially if the programs can be shown to support national mandates such as I[nformation] L[iteracy] and lifelong learning" (Grassian and Kaplowitz, 2001: 266).

EDUCATION AND OUTCOMES-BASED LEARNING

Since the 1980s, educational reforms that focused on the development of critical thinking skills have changed the way educational institutions are assessing their students in general, and libraries are no exception (Gratch-Lindauer, 2001). The 1983 report *A Nation at Risk* (National Commission for Excellence in Higher Education. U.S. GPO) called for the assessment of teaching and learning in colleges and universities. This report has been credited with spawning a nationwide reassessment of how students learn and how to best prepare students to be lifelong learners (Meulemans 2002: 62–63). "Learning in the twenty first century is significantly different from learning in the previous days. Learning is to be considered learner-centered, a lifelong process and the means to cope with continuous or radical changes. . . . Learning has become more self-directed, collaborative, intertwined with personal life and work, more resource based, calls for perpetual access and usage of information and learning resources" (Sacchanand, 2002).

For libraries, implementation of these goals has manifested itself in the area of library instruction. Librarians have been cognizant of the need for students to be lifelong learners (from the early days of library instruction), but the report and its repercussions have intensified activity in this area. In 1988 Kascus and Aguilar wrote, "Off-campus library services have spawned much creative energy toward solving the physical problems of access and delivery. In planning for future off-campus library services, academic libraries should emphasize helping off-campus students to become independent self-directed learners" (1988: 36).

The philosophical move in the 1980s and 1990s from library instruction to information literacy instruction and learning-based outcomes has had a great impact on how libraries assess library instruction. In the past, assessment in libraries has been very much an inputs/outputs-based gathering of statistical data (Dugan and Hernon, 2002; Knight, 2002: 45; Kyrillidou, 2002; Ratteray, 2002). However, such measures demonstrate neither student learning nor how the library plays an integral role in the learning process (Dugan and Hernon, 2002; Kapoun, 2004; Meulemans, 2002). Outcomes, as opposed to outputs, are defined by the Institute of Museum and Library Services as "benefits of changes for individuals or populations after participating in program activities, including new knowledge, increased skills, changed attitudes or values, modified behavior, improved condition, or altered status. . . . While outcome measurement may at first seem very different from the traditional program or service model, it in fact incorporates all of the elements of traditional library measurements (input activities, outputs) while adding only the element of outcomes" (IMLS. "Perspectives on Outcome Based Evaluation for Libraries and Museums," p. 20; in Knight, 2002: 45).

Outcomes-based learning, therefore, requires the institution to focus its attention on the student's learning experience (Smith, 2000). Assessment has therefore moved away from counting titles and numbers of students attending library instruction sessions to the assessment of library instruction programs (Lindauer, 1999; in Knight, 2002).

DISTANCE LEARNERS AND DISTANCE LEARNING PROGRAMS

Distance learning is the fastest-growing form of providing instruction (Thompson, 2002). The current statistics indicate that the number of students who are involved in distance learning in some form has been on the rise for some time and that this number will continue to grow (Johnstone and Krauth, 2002; O'Hanlon, 2001; Kaufmann, 2003; Lindsay, 2004; Viggiano, 2004). As this number grows, and more programs are made available to distant users, the need for library services grows, and it will therefore become even more important for distance users to be able to navigate the ever-growing number of online resources effectively. The increasing number of students acquiring an education through distance learning programs "has been one of the driving factors in how we provide library services to them and, in consequence, how well we are doing it" (Riedel, 2002).

The students enrolled in these programs are generally older adults who are highly motivated and like to see how what they learn translates into actual practice (Niemi, Ehrhard, and Neeley, 1998; Lindsay, 2004). They want to know that what they are learning has practical application.

ACCREDITATION AND ACCOUNTABILITY

More and more, institutions of higher learning are being asked to provide evidence that their programs are successful in producing highly employable students (Rader, 1998). There are constituents or stakeholders (parents, governing boards, federal and state agencies) who have been calling for increased accountability for a number of years (Colburn and Cordell, 1998; Dugan and Hernon, 2002; López, 2002; Pausch and Popp, 1997). Economic pressures have forced many educational institutions to do more with less. Putting resources into programs that provide evidence of outcome is a priority for many, as is the need to prove their usefulness to federal, state, and local agencies (Blixrud and Doles, 2005; Grassian and Kaplowitz, 2001; Rader, 1998).

In the United States one method of providing this evidence is through the accreditation process. Accreditation is "the oldest and best known seal of collegiate quality" (Baker, 2002: 3). It serves two main purposes: "quality assurance and institutional improvement" (Dalrymple, 2001: 24). The 2005 *Bowker Annual* cites accreditation as the driving force for change in how libraries look at performance measures (Blixrud and Doles, 2005). In distance education the assessment movement began in the late 1970s, when the Council of Post-Secondary Education reported on the inferior quality of distance education programs (Kascus and Aguilar, 1988). This in turn led many of the accrediting agencies to revise their standards regarding extended education courses and, in consequence, the libraries providing services to those programs (Simmons, 1991).

All accreditation agencies in the United States have changed their standards regarding libraries over the years, specifically moving away from requiring inputs and outputs to emphasizing outcomes, in the case of library services, an emphasis on information literacy skills (Ratteray, 2002). In her excellent 2002 analysis of regional accreditation standards, Gratch-Lindauer notes that "all of the regional accreditation commissions' standards stress that the improvement of student learning and institutional effectiveness is the primary reason for assessment activities" (14). Many of the standards were revised in the late 1990s. In general, the changes to the text in these documents have become "less prescriptive and less concerned with measuring specific library and learning resources inputs" (15) and more focused on assessing student learning than in the past. There is less text on libraries and information resources than in previous versions of the standards, but the emphasis is more on information literacy. While these changes have caused some concern among librarians that the library is being deemphasized, Gratch-Lindauer argues that these changes actually strengthen the library role and that the connections among library use, information resources, and a successful learning environment are made more evident (Hardesty, 2001; Meulemanns, 2002). Moreover, all the standards require that distance education programs provide evidence of how student and faculty will be provided access to resources and how library services will be evaluated (Gratch-Lindauer, 2002).

In addition to providing the standards, the eight accrediting agencies have also collaboratively written *Best Practices for Electronically Offered Degree and Certification Programs* (Commission on Colleges. Southern Association of Colleges and Schools. December 2002). This document also clearly states the importance of library services to distance users (Section 4c, 11) but also the need to evaluate and assess the programs.

> Both the assessment of student achievement and evaluation of the overall program take on added importance as new techniques evolve. For example, in asynchronous programs the element of seat time is essentially removed from the equation. For these reasons, the institution conducts *sustained, evidence-based and participatory inquiry* [emphasis added] as to whether distance learning programs are achieving objectives. The results of such inquiry are used to guide curriculum design and delivery, pedagogy, and educational processes, and may affect future policy and budgets and perhaps have implications for the institution's roles and mission. (Section 5. "Evaluation and Assessment," 12)

Because accreditation is usually done at the institutional level (although there is also programmatic assessment), there are no accrediting agencies specifically for libraries (Dalrymple, 2001). It is therefore extremely important for librarians to be involved in accreditation teams at the institutional level (López, 2002). Libraries are judged by how well they help the institution meet its mission statement. As institutions are asked to provide evidence of learning outcomes, so are libraries (Pausch and Popp, 1997). "The current increase," writes Dalrymple, "in off-campus instruction and virtual universities has underscored the need for thoughtful and informed librarian participation in both the setting of standards and the review process on both the institutional and programmatic levels" (2001: 26).

LIBRARY COMMUNITY

The library community itself has actively embraced the educational goals of life-long learning, and library associations have also set rigorous new guidelines and standards for assessing programs and services to distance learners. These are in part a reaction to or consequence of the other factors listed above. In addition to the *Information Literacy Competency Standards for Higher Education*, the most significant document of this type for distance education librarians is the ACRL "Guidelines for Distance Learning Library Services," first formulated in 1967, which lists "lifelong learning skills through bibliographic instruction and information literacy" as a primary outcome for distance learning library services (Frederikson, 2002: 337).

The ACRL "Guidelines for Distance Learning Library Services" "set out the challenge to libraries to provide services to distance learners equivalent to those provided to on-campus students" (Riedel, 2002). It is the parent institution that has been given the responsibility of providing library services to the distance learner. This includes teaching not only the ability to access or acquire the resources students need to complete their course work but also the skills to use the resources correctly. Distance librarians therefore have the challenge of proving that the programs and services, including library instruction, offered off-campus are equitable to those offered on-campus.

TECHNOLOGY

One reason for an increased interest in library instruction for distance learners in the last ten to fifteen years has been the technology that now allows libraries to provide instruction to distant students and faculty in whole new ways, from streaming video to online Web-based tutorials and course management systems (Argentati, 1999). The impact that, for example, the Internet, proxy servers, full-text networked resources, electronic document delivery services, and speedier interlibrary loan services have had on library services to distance users is tremendous, and it has brought the issue of information literacy for distance users to the forefront, while access to resources, though still significant, has become less of an issue. DeWald et al. agree that new technologies, such as the Internet and online library catalogs, make it necessary that students can access and use the resources in an effective manner (2000). Some have even made the case that information literacy is more important for distance learners than for on-campus students because of the computer skills necessary to effectively access the resources and services. As Johnstone and Krauth wrote in their white paper *Information Literacy and the Distance Learner*, "All learners need to be taught information literacy skills, both for their current academic program and for lifelong learning. These skills are as important for distance learners as they are for students in a traditional campus setting" (2002: Section 1, Para. 1). As library instruction has become more available and necessary to distance learners, the question of assessment, specifically how to assess student learning, also has, naturally, become a point of discussion (Pausch and Popp, 1997; Shklanka, 1990).

TYPES OF ASSESSMENT

Regional accreditation standards provide one set of guidelines or standards from which goals and objectives can be derived. Distance education librarians planning assessment of a library instruction program have, in addition to these documents, a number of useful guidelines to assist them in developing a successful assessment program for library instruction. First and foremost are the *Information Literacy Competency Standards for Higher Education* guidelines (ACRL, 2000) and the "Guidelines for Distance Learning Library Services" (ACRL, 2000). Both documents provide a set of guidelines librarians can use to develop outcomes (Frederikson, 2002). In addition to these documents, several others have developed out of the initial guides, including the *Objectives for Information Literacy Instruction: A Model Statement for Academic Librarians* (ACRL, 2001) and *Characteristics of Programs of Information Literacy That Illustrate Best Practices* (2001). Each document further develops the goals and objectives of information literacy and recommends the best practices for accomplishing these goals. All these documents can serve as guides for libraries developing their own goals and objectives.

Learning outcomes are not the only important area of assessment. Other vital areas include "personal experiences that contribute directly to the development of information literate individuals, such as specific indicators that capture the quality of the learning environment and learner self-assessment of skills and instruction/learning satisfaction ratings" (Gratch-Lindauer 2004: 123). Institutions doing assessment will need to use a combination of qualitative and quantitative measures and then compare the data they have collected to provide a truly comprehensive assessment (Dugan and Hernon, 2002; Fister, 2003; López, 2002).

CURRENT SITUATION

There has been "a dramatic increase in assessment activities and by a shift from just plain descriptive library statistics (input and output measures) to a search for quantitative and qualitative performance measures for services, values and cost effectiveness" (Blixrud and Dole, 2005: 273), and the emphasis on continual, standardized, outcomes-based assessment is certainly present in the literature. Implementing a successful assessment program is undoubtedly a challenge and requires a significant commitment of resources (Frederikson, 2002; Young and Blixrud, 2003). Other potential obstacles are lack of time, staff, and/or financial resources. Gratch-Lindauer (2004) notes that many librarians see assessment as difficult and time consuming and therefore "assessing the outcomes is often relegated to second place," despite the fact that most librarians, as evidenced by the literature, agree that learning-based outcomes are essential (122). Librarians do not always feel adequately trained to do assessment (Gratch-Lindauer, 2001).

In 1994 the ACRL surveyed a number of institutions in the Middle States accreditation region and concluded that "only a limited number had 'functional' information literacy programs, and there was very little assessment" (Ratteray 2002: 368). Other studies that have been done generally concur with this conclusion.[4]

In the 2001 edition of the publication *Academic Library Trends and Statistics*, published annually by the ACRL, an additional survey was included regarding trends in distance library learning services. Of the 503 libraries surveyed that offered distance learning, only 10.9% rated their library services to distance learners at more than adequate. Over 80% rated it "Adequate" or "Somewhat Adequate." Unfortunately, the survey did not inquire about assessment itself; however, the 2003 edition of this publication includes the survey Trends in Information Literacy Assessment. While 69.2% reported that their "librarians and faculty have developed information literacy instruction that is taught as an integral part of one or more courses" (159) only 14.3% indicated that they assessed students' information literacy skills at the time of graduation (160).

There is, unfortunately, no thorough survey or study of how library instruction programs serving distance learners perform assessment.[5] There are, however, many examples of institutions that are actively working on the integration of information literacy into the curriculum and on using appropriate assessment tools.[6] In some cases, the process has only begun and the results have not yet been reported (Kapoun, 2004: "Observations," Para. 8), but in other cases these are full-fledged active assessment programs. Anne Marie Johnson and Sarah Jent reviewed the 2003 literature on information literacy in 2003 and found that "assessment continues to be an important topic. Many articles now include a section on assessment of the particular instruction effort being conveyed." *Assessing Student Learning Outcomes for Information Literacy Instruction in Academic Institutions* (Avery, 2003) was also published this year and contains a wealth of information both practical and theoretical on the topic. They also found that "other favored themes included using course management software to provide various kinds of information literacy instruction" (2004: 413). In fact, an entire issue of *Reference Services Review* (vol. 32, issue 4. Special Issue: LOEX-of-the-West 2004 plus Library Instruction and Information Literacy, 2003) is dedicated to information literacy and library instruction.

Libraries are looking increasingly to technology as a cost-effective method for providing instruction to a large number of groups or, in the case of distance learners, to help overcome the distance and time issues. Computer-assisted instruction is not exempt from assessment, but "must take into account the special requirements of the medium and the difficulties inherent in the lack of face-to-face instruction" (Pausch and Popp, 1997, "Assessment Methods and Libraries," Para. 5).

As many authors in this field agree, it is incumbent upon librarians to educate themselves about assessment, about how assessment works on their campus, and about how they can better contribute to student learning–based outcomes. Librarians need to be sure not only that they gather the relevant information but that they produce it in a way that nonlibrarians will be able to understand (Gratch-Lindauer, 2002; Knight, 2002; López, 2002).

FUTURE

What does the future hold for the assessment of information literacy instruction? Standardized assessment is looming large. There are already several instruments available to assess student learning, including the College Student Experiences Questionnaire (CSEQ) and LibQUAL, but these measure overall library satisfaction and are not focused on assessing learning outcomes.

There are several projects under way that look to standardizing information literacy assessment. One of these is SAILS, the Standardized Assessment of Information Literacy Skills, developed at Kent State University and, at the time of this writing, in its final test phase. The purpose of SAILS is to "develop an instrument for programmatic level assessment of information literacy skills that is valid and credible to university administrators and other academic personnel" (Antonisse and Dillon, 2005: "SAILS," Para. 1). How well the SAILS test will help in assessing outcomes-based learning remains to be seen. There are skeptics who are concerned that "the assessment tool is based on multiple choice tests and these don't necessarily work well for assessing outcomes" (Fister, 2003: 3).

The other project is the Educational Testing Service's National Higher Education Information and Communication Technology (ICT) Initiative. The Educational Testing Service (ETS) in conjunction with seven academic institutions, including California State University, the California Community College system, University of Texas system, the University of Washington, University of California, Los Angeles, and the University of Louisville, formed the National Higher Education ICT Initiative (Educational Testing Service, 2002).

CONCLUSION

As the lines between on-campus and distance learning become more blurred and as more librarians turn to online alternatives as opposed to the face-to-face one-shot instruction, assessment will become even more important. The outside factors that influence assessment outlined above will not disappear. A thorough understanding of these factors can only be beneficial to the library in its effort to demonstrate the validity of its information literacy programs (Meulemanns, 2002). Librarians and educators alike are asking if online instruction can provide a level of instruction equitable to face-to-face instruction so that distance students achieve the same learning goals as those of on-campus students. The results so far have not been all that promising (Drabbenstott, 2003), but there are many opportunities to develop better online delivery of instruction in the future. Only rigorous assessment programs will provide the answer.

ENDNOTES

[1] In 1978, for example, a study conducted of eighteen institutions in Westchester County, New York, including Cornell, Adelphi, and New York University, found that only one institution provided library orientation for off-campus students (*A Study of Collegiate Off-Campus Centers in Westchester County*. 1978. ERIC Document Reproduction Service No. ED 160004). In 1983 the University of Wyoming sponsored a meeting among University of Wyoming and other regional academic, college, and public libraries libraries to discuss the issues surrounding service to distance students in a widespread area (Johnson, J., ed. 1983. *Library Services to Off-Campus Students* [Articulation conference conducted at Casper College, Casper, WY, on November 10–11. (ERIC Document Reproduction Service No. ED 256347]).

A 1985 survey of Ohio colleges uncovered that "library services actually provided for off-campus students ranges from sophisticated systems to nothing at all" (37) (Evans, David C. 1986. "Off-Campus Library Services in Ohio." In *Off-Campus Library Services Proceedings*. Edited by B. Lessin. Mt. Pleasant, MI: Central Michigan University Press).

[2] One author surveyed various libraries regarding their understanding and use of the ACRL guidelines as a basis for the revision of the guidelines. In that survey the author notes, "Some libraries have already expressed desire for an instrument like the [ACRL] guide in order to review the efficacy of their extended campus library services operation . . ." (206). (Hodowanec, George V. 1983. "Emporia State University Review And Revision: The Preparation of the 'Guidelines for Extended Campus Services.'" In *Off-Campus Library Services Proceedings*. Edited by B. Lessin. Mt. Pleasant, MI: Central Michigan University Press).

[3] The second OCLS proceedings contain an article on how to conduct a program review, but it does not deal specifically with instruction. (Garten, Edward. 1986. "The Design and Conduct of Off-Campus Library Program Reviews Based on Effectiveness Models." In *Off-Campus Library Services Proceedings*. Edited by B. Lessin. Mt. Pleasant, MI: Central Michigan University Press).

[4] A 1999 survey by the Western Cooperative of Education Telecommunications, which was mailed out to over one thousand institutions of higher education in fourteen states revealed that almost one-third of the institutions offering distance education courses "provided no special access to library service for distance learners. While more than half (59%) offered access to online catalogs, periodical indexes and bibliographic databases, 58% did not provide distance learners with "special training on how to access research materials electronically at a distance" (7–8). The report also indicates that some of the institutions have "developed training videos, and a few have instructions available on their Web sites. Four mentioned that they had undergraduate courses on this topic, but only one requires all students to take the course" (8). Assessment of student support services, which included library services, took place at more than three-fourths (76%) of the institutions, but only

half (48%) conducted systematic reviews of services and polices (15). Unfortunately, the report does not provide any information about assessment of learning outcomes (Dirr, Peter J. 1999. *Putting Principles into Practice: Promoting Effective Support Services for Students in Distance Learning Programs: A Report on the Findings of a Survey*. December 1999. Available: www.wcet.info/projects/studentservices/appendices.pdf (accessed March 19, 2006).

An Association of Research Libraries survey on evaluating library instruction, published as SPEC Kit 279: *Evaluating Library Instruction* (Washington, DC: Association of Research Libraries, December 2003), reported that "barely two-thirds of the responding libraries (42 or 63%) formally assess the effectiveness of their library program. At the majority of these libraries, assessment of library instruction is voluntary and anonymous for both the participants and the faculty" (14). The report goes on to say that "despite all the indications that library instruction programs are being measured and that the data are being used in a variety of ways, 33 respondents (57%) indicated that the current assessment tool was not able to provide adequate information about the success of the instruction program in the previous year. . . . several [respondents] lamented that they did not have a good method for assessing the impact of library instruction on student learning" (15).

Jim Kapoun (instruction coordinator, Minnesota State University, Mankato) reported in 2004, and as the two surveys mentioned above and others indicate, that many libraries are not yet assessing their programs based on outcomes-based student learning (Kapoun, 2004: "Observations," Para. 1).

[5] See Snyder, Carolyn C., Howard Carter, and Jerry C. Hostetler. 2004. "Distance Education Support in University Libraries." *Journal of Library and Information Services in Distance Learning* 2: 15–30. This article updates the Association of Research Libraries' SPEC Kit 216: *Role of Libraries in Distance Education* (Washington, DC: Association of Research Libraries, 1996) and provides useful general statistics about library support for distance learners.

[6] Lindsay 2004. See also Buchanan, Lori, DeAnne L. Luck, and Ted C. Jones. 2001. "Integrating Information Literacy into the Virtual University: A Course Model." *Library Trends* 51 (Fall): 144–166.; Fishman, D., et al. 2005. "Information Literacy and the Distant Student: One University's Experience Developing, Delivering, and Maintaining an Online, Required Information Literacy Course." *Internet Reference Services Quarterly* 9, 1/2: 21–36.; Flaspohler, M. R. 2003. Information Literacy Program Assessment: One Small College Takes the Big Plunge. *Reference Services Review* 31, 2: 129–140.; Jerabek, J. A., and L. M. McMain. (2004). Assessing Minds Want to Know: Developing Questions for Assessment of Library Services Supporting Off-Campus Learning Programs. *Journal of Library Administration* 41, 1/2: 303–314.; Joint, N. 2003. "Information Literacy Evaluation: Moving Towards Virtual Learning Environments." *The Electronic Library* 21 (2003): 322–334; Maki, P. L. 2002. "Developing an Assessment Plan to Learn about Student Learning." *The Journal of Academic Librarianship* 28, 1/2: 8–13. O'Connor, L. G., C. J. Radcliff, and J. A. Gedeon. 2001. Assessing Information Literacy Skills: Developing a Standardized Instrument for Institutional and Longitudinal Measuring. In *Crossing the Divide: Proceedings of the ACRL Tenth Conference, March 15–18, 2001, Denver Colorado*. Chicago: American Library Association; O'Hanlon, N. 2001. "Devel-

opment, Delivery, and Outcomes of a Distance Course for New College Students." *Library Trends* 50 (Summer): 8–27; Reynolds, L. 2001. "Model for a Web-based Information Literacy Course: Design, Conversion and Experiences." *Science and Technology Libraries* 19: 165–178; Samson, S. 2000. What and When Do They Know? Web-Based Assessment. *Reference Services Review* 28: 335–342.

Another excellent source for finding articles on library services for distance learners is Slade, Alexander. *Library Services for Distance Learning: The Fourth Bibliography.* Available at: http://uviclib.uvic.ca/dls/bibliography4.html.

REFERENCES

Antonisse, Peggy, and Irma Dillon. 2005. *Report of the University of Maryland Libraries and the Professional Writing Program Participation in the ARL/Kent State University SAILS Project.* Available: www.lib.umd.edu/UES/Sailsananalysis.doc (accessed September 15, 2006).

Argentati, Carolyn. 1999. "Library-University Partnerships in Distance Learning." Paper presented at the *IFLA Council and General Conference. Conference Programme and Proceedings, 65th, Bangkok, Thailand, August 20–28, 1999.* ED 441 406.

Avery, Elizabeth F., ed. 2003. *Assessing Student Learning Outcomes for Information Literacy Instruction in Academic Institutions.* Chicago: Association of College and Research Libraries.

Baker, Ronald L. 2002. "Evaluating Quality and Effectiveness: Regional Accreditation Principles and Practices." *Journal of Academic Librarianship* 28, no. 1: 3–7.

Blixrud, Julia C., and Wanda Dole. 2005. "Library Assessment and Performance Measures: An Overview." In *The Bowker Almanac: Library and Book Trade Almanac.* 50th ed. Edited by Dave Bogart. Medford, NJ: Information, Inc.

Colborn, Nancy W., and Roseanne M. Cordell. 1998. "Moving from Subjective to Objective Assessment of Your Instruction Program." *Reference Services Review* 26, no. 3: 125–137.

Commission on Colleges. Southern Association of Colleges and Schools. 2002. *Best Practices for Electronically Offered Degree and Certification Programs* (Commission on Colleges. Southern Association of Colleges and Schools. Available: www.wcet.info/resources/accreditation/Accrediting%20-%20Best%20Practices.pdf (accessed September 15, 2006).

Dalrymple, Prudence. 2001. "Understanding Accreditation: The Librarians' Role in Educational Evaluation." *Portal: Libraries and the Academy* 1: 23–32.

DeFranco, Francine, and Richard Bleiler. December 2003. *SPEC Kit 279, Evaluating Library Instruction.* Washington, DC: Association of Research Libraries/Office of Leadership and Management Services.

Dewald, Nancy H. 1999. "Web-Based Library Instruction: What Is Good Pedagogy?" *Information Technology and Libraries* 18, no. 1: 26–31.

Dewald, Nancy H., et al. 2000. "Information Literacy at a Distance: Instructional Design Issues." *Journal of Academic Librarianship* 26, no. 1: 33–44.

Drabenstott, Karen M. 2003. "Interactive Multimedia for Library-User Education." *Portal: Libraries and the Academy* 3, 4: 601–613.

Dugan, Robert E., and P. Hernon. 2002. "Outcomes Assessment: Not Synonymous with Inputs and Outputs." *Journal of Academic Librarianship* 28, no. 6: 376–380.

Educational Testing Service. 2003. *Succeeding in the 21st Century: What Higher Education Must Do to Address the Gap in Information and Communication Technology Proficiencies.* Available: www.calstate.edu/LS/ICTwhitepaperfinal.pdf (accessed September 15, 2006).

Fister, Barbara. 2003. "What Do They Know? Assessing the Library's Contribution to Student Learning." *Library Issues* 23, no. 3: 1–4.

Frederickson, Linda. 2002. "Grading Ourselves: Using the ACRL Guidelines for DLS to Develop Assessment Strategies." *Journal of Library Administration* 37: 333–339.

Grassian, Esther S., and Joan R. Kaplowitz. 2001. *Information Literacy Instruction: Theory and Practice.* New York: Neal-Schuman.

Gratch-Lindauer, Bonnie. 1998. "Defining and Measuring the Library's Impact on Campuswide Outcomes." *College & Research Libraries* 59: 546–570.

Gratch-Lindauer, Bonnie. Fall 2001. *ARL E-Metrics Project 2001. Analysis of Accreditation Standards of the Six Regional Higher Education Commissions for Senior College and Universities.* Available: www.arl.org/stats/newmeas/emetrics/Gratch-Lindauer.pdf. (accessed December 15, 2006).

Gratch-Lindauer, Bonnie. 2002. "Comparing the Regional Accreditation Standards: Outcomes Assessment and Other Trends." *Journal of Academic Librarianship* 28, no. 1–2: 14–25.

Gratch-Lindauer, Bonnie. 2004. "The Three Arenas of Information Literacy Assessment." *Reference & User Services Quarterly* 44, no. 2: 122.

Hardesty, Larry. 2001. "Academic Libraries and Regional Accreditation." *Library Issues* 21: unnumbered.

Johnson, Anna, and Sarah Jent. 2004. "Library Instruction and Information Literacy—2003." *Reference Services Review* 32 (Winter): 413–442.

Johnstone, Sally M., and Barbara Krauth. 2002. *Information Literacy and the Distance Learner.* White paper prepared for UNESCO, the U.S. National Commission on Libraries and Information Science, and the National Forum on Information Literacy, for use at the Information Literacy Meeting of Experts, Prague, Czech Republic. U.S. National Commission on Libraries and Information Science. Available: www.nclis.gov/libinter/info litconf&meet/papers/johnstone-fullpaper.pdf (accessed September 15, 2006).

Kapoun, Jim. 2004. "Assessing Library Instruction Assessment Activities." *Library Philosophy and Practice* 7. Available: www.webpages.uidaho.edu/~mbolin/kapoun2.htm (accessed September 15, 2006).

Kascus, Marie, and W. Aguilar. 1988. "Providing Library Support to Off-Campus Programs." *College and Research Libraries* 49, no. 1: 29–37.

Kaufmann, Frances G. "Collaborating to Create Customized Library Services for Distance Education Students." *Technical Services Quarterly* 21: 51–62.

Kirk, Tom G. 1999. "Course-Related Bibliographic Instruction in the 1990s." *Reference Services Review* 27: 235–241.

Knight, Lorrie A. 2002. "The Role of Assessment in Library User Education." *Reference Services Review* 30, no. 1: 15–24.

Kyrillidou, Martha. 2002. "From Input to Output Measures to Quality and Outcomes Measures, or, from the User in the Life of the Library to the Library in the Life of the User." *Journal of Academic Librarianship* 28: 42–46.

Lessin, Barton M. 1991. "Library Models for the Delivery of Support Services to Off-Campus Academic Programs." *Library Trends* 39, no. 4: 405–423.

Lindsay, E. B. 2004. "Distance Teaching: Comparing Two Online Information Literacy Courses." *Journal of Academic Librarianship* 30: 482–487.

López, Cecilia L. 2002. "Assessment of Student Learning: Challenges and Strategies." *Journal of Academic Librarianship* 28: 356–367.

Meulemans, Yvonne N. 2002. "Assessment City: The Past, Present, and Future State of Information Literacy Assessment." *College and Undergraduate Libraries* 9, no. 2: 61–74.

Niemi, John A., B. J. Ehrhard, and L. Neeley. 1998. "Off-Campus Library Support for Distance Adult Learners." *Library Trends* 47, no. 1: 65–74.

Pausch, Lois M., and M. P. Popp. 1997. *Assessment of Information Literacy: Lessons from the Higher Education Movement.* Available: www.ala.org/ala/acrlbucket/nashville1997pap/pauschpopp.htm (accessed September 15, 2006).

Rader, H. B. 1998. *Faculty-Librarian Collaboration in Building Curriculum for the Millennium—the US Experience.* Paper presented at the 64th IFLA General Conference, August 16–August 21, 1998. Available: www.ifla.org/IV/ifla64/040-112e.htm (accessed September 15, 2006).

Ratteray, Oswald M. T. 2002. "Information Literacy in Self-Study and Accreditation." *Journal of Academic Librarianship* 28, no. 6: 368–375.

Riedel, Tom. 2002. "Added Value, Multiple Choices: Librarian/faculty Collaboration in Online Course Development." *Journal of Library Administration* 37: 477–487.

Rose, Amy D. and M. A. Leahy. 1997. *Assessing Adult Learning in Diverse Settings: Current Issues and Approaches.* San Francisco: Jossey-Bass.

Sacchanand, Christina. 2002. *Information Literacy Instruction to Distance Students in Higher Education: Librarian's Key Role.* Paper presented at the 68th IFLA Council and General Conference, August 18–24, 2002, Glasgow, Scotland. Available: http://eprints.rclis.org/archive/00005249/01/113-098e.pdf (accessed September 15, 2006).

Shklanka, O. 1990. "Off-campus Library Services: A Literature Review." *Research in Distance Education* 2: 2–11.

Simmons, Howard L. 1991. "Accreditation Expectations for Library Support to Off-Campus Programs." *Library Trends* 39, no. 4: 388–404.

Smith, Kenneth R. 2000. *New Roles and Responsibilities for the University Library: Advancing Student Learning through Outcomes Assessment.* Paper prepared for the Association of Research Libraries. Available: www.arl.org/stats/newmeas/outcomes/HEOSmith.html (accessed May 4, 2000).

Snyder, Carolyn, et al. October 2001. *SPEC Kit 265, Instructional Support Services.* Washington, DC: Association of Research Libraries/Office of Leadership and Management Services.

Thompson, Gary B. 2002. "Information Literacy Accreditation Mandates: What They Mean for Faculty and Librarians." *Library Trends* 51 (Fall): 218–241.

Viggiano, Rachel G. 2004. "Online Tutorials as Instruction for Distance Students." *Internet Reference Services Quarterly* 9, no. 1/2: 37–54.

Young, Sheila, and J. C. Blixrud. 2003. "Research Library Involvement in Learning Outcomes Assessment Programs." *ARL Bimonthly Report 230/231* (2003, October/December). Available: www.arl.org/newsletr/230/learnout.html (accessed September 15, 2006).

►Index

Page numbers in italics represent when the terms appear in figures.

A

AASL. *See* American Association of School Librarians

Abelson, Hal, 67

Academic departments, establishing lines of communication with, 22

Academic librarians, transforming role of, 57

Academic Library Trends and Statistics, 204

Access
guidelines, 190
library instruction and, 5, 6

Accountability, accreditation and, 200–201

Accreditation
accountability and, 200–201
assessment tools and, 24
library assessment and, 198

Accrediting agencies, information literacy skills and, 162

ACRL. *See* Association of Research and College Libraries

ACRL standards
for information literacy, 5
utilization of, in instruction programs, 6, 7

Active learning, 10

Active learning assignment, 187

Adaptive technologies, 190

Administrators
distance learning policy setting and, 32
four realities needing recognition by, 27–28
as target market for off-campus library instruction services, 162–163

Adobe Acrobat Reader, 102

Adobe Professional, 183

Adult learners
assessment of prior learning and, 187
distance education and, 74–75
learning theory and, 4–5

Adult-oriented assessment, 190

Advisers, communicating with, 23

Aguilar, W., 196, 199

AIM, 89

"Alternative Assessment Techniques in the Language Arts" (Indiana University Web site), 190

Ambrose, Stephen, 73

American Association for Higher Education Web site, 185

American Association of Colleges of Nursing, 93

American Association of School Librarians, 198

American Cancer Society Web site, 96

American Diabetes Association Web site, 96

American Heart Association Web site, 96

American Library Association, 198

Andragogy learning theory, 5

ANGEL, 156

Animation, 23, 52

Annotated bibliographies, 132

Apache, 67

APA source citations, 51, 109, 110

Application sharing
with virtual classroom, 140
with virtual reference, 140

Archives, digitizing projects and, 88

ARL. *See* Association for Research Libraries

Armstrong, Gary, 161, 163

▶About the Editor

<hr/>

Susan J. Clayton is the editor of this collection as well as a chapter contributor. She is the Off-Campus Services Librarian at the University of Redlands in Redlands, CA, and is the library liaison to the School of Business and the School of Education. In her previous position, Susan was the media librarian at Finger Lakes Community College near Rochester, NY. Susan received her master of library science degree from the University of Michigan and her bachelor of arts in German from the University of California at Davis.

▶ About the Contributors

<hr>

Jackie AlSaffar is a Reference Librarian at Buena Vista University in Storm Lake, Iowa. She also serves as liaison to the fourteen BVU Centers located throughout the state as well as to the institution's online students. She is a member of the University's Copyright Review Team and has presented on copyright issues at conferences. She was previously the Collection Development Librarian at Doane College in Crete, Nebraska.

Stefanie Buck is the Librarian for Extended Education and Summer Programs at Western Washington University in Bellingham, WA. She has also worked for the Bill and Melinda Gates Foundation and overseas at the International University Bremen in Bremen, Germany. She has an MLS and an MA in history from the University of Hawaii.

Nicole A. Cooke began her career as a young adult librarian, has worked as a medical librarian, and in her current position is an Assistant Professor/Reference Librarian at Montclair State University (NJ). At the university, she is able to combine her love of reading and research with her teaching and training skills to assist students with their coursework. Nicole has completed a second master's degree in adult education (along with a certificate in distance education), completely online through Penn State University's World Campus; through her online studies, she has gained a unique perspective and appreciation for distance learners. Nicole's professional involvements are many and varied. Her vita can be found at http://nicolecooke.info.

Luann DeGreve is the Assistant Director for Collection Services at the Benedictine University Library. She is responsible for overseeing all collection services functions, including acquisitions, cataloging, collection management, periodicals, government documents, and special collections. Prior to joining Benedictine University, Luann was the Interlibrary Loan/Serials Librarian at Quincy University and a junior high social studies teacher in Indiana. Luann received her bachelor of arts in history from Butler University of Wisconsin–Stevens Point, her master of library science from Indiana University, and her master of arts in history from Purdue University.

Ulrike Dieterle holds degrees from the University of Cincinnati (MA in German) and the University of Alabama at Tuscaloosa (MLS). She is currently Distance Services and Outreach Coordinator at Ebling Library, Health Sciences Learning Center,

University of Wisconsin–Madison. Before developing this new position, she served as Head of Access Services. Ulrike has nineteen years of experience in health sciences, general academic, and law libraries and a previous career in teaching.

Denise K. Dipert graduated from the University of Illinois at Champaign-Urbana and pursued graduate studies in English literature at the University of Wisconsin–Madison. She taught high school English before entering the field of library science. Denise received an MA in library and information studies from the University of Wisconsin–Madison. She has been employed as a special librarian at the UW School of Nursing for the past twenty years and is enjoying the opportunity to work closely with both School of Nursing faculty and other health science librarians.

Lani Draper graduated from Stephen F. Austin State University in Nacogdoches, TX, and received her MLIS from the University of Texas. She worked as a children's librarian for Harris County Public Library in Houston, TX. Since 2002, Lani has worked for SFASU in Nacogdoches in various positions including Social Science Librarian, Web Content Specialist, and Distance Education Liaison.

Naomi Eichenlaub is a librarian at Royal Roads University Library, where she works in the areas of reference and cataloging. She has been at RRU since graduating with her MLIS from the University of British Columbia School of Library, Archival and Information Studies in 2001.

Jack Fritts is Director of Library Services at Benedictine University in Lisle, IL. He is the past chair of the Distance Learning Section of ACRL and has been involved in distance learning librarianship for many years. Jack has previously served as Executive Director of the Southeastern Wisconsin Information Technology Exchange consortium and in several roles as a faculty member at National-Louis University. He completed his bachelor of arts degree in elementary education and has a master of education degree at National College of Education. Jack also earned the master of arts in library and information science at Dominican University.

John-Bauer Graham graduated from Auburn University with a BA in history, received an MA in history, and then received an MLIS from the University of Alabama. He is currently pursuing a doctorate in higher education administration from the University of Alabama. John is an Assistant Professor of Library Science for Jacksonville State University's Houston Cole Library, where he served as the Instructional Services Coordinator for five years and was recently appointed Head of Public Services. He serves on the editorial board for the *Journal of Academic Librarianship*. A list of publications and presentations can be found at www.jsu.edu/depart/library/graphic/jgraham.htm.

Ladonna Guillot received her BS in secondary education from Louisiana State University and her MLIS from the same institution. She currently serves as Health Sciences Librarian at Southeastern Louisiana University and head of the nursing library located in Baton Rouge, LA. Ladonna's previous experience includes hospital, academic, and school librarianship in Baton Rouge. She works closely with the Distance Learning Librarian to serve nursing faculty and students across two campuses and distance learners in a four university consortium pursuing a master of science degree in nursing.

Sandra Lee Hawes has been the Distance Learning Reference Librarian at Saint Leo University since 2002. She has a bachelor of science degree in elementary and early childhood education from George Mason University in Fairfax, VA; a master of arts degree in library and information science from the University of South Florida; and a master of arts in educational leadership from Saint Leo University. Before becoming a librarian, Sandra worked for eighteen years as a classroom teacher in Virginia and Florida. She currently is involved in a library resources and services research project to survey distance learning and off-campus adjunct faculty at Saint Leo University in an effort to streamline and improve faculty awareness and student use of the library.

Karen Elizabeth Jaggers graduated from the University of Texas (Austin) and received her MLS from North Texas State University. Formerly the Head of the Distributed Library Services department of Northern Arizona University, Karen is a reference librarian in NAU's southern region and a member of the Education Team, which works with faculty and students at the Flagstaff campus and within the distance education programs. She has worked in providing library services to remote users since 1986.

Paula A. Jarzemsky earned her nursing degrees from Rush University (BSN) and the University of California San Francisco (MSN). She is currently a Clinical Associate Professor at the University of Wisconsin–Madison and has taught in the first-year clinical courses for undergraduate nursing students since 1992.

Denise Landry-Hyde currently serves as a Reference/Distributed Learning Librarian at Bell Library, Texas A&M University–Corpus Christi, where she has worked since January 1993. Other positions she has held are Reference as well as Information Literacy Coordinator. Denise began her professional life as a teacher. Most of her library experience has been in university/research libraries, but she has also worked in an online newspaper library, as researcher for development in a university foundation, and in a one-person library in a Marine Science Center. Along the way, she worked part-time in the retail side of the book trade, as an intern at a public library; and she fulfilled a practicum in a business and industry association library. An MLS graduate of LSU, Denise loves the diversity in this profession.

Kate Manuel was the Coordinator of the Library Instruction Program at New Mexico State University (NMSU) Library From 2001–2004. She is currently a student in the Technology Law Program at George Mason University School of Law. She is also teaching online as an adjunct professor for University of Maryland University College (UMUC) and coauthoring a book on research methodologies for Neal-Schuman.

Jill Markgraf, associate professor, has been the Coordinator of Distance Education Library Services and Reference Librarian at the University of Wisconsin–Eau Claire since 1998. Prior to coming to Eau Claire, she was a librarian at Michigan Technological University, the University of Mississippi Medical Center, and the University of Florida, specializing in areas of distance education, reference librarianship, and library instruction. Jill holds an MA in library and information studies and a BA in journalism and mass communication from the University of Wisconsin–Madison.

Dana McFarland has been University Librarian at Royal Roads University, a primarily e-learning university, since 1997. Formerly she worked at the Education Library of the University of British Columbia. Dana has also been a college instructor in history. Her interests include innovations in information literacy and library services for e-learning environments.

Lisa T. Nickel graduated from Rutgers University with a BA in history and received her MA in library and information science from the University of South Florida. Currently the Distance Education Librarian at the J. Murrey Atkins Library at University of North Carolina–Charlotte, Lisa was previously a Reference/Instruction Librarian at the University of South Florida. Lisa attended the ACRL Institute for Information Literacy Immersion Program and is active in both ALA and ACRL. She presents and publishes on distance education and instruction topics. Her vita and presentations can be found linked from http://library.uncc.edu/distance.

Jodi Poe graduated from Jacksonville State University with a BS in accounting and an MLIS from the University of Alabama. Jodi is an Assistant Professor and Assistant Librarian for Jacksonville State University's Houston Cole Library, where she serves as the Distance Education Librarian and Electronic Resources Manager. A list of publications and presentations can be found at www.jsu.edu/depart/library/graphic/jpoe.htm.

Srivalli Rao is Associate Professor and Branch Librarian at the White Plains Campus of Mercy College Libraries in New York state. She is also the Coordinator of the Library and Information Science Program for the Division of Libraries at the college. She has been involved with distance education since the mid-1990s and has developed and teaches the online course "Using Electronic Resources for

Research" to distance education students at Mercy College. This course was recently chosen by the college for embedding and testing general education competencies for a cohort of overseas students, making it a mandatory course for these students.

Sandra Rotenberg is an Access Services Librarian at Solano Community College in California. She graduated from the University of California at Berkeley and received her master of library and information science degree from San Jose State University. Solano Community College is her first professional position; prior to that Sandra worked at the Oakland Public Library in a variety of positions, including technical support, cataloging, circulation, and a bit of everything in the branches. In addition to her other duties at Solano Community College, she teaches an online library instruction course at least once each semester, as well as serving as an "embedded" librarian in other online courses.

Beth Stahr received her BS in engineering from Purdue University and her MLS from Syracuse University. She serves as the Distance Learning Librarian at Southeastern Louisiana University in Hammond, LA. She also serves as local administrator for a virtual reference service and administers the plagiarism detection service for her institution. Beth works closely with the Intercollegiate Consortium for the Master of Science in Nursing and provides bibliographic instruction to students at remote-site locations and in electronic environments. She formerly served as president of an international certifying body for genealogists and has published in both library science and genealogy.

Gretel Stock-Kupperman is the Assistant Director for Public Services at the Benedictine University Library. She is responsible for overseeing all user services functions, including reference, instruction, access services, interlibrary loan, and public relations. Gretal also serves as liaison to the College of Business and the Fine Arts department. Prior to joining Benedictine University, she was a Senior Research Manager at a boutique executive search firm in Chicago. Gretel received her bachelors of art degree from the University of Wisconsin–Stevens Point and her master of library science from the University of Illinois at Urbana-Champaign.

Marthea Turnage graduated from Texas Woman's University with a BS and an MLS. Marty has worked at the Ralph W. Steen Library for many years and had the opportunity to work in a variety of positions in both technical services and public services. Currently, she is a Reference Librarian with subject specialties in business, law, Web content management, and distance education. Marty has published in the *Texas Library Journal, Handbook of Texas, Advances in Library Resource Sharing, Research Strategies*, and *Internet Reference Services Quarterly*.

SEP 1 2 2007